LOST
HERO

LOST HERO

THE MYSTERY OF
RAOUL
WALLENBERG

FREDERICK E. WERBELL AND

THURSTON CLARKE

McGraw-Hill Book Company
New York * St. Louis * San Francisco
Hamburg * Mexico * Toronto * London * Sydney

1 2 3 4 5 6 7 8 9 D O D O 8 7 6 5 4 3 2 1

ISBN 0-07-069410-9

LIBRARY OF CONGRESS CATALOGING IN PUBLICATION DATA

Werbell, Frederick E.
    Lost hero.
    1. Wallenberg, Raoul.   2. World War, 1939–1945—
Civilian relief—Hungary.   3. Jews—Hungary—History
—20th century.   4. Holocaust, Jewish (1939–1945)—
Hungary.   5. Hungary—History—1918–1945.   6. Diplo-
mats—Sweden—Biography.   I. Clarke, Thurston.
II. Title.
D809.S8W328   940.54′779439′0924   [B]   81–12417
ISBN 0–07–069410–9   AACR2

Book design by Janice Stern

For my grandfather, Rabbi A. I. Jacobson,
for his untiring efforts on behalf of the many
survivors of the Holocaust who found a
new home in Sweden.

FREDERICK E. WERBELL

For Robert Fletcher and Ben Stickney

THURSTON CLARKE

Contents

Introduction

Raoul Wallenberg was one of World War Two's most heroic figures, and one of the Cold War's most mysterious victims.

His heroism was unique. At the behest of the United States government and the World Jewish Congress, the Swedish government sent him to Budapest in 1944 as an accredited diplomat but with the specific assignment of rescuing as many Jews as possible from Hitler's "Final Solution." During the five months he stayed in Budapest he saved approximately thirty thousand Jews. He bribed and intimidated leading German and Hungarian fascists, created a special passport which placed thousands of Jews under Swedish protection, and literally snatched people from trains taking them to Nazi death camps.

Wallenberg's courage, determination, and his numerous successes stand in sharp contrast to the abysmal failure of the Allied governments to rescue Jews from the Holocaust. Wallenberg was the exception to an embarrassing rule—an exception that highlights Allied failures and makes them appear even more shameful; an exception that forces speculation as to how many Jews might have escaped the Final Solution if more had acted as he did; an exception that, despite the horrors of the Holocaust, makes it impossible to despair of humanity.

The Russians arrested Wallenberg in January 1945, as soon as they liberated Budapest from Nazi rule. The precise reasons for his arrest have never been announced. It appears, however, that he was considered to be an American spy and a threat to Soviet plans to install a communist government in Hungary after the war. It is not unreasonable to place him among the Cold War's earliest victims.

Wallenberg has never been released. Soviet officials first confirmed, then denied, and then confirmed again his presence in their country. The current Soviet explanation is that in 1947 he died of a heart attack in a Moscow prison. There is convincing evidence that this explanation is a lie.

During his decades of unjust imprisonment Wallenberg has become a potent and, from the Russian point of view, dangerous symbol of the arbitrariness and cruelty of the Soviet system. Here was a neutral diplomat, whose heroism was well known to the Russian authorities, arrested without explanation, charged with no crime, forbidden to contact his government or his family, and held incommunicado for years—a man who, like the Jews he failed to save who disappeared into the "night and fog" of Nazi extermination camps, had himself vanished into the "night and fog" of the Soviet Gulag.

During the last five years there has been a significant increase in international interest in the Wallenberg case. Former President Carter has asked Soviet leaders for an explanation of his whereabouts; Prime Minister Begin of Israel has presided over a ceremony in his honor at Jerusalem's memorial to the victims of the Holocaust; a group of distinguished British parliamentarians have nominated him for a Nobel Peace Prize; an American congressman has introduced a bill that would make him an honorary American citizen; a million-dollar reward has been offered for information leading to his release, presuming he is still alive; and there have been books and magazine articles written about him.

These books and articles have tended to concentrate on the

postwar search for Raoul Wallenberg: on the attempts of his friends, family, and government to secure his release, and on the credibility of evidence and witnesses that place him in a specific Soviet prison at a specific time. This information is undeniably important, and much of it is included in Part IV of this book, but it is, nevertheless, merely a tragic appendix to a heroic life, not what makes this life so notable.

We have placed the emphasis of this book on Wallenberg the man: on who he was, what he did in Budapest, and what he suffered during his imprisonment. The principal events in his life have been reconstructed from interviews, official Swedish papers, and other published sources. Only in the last part of the book do we describe the search for Raoul Wallenberg, and in this part we present new, previously secret information which casts new light on the failure of the Swedish government to pursue his case more energetically, and on the question of whether or not, thirty-six years after his arrest, he is still alive in a Soviet prison.

PROLOGUE

FEBRUARY 6, 1957.

MOSCOW.

THE KREMLIN.

OFFICIAL SOVIET MEMORANDUM ON RAOUL WALLENBERG
RELEASED TO *TASS* AND SIGNED BY DEPUTY FOREIGN MINISTER
GROMYKO (Until this date the Soviet government had denied
even arresting Wallenberg.):

*At the request of the government of the kingdom of Sweden,
the competent Soviet authorities were charged with undertaking a thorough examination of the Wallenberg file received
by the Soviet Foreign Ministry from Sweden in March, April,
and May 1956. . . .*

*However, in the course of their research, the Soviet authorities had the occasion to examine the files of prison infirmaries.
They discovered in Lubyanka [in Moscow] a handwritten report which may refer to Wallenberg. This report is addressed
to Abakumov, minister for state security, from A. L. Smoltsov,
the head of the prison hospital service. It is dated July 17,
1947: "I am writing to inform you that the prisoner Walenberg
[sic], known to you, died suddenly in his cell last night. He
was apparently the victim of a myocardiac infarction.. . . ."*

JANUARY 3, 1979.

STOCKHOLM.

SWEDISH MINISTRY FOR FOREIGN AFFAIRS.

AIDE-MÉMOIRE HANDED BY LEIF LEIFLAND, PERMANENT UNDERSECRETARY OF STATE, TO EVGENIY RYMKO, CHARGÉ D'AFFAIRES OF THE SOVIET UNION:

In the continuing efforts to shed light upon the fate of Raoul Wallenberg, information has now reached the Swedish authorities to the effect that Wallenberg was alive as recently as 1975. . . .

In view of the information which has now come to light the Swedish government requests the government of the Soviet Union to initiate a prompt investigation for the purpose of establishing whether Wallenberg was present in the abovementioned at the times stated.

JANUARY 24, 1979.

STOCKHOLM.

MINISTRY FOR FOREIGN AFFAIRS.

AIDE-MÉMOIRE HANDED BY EVGENIY RYMKO, CHARGÉ D'AFFAIRES OF THE SOVIET UNION, TO SVEN HIRDMAN, DIRECTOR, MINISTRY FOR FOREIGN AFFAIRS:

The government of the Soviet Union officially informed the Swedish government as early as 1957 that a thorough and exhaustive investigation had revealed that Raoul Wallenberg died in July 1947.

The renewed investigation of documents relating to this case carried out at the request of the Swedish government in 1965 confirmed that there is no, nor can there be any, new information as regards the fate of Raoul Wallenberg.

This conclusion was definitively confirmed by the findings of an examination of the information supplied by the Swedish government in its request of January 3 this year. The assertions that Raoul Wallenberg was in the Soviet Union as recently as 1975 are not true to the facts.

OCTOBER 13, 1979.
WASHINGTON, D.C.
THE WHITE HOUSE OVAL OFFICE.
PRESIDENT CARTER RESPONDS TO A QUESTION DURING "ASK
THE PRESIDENT" ON NATIONAL PUBLIC RADIO.

QUESTION [Annette Lantos of Hillsborough, California]:

*Mr. President, when my husband and I were youngsters
in Hungary during World War Two, our lives were saved
through the intervention of a Swedish diplomat named Raoul
Wallenberg. We later learned that Mr. Wallenberg, who also
saved the lives of thousands of other Jewish people like us,
was acting on behalf of the American State Department, but
unfortunately Mr. Wallenberg was arrested at the end of the
war by the Russians and has been in Russia ever since and
although the Russians claim that he died, there is an overwhelming amount of evidence which indicates that he is still
alive in a Soviet prison. Could you do something, Mr. President, to help him get released?*

MARCH 19, 1980.
LONDON.
THE HOUSE OF COMMONS.
FROM *THE TIMES*, LONDON, MARCH 20, 1980:

Renewed interest in Mr. Wallenberg's fate has led to the formation of an all-party committee of British MP's to support international efforts to have the case investigated.

This was announced at the House of Commons this week by the committee's sponsors, Mr. Greville Janner, Labour MP for Leicester, West, and Mr. Winston Churchill, Conservative MP for Stratford, who also plan to nominate Mr. Wallenberg for the Nobel Peace Prize.

PART ONE

DIPLOMAT

1

July 1944

THE ARIZONA NIGHTCLUB,
BUDAPEST

Wallenberg found it impossible *not* to stare at Eichmann. Even if he looked over Eichmann's shoulder or turned away from the small round table where they sat discussing the price of a Jewish house or the price of a Jewish life, he could still, through the haze of cigarette smoke, see his black uniform, the death's head insignia on his epaulets, his thin lips, sharp nose, and the twitch that contorted his mouth—all reflected, re-reflected, and re-re-reflected in the huge mirrors lining the walls of the Arizona nightclub.

Everywhere images bounced back and forth between these mirrors. An infinity of doppelgängers shadowed Eichmann, Wallenberg, and everyone in the nightclub. The hostesses in long gowns at the wood-paneled bar; the chorus line of plump Hungarian blondes; the girls in bathing suits who descended from the ceiling on chandeliers at the finale of the stage show; the girls who frolicked in the fake waterfall, jumped through hoops of fire, and pelted each other with artificial snowballs; the waiters in tails carrying trays of Tokay wine and black-market cognac; the black-marketeers who called one another on the telephones mounted on each table to quote prices for nylons, whiskey, and counterfeit baptismal certificates; the Hungarian aristocrats huddling in booths drinking too much, trying to forget the Allied bombing raids and the Russian assault on the crucial Carpathian mountain passes; the gypsies playing waltzes and czardas on violins; and the green-shirted Hungarian fascists, the gendarme officers in their musical comedy uniforms, and the black-uniformed SS fox-trotting around the revolving glass dance floor with the Hungarian hostesses: all were duplicated and triplicated in the Arizona's mirrors.

Eichmann had proposed this meeting; Wallenberg had readily accepted. He had been stalking Eichmann since arriving in Budapest several weeks before. Twice he had bribed the Arizona's headwaiter to seat him at a table next to Eichmann; twice he had listened as Eichmann and his aides ordered brandy, requested songs from the band, and pried information from the club's owner, Miss Arizona—a large middle-aged woman who, dressed in a blond wig and tight sequined gown, sang "Stormy Weather," introduced the acts, performed Mae West imitations, and spied for the Allies and the Gestapo. Eichmann had learned that her husband was Jewish and had proposed a bargain: the life of her husband, who was in Gestapo custody, in exchange for information about her patrons.

The leaders of Budapest's Jewish community had already told Wallenberg that Eichmann and other SS officers sometimes appeared open to negotiations. In April, Eichmann had proposed a deal to one of Budapest's Jewish leaders, Joel Brand. He would "sell" a million Jews to the Allies for trucks and other goods. He permitted Brand to leave Hungary to present his offer to the Allies. The British, however, believing Brand to be a German agent, arrested him, held him in Cairo for months, and refused to consider Eichmann's offer.

Negotiations with Eichmann were the pretext for tonight's meeting. Wallenberg needed more buildings in which to house his expanding offices, his Jewish employees, and the ever-increasing numbers of Jews holding the special Swedish pass he had devised to protect them.

For Eichmann, the question of Swedish buildings was unimportant. When the time came to deport Budapest's Jews it would make no difference where they lived, or so he thought. In the meantime, if he could sell back to the Jews the houses he had already confiscated from them, so much the better. He also wanted a chance to probe, to spar with this new Swedish diplomat. Now he had it.

"How many of these houses do you require, Mr. Secretary?" he asked. He was polite, businesslike.

"Eventually, at least forty," Wallenberg said.

"Fine. I have that many under my control. How much are you willing to pay?"

"For all forty, two hundred thousand dollars, payable in Swedish kroner."

Eichmann feigned shock. "But, Mr. Secretary. You can't be serious. Why, the Americans once offered us two million dollars for the Jews from Slovakia. Why should the Hungarian Jews be worth less?"

In fact, as Eichmann and Wallenberg both knew, they were worth much more. The 175,000 Jews living in Budapest and the 50,000 working in labor battalions in the provinces had had a scarcity value that made them virtually priceless. They represented the only large, thriving Jewish community left in Europe. The "Final Solution" would not be final, Europe not truly "Judenrein," until they were deported "to the east" where they could receive the same "special treatment" meted out to 430,000 provincial Hungarian Jews between March and July of 1944.

Until March 1944, Hungary had been a relative haven for Jews. Its prewar Jewish population of 400,000 had been almost doubled by refugees fleeing neighboring countries and by Jews living in territories annexed by Hungary when it joined the Axis. During the first four years of the war these Jews remained safe. Although Hungary joined the German attack on Russia and was technically at war with the other Allied powers, it managed to maintain its internal sovereignty and resist German demands to deport its Jews.

The Hungarians resisted on practical and sentimental grounds. Jews owned and managed most of the Hungarian industry, and it was feared that their removal would precipitate an economic disaster. (One German businessman reported back to Berlin in 1943 that the Christian Hungarians had neither the brains nor the capital to compensate for the elimination of the Jewish industrialists.) Furthermore, a greater percentage of Jews in Hungary than in other European countries had converted to Christianity. They and many others who had become assimilated into Hungarian culture, or "Magyarized," played a leading role in the country's economic, political, and artistic life.

Hungary would not deport its Magyarized Jews, but it would persecute them. Since 1938 fascist-dominated Hungarian governments had passed laws restricting the numbers of Jews allowed to enter the professions, liquidating their agricultural holdings, and segregating them from public social gatherings. In 1941, twenty thousand Polish, Rumanian, and Czechoslovakian Jews residing in Hungary were deported to Poland and murdered by Einsatzengruppen—German death squads. The following year, fifty thousand Hungarian Jews were drafted into work brigades and sent to clear mines and build earthworks on the eastern front. Only ten thousand returned.

Still, the government of Prime Minister Miklós Kállay resisted the wholesale deportation of men, women, and children. Throughout 1942 and 1943 the Germans increased pressure on their ally to "solve" its "Jewish problem." Kállay told one German that he could not send Magyarized Jews to Germany unless he knew their fate and could be sure that they would be "given a chance to exist." To appease the Nazis he offered to deport the 300,000 non-Magyarized Jews remaining in Hungary.

Eichmann argued successfully against accepting the Hungarian offer. He advised: "Experience has proved a partial action requires no less effort in preparation and execution than a total measure against all the Jews of a country." Hence deporting only the foreign Jews residing in Hungary would mean "putting into motion the whole evacuation apparatus" without conclusively solving Hungary's "Jewish problem." He concluded, "We had better wait till Hungary is ready to include all its Jews in the necessary measures.

In March 1944, Hitler made certain that Hungary was ready. He considered its refusal to surrender its Jews proof of its traitorous intentions. He also knew that after recent German defeats on the eastern front, Hungarian diplomats in neutral countries had broached the subject of a separate armistice with the Allies. A Hungarian armistice would cut Germany's lines of communication with its other Eastern European Allies—Rumania and Bulgaria—and weaken its ability to withstand the Russian onslaught.

On March 18, 1944, Hitler summoned the Hungarian regent, Miklós Horthy, to Klessheim Castle, and gave him an ultimatum: Dismiss the Kállay government and replace it with one under strict German supervision or accept total German occupation and the status of an occupied enemy. Horthy chose the first course. As he and Hitler spoke, German troops marched into Hungary.

The only Hungarian to oppose the German occupation was Endre Bajcsy-Zsilinszky, a member of the parliament. A month before, he had written to Prime Minister Kállay advocating armed resistance to a German invasion. He argued that a forceful occupation would be better than one borne "with meekness and patience; because the forceful occupation will win the honor and future of the country maybe by suffering, possibly by grave torments, blood and destruction to our fatherland, but it will separate us from the fate of the German Reich."

When a squad of SS soldiers approached Bajcsy-Zsilinszky's apartment house, he fired at them with a revolver. When he fell wounded after a brief exchange, Hungarian resistance to the German occupation ended.

Prime Minister Kállay took refuge in the Turkish Embassy, and the pro-German Döme Sztójay, formerly the Hungarian ambassador to Berlin, succeeded him. Hungary's real ruler, however, was the Reich plenipotentiary, Dr. Edmund Veesenmayer. German advisors quickly established a shadow government, and German orders, particularly in regard to the Jews, began to be executed. Hours after the coup, Adolf Eichmann arrived in Hungary at the head of a mile-long military column known as Sondereinsatzkommando Eichmann (Special Operations Group Eichmann).

When Himmler had learned that the occupation of Hungary was imminent he had given the order "Send down to Hungary the 'Master' in person." Adolf Eichmann—"the 'Master' in person"—had immediately summoned his aides to an Austrian village near the Hungarian border.

He summoned Dieter Wisliceny and Alois Brunner from Slovakia and Greece, Franz Abromeit from Yugoslavia, Theodor Dannecker from Paris, Herman Krumey from Vienna, and Sigfreid Seidel from his position as commandant of the "model" Thereinstadt concentration camp. From Berlin came Rolf Gunter, his chief deputy; Franz Novak, his deportation officer; and Otto Hunsche, his legal expert. They could assemble so quickly because they had completed their mission elsewhere in Europe; under the Master's direction they had organized the collection and transportation of millions of Jews to the Nazi extermination camps.

Although only holding the rank of Lieutenant Colonel in the SS, Eichmann deserved Himmler's compliment; he was indeed the "Master" of the Jewish question. As head of the Gestapo's Section IV B4—Jewish affairs—he had been instrumental in planning and executing every stage of Germany's persecution and elimination of European Jewry.

After the German occupation of Austria in 1938, he had invented the assembly-line procedure by which Jews entered a huge shed where, in less than an hour, they were stripped of their possessions, homes, and citizenship and given exit visas that expired in twenty-four hours. He also introduced these Jewish asset-stripping factories to Prague and Berlin.

In 1942, he prepared the agenda for the Wannsee Conference

at which it was decided to exterminate Jews in gas chambers. He organized the pace and timing of shipments of Jews to the killing centers and became a genius at coordinating the arrivals of the deportation trains so that the gas chambers could operate at maximum capacity and efficiency.

He believed he was an idealist performing a historic mission. The commandant of Auschwitz, Rudolf Hoess, said he was "absolutely devoted to his mission, and believed that the extermination was necessary in order to save the German people."

After the war, Eichmann told a former Dutch Nazi who tracked him down in Argentina: "To be frank with you, had we killed all of them, the ten point three million, I would be happy and say, 'All right, we managed to destroy an enemy.' "

He destroyed his enemy without pity or remorse. According to his aide, Dieter Wisliceny, "Eichmann was very cynical in his attitude to the Jewish question. He gave no indication of any human feeling toward these people. He was not immoral: he was amoral and completely ice-cold in his attitude."

He was determined to kill every Jew in Europe. "Eichmann was sharply opposed to every suggestion to sift out the Jews capable of work from those deported," Rudolf Hoess wrote in his diary. "He regarded this as a constant danger to his plans for the Final Solution, in view of the possibility of mass escapes or some other event that might permit the Jews to remain alive. . . . He showed himself to be completely obsessed with the idea of destroying every single Jew he could lay his hands on."

The German occupation of Hungary gave Eichmann an opportunity to lay his hands on 700,000 Jews, about one-seventh as many as the Germans had killed during the preceding five years. Eichmann would have to kill the Hungary Jews quickly. The Soviet Army had almost reached the Carpathian passes that lead to the Hungarian plains and Budapest.

"Comb the country from east to west!" Himmler ordered. "Send all the Jews to Auschwitz as quickly as possible. Begin with the eastern provinces, which the Russians are approaching.

See to it that nothing like the Warsaw ghetto revolt is repeated in any way."

Eichmann was ecstatic. The Hungarian Jews represented a challenge—a "fantastic opportunity," he told an aide. Never before had he been faced with transporting so many Jews so quickly. If he succeeded, he would set a record for dispatching people to their deaths unequaled in history.

Eichmann's Jewish "actions" all had four stages: marking, collection, isolation in ghettos, and deportation. The day after arriving in Hungary he initiated the first stage. At his request, the government promulgated a law requiring all Jews to wear a "canary-yellow" Star of David badge on the left-hand breast pocket of their outergarments. Subsequent laws forbade Jews from owning radios or telephones, required them to remain indoors except for three hours every day, and banned them from most restaurants, stores, and cinemas. The government confiscated Jewish stores, enterprises, and bank accounts, and closed pawnshops. It was feared that Jews might pawn their possessions and use the proceeds to escape. The Hungarian press announced that it was "the patriotic duty of every Hungarian to denounce any Jews who did not comply with or tried to evade the new regulations," and that "of all the orders of the government, hardly another one was acclaimed with such enthusiasm by the broad public as that restraining the rights of the Jews."

Eichmann started collecting Jews in the middle of April. Hungarian gendarmes, acting under the guidance of his SS unit, woke Jews in the early morning hours, ordered them to pack (valuables were to be left behind), and herded them into instant ghettos—schools, synagogues, and community centers. Here they remained for several weeks without sufficient food, medical attention, or sanitary facilities.

Few Jews actively resisted the roundups. In March, Eichmann had ordered the Jews to form a "Jewish Council," composed of leading members of the Jewish community. On March 31 he had met with its principal members—Samu Stern, Dr. Ernö Petö,

Dr. János Gábor, and Dr. Károly Wilhelm—to reassure them that his main purpose in Hungary was to increase the efficiency and output of the war industries. The Jews would work but not be harmed. Families would be deported, he said, "out of consideration for the close family life of the Jews."

He warned that "I am not an adherent of violence because I value manpower, but any opposition will be broken. If you think of joining the partisans or applying their methods, I shall have you mercilessly slaughtered. After the war the Jews will be free; all the Jewish measures will, anyway, be abandoned, and the Germans will again be good-natured as before. . . ."

The members of the Jewish Council wanted to believe Eichmann and he made it easy to do so. He was polite and solicitous. "I will visit your museum soon," he told them, "because I am interested in Jewish cultural affairs. You can trust me and talk freely to me—as you see, I am quite frank with you. If the Jews behave quietly and work, you will be able to keep all of your community institutions."

The first trains left for Auschwitz on May 15. Hungarian gendarmes under Eichmann's direction marched the Jews from their ghettos to the nearest train station, searched and tortured them to make them reveal the location of any hidden valuables, and then shoved eighty to a hundred into each freight car. "Pack them in like herrings," Eichmann ordered. At least a tenth died before leaving Hungarian territory.

The Master himself accompanied the first train to Auschwitz. He had ordered a new rail spur constructed so that the Hungarian trains could unload within two hundred yards of the gas chambers. Time was crucial. He did not want to waste it by marching his Jews through the camp.

Eichmann's huge transports strained the camp's capacity. Between May 15 and the end of June as many as five trains a day, each carrying an average of ten thousand Jews, pulled into the new spur. Commandant Hoess increased the number of men in the death squads from two hundred to six hundred and placed them on a twenty-four-hour schedule. The gas chambers and ovens operated day and night and still Eichmann had shipped so many Jews that thousands could not be accommodated. These were thrown, still alive, onto huge bonfires.

By the thirtieth of June a total of 147 trains had delivered 437,000 Hungarians to Auschwitz and other camps. In less than two months Eichmann had cleansed the Hungarian countryside of Jews. "It went like a dream," he boasted to an aide.

He reported to Berlin: "The complete liquidation of the Hungarian Jews is an accomplished fact. Technical details will only take a few more days in Budapest." In all of Europe only one large Jewish community survived, that of Budapest. It was next.

Eichmann scheduled his Budapest action for July 6. It would be the last, most grandiose action of his career: the largest one-day roundup of Jews ever attempted. He had already gathered the Jews into special houses marked with a yellow Star of David, reserved Budapest's buses and trams, brought Lieutenant-Colonel László Ferenczy and his gendarmes in from the countryside, and recruited the city's postmen and chimney-sweeps to guide the gendarmes to the Jewish houses. In a single day he planned to round up the city's Jews and intern them on an island in the Danube. From there he would dispatch them to Auschwitz in batches of ten thousand. By the end of July, Hungary would be "Judenrein."

At the last minute the Hungarian regent, Admiral Miklós Horthy, canceled the roundup and announced an indefinite suspension of the deportations. The gendarmes returned to the countryside and László Baky and László Endre, the two Hungarian ministers who had helped Eichmann orchestrate his Jewish actions, went on leave. Eichmann was furious. "In all my long practice, this is the first time such a thing has happened to me!" he shouted at Colonel Ferenczy. "This won't do at all! It's contrary to all agreements. I can't get over it!"

The object of Eichmann's rage, Admiral Horthy, was a member of one of Hungary's most aristocratic families. He had served with distinction in the Austro-Hungarian Navy during the First World War and afterward was named to be Hungary's regent. In theory he was holding the Hungarian crown in trust for a monarch, but in fact the monarch was nonexistent. There was no authentic Hungarian royal family, and the Magyars would not accept an exiled Hapsburg as king. Although Hungary was supposed to be a constitutional monarchy, Horthy had persuaded the parliament to vote him considerable powers, particularly over the security forces and army. He was a fanatic anti-communist and despite his personal dislike of Hitler had joined Germany in what he termed its "crusade against Bolshevism." The German envoy, Edmund Veesenmayer, referred to the seventy-six-year-old Horthy as being "weak and vacillating." There were suggestions that he was becoming senile.

Horthy was an anti-Semite. He had approved the anti-Jewish laws of the 1930s and even his son later admitted that anti-Semitism had permeated their household. He once told his chief of gendarmes, "I do not care what happens to the 'little' Jews but I certainly don't want the valuable and wealthy ones taken out of the country." He did not stop Eichmann's deportations out of affection for his Jewish subjects, but out of fear.

He feared that László Baky, one of Sztójay's pro-German ministers, planned to use the Jewish action to camouflage a Nazi-inspired coup d'etat. He also feared that the recent Allied landings in Normandy and Russian victories in the east had made Germany's defeat inevitable.

He was influenced further by protests against the deportations made by the king of Sweden, the Pope, and the Red Cross, and by threats made by Britain and the United States to hold trials for war criminals.

The international protests and detailed reports of the Nazi extermination camps handed to Hungarian diplomats in neutral capitals made it impossible for Horthy to delude himself that Hungary's Jews were working as laborers in Germany. As Angelo Rotta, the papal nuncio in Budapest who had already done much to help the Jews, had told him, "The whole world now knows what 'deportation' means in practice."

In fact, the "whole world" had known the fate of Jewish deportees for some time. Yet, until 1944, the Allied governments had not taken concerted or effective measures to halt the deportations or aid those who escaped them. Their response, and in particular the response of the United States, was characterized by apathy and inaction.

During the previous eleven years of Nazi persecutions the United States had issued only 165,000 immigrant visas to European Jews. Instead of loosening immigration restrictions for Jewish refugees, the American government had tightened them. Jews were denied visas because they were penniless, even though the Germans had confiscated their assets, and because they were technically "enemy aliens," even though the Germans had stripped them of their citizenship. These harsh criteria, inspired in part by anti-Semitism, ensured that American immigration quotas remained unfilled even when the fate of European Jewry was widely known.

Since the beginning of the war neutral diplomats, newsmen, and eyewitnesses had supplied the Allies with uncontestable evidence of Nazi atrocities against Jews. The murder of 250,000 Jews in Poland, the liquidation of Polish ghettos, and the shipment of 380,000 Jews to the extermination camp at Treblinka were all reported, and then buried in diplomatic files. During the first three years of the war, official Allied publications avoided stating that the Jews were the principal targets of German atrocities. To do so, it was feared, would lend credence to Nazi allegations that the Allies were fighting a "Jewish war."

In August 1942 the Allies received the first evidence that the Nazis planned to systematically murder Jews in special camps. Gerhart Riegner, the representative of the World Jewish Congress in Switzerland, learned from a German industrialist that Hitler had ordered the construction of enormous gas chambers.

It was not until five months later, in December 1942, that

the Allies publicly admitted that the Jews were victims of a coordinated and organized Nazi campaign of extermination. British Foreign Secretary Anthony Eden informed the House of Commons that the Nazis "are now carrying into effect Hitler's oft repeated intention to exterminate the Jewish people of Europe."

Even after acknowledging the existence of the Final Solution, Allied and neutral governments and even international agencies such as the Red Cross failed to mount an effective campaign to rescue the Jews. Britain continued to impose tight restrictions on Jewish immigration to Palestine, and American consulates continued enforcing their strict visa regulations.

When an American rabbi, Stephen Wise, devised a plan for saving seventy thousand Jewish lives by paying bribes to Nazi officials through Swiss bank accounts, the State Department took months to weigh the plan before finally giving its approval. The British Ministry of Economic Warfare immediately vetoed it, explaining, "The British Foreign Office is concerned with the difficulty in disposing of any considerable number of Jews should they be released from enemy territory." The British were worried that these Jews would slip into Palestine and upset the delicate relations there between Arabs and Jews.

The International Red Cross argued that to intervene on behalf of the Jews would constitute interference in the internal affairs of a belligerent nation. When Eichmann started his campaign against Hungarian Jewry, the Vatican and neutral and Allied nations begged the Red Cross to increase its staff in Budapest. The president of the International Red Cross refused, saying that "under the present circumstances such a mission might be considered as unrelated to the Committee's traditional and conventional competence (the treatment of prisoners of war and interned civilians)." The Red Cross could only help war victims "without intruding into the domestic policy of any of those states."

When, in 1943, the British proposed a conference in Bermuda to devise methods of aiding and rescuing victims of Nazi persecution, six weeks passed before the American State Department agreed to attend. At the time, Nazi extermination camps were murdering an average of fifteen thousand people a day. When the conference finally convened, it did nothing to alleviate Jewish suffering. Its principal result was to demonstrate to the Germans that stopping the Final Solution was low on Allied priorities.

Throughout the last three years of the war, Jewish leaders suggested paying ransom to free groups of Jews, granting mass visas to all refugees, and bombing Auschwitz and the rail lines leading to the gas chambers. All these proposals were rejected. The most common excuse given was that winning the war as quickly as possible was the best way to stop Nazi atrocities. Bombing Auschwitz would divert resources; paying ransom would strengthen the enemy. These arguments were made in good faith by Allied patriots, in bad faith by Allied anti-Semites.

The Allied reaction to the Final Solution persuaded Josef Goebbels to write in his diary, "Fundamentally, however, I believe both the English and the Americans are happy that we are exterminating the Jewish riffraff."

In January 1944, American policy changed dramatically. Secretary of the Treasury Henry Morgenthau received a report from the Treasury Department's general counsel entitled "The Acquiescence of This Government in the Murder of the Jews." The report charged that "[State Department officials] have not only failed to use the governmental machinery at their disposal to rescue Jews from Hitler, but have even gone so far as to use this governmental machinery to prevent the rescue of these Jews. . . . In their official capacity [they] have gone so far as to surreptitiously attempt to stop the obtaining of information concerning the murder of the Jewish population of Europe."

Several days later Morgenthau presented President Roosevelt with a summary of the report which concluded: "The matter of rescuing the Jews from extermination is a trust too great to remain in the hands of men who are indifferent, callous, and perhaps even hostile. The task is filled with difficulties. Only a fervent will to accomplish, backed by persistent and untiring effort, can succeed where time is so precious."

If he had known Raoul Wallenberg, Morgenthau could not have described his qualities more accurately.

A week later Roosevelt established the War Refugee Board, charging it with "the rescue, transportation, maintenance and relief of the victims of enemy opposition and . . . the establishment of havens of temporary refuge for such victims." Finally, at this late hour, the American government would try to save what little remained of European Jewry, and of America's honor.

The Board was headed by John Pehle, a thirty-four-year-old Treasury lawyer. Despite its small budget and staff, and the late date at which it commenced its efforts, it had some remarkable success. It freed entry visas for the handful of Jews remaining alive in Germany, granted visas to Jewish children stranded in Switzerland, and arranged for Jewish refugees trapped in Spain to make their way to North Africa. Representatives of the Board dispatched to neutral capitals threatened Axis diplomats with war crimes trials and urged neutral diplomats to take a more active role in protecting the Jews who survived.

The War Refugee Board representative in Ankara, Ira Hirschmann, used the threat of postwar retaliation to persuade the Rumanian government to empty its concentration camps in Transnistria and return the surviving 18,000 Jews (out of an original 185,000) to their homes. The Transnistrian camps lay in the path of a retreating German Army, and without Hirschmann's intervention these Jews would certainly have been slaughtered.

The Board's first attempts to duplicate Hirschmann's success in Hungary failed. Following the Nazi occupation of March 18, the Hungarian government had less independence than the Rumanians. Throughout the spring of 1944, Hungarian diplomats in neutral countries resisted the Board's tactics of pressure and blackmail.

During March and April, while Eichmann was marking the

Hungarian Jews and gathering them into ghettos, President Roosevelt and Cardinal Spellman of New York appealed to Hungarian Christians to protect their nation's Jews. The British government warned that the RAF would hit residential neighborhoods if Jews were collected into ghettos, and in April the RAF and the American Air Force began bombing Budapest. The War Refugee Board urged the Pope to threaten the Nazis and their Hungarian accomplices with excommunication. For a month the Pope stalled. Finally he sent a message to Admiral Horthy that arrived after the majority of Hungary's Jews had been sent to Auschwitz.

When it became clear that these long-distance threats were not working, the Board decided to mount a direct rescue operation from within Hungary. Because the United States and Hungary were at war, the Board could not send an American to Budapest. Because the Swedish government had been the most receptive to pleas to increase its diplomatic representation in Hungary, the Board's representative in neutral Sweden, Iver Olsen, was ordered to find a Swedish citizen who could be sent on a mission to rescue Hungarian Jews. He would go to Budapest as a Swedish diplomat but with American funds and support.

Iver Olsen received his instructions from Washington on the morning of June 12. He immediately walked out of the offices of the American Embassy, down the hall, and into the headquarters of the Middle European Trading Corporation. Olsen knew its director, Kalman Lauer, a small, corpulent middle-aged man with fiery black eyes, a Hungarian Jew whose wife's parents were trapped in Budapest. Olsen explained the type of mission the Board wished to mount in Budapest. Did Lauer know someone who was qualified to be a Swedish diplomat and who was also willing to undertake such a dangerous assignment?

Without hesitation Lauer suggested his thirty-one-year-old associate, Raoul Wallenberg. He spoke fluent German and had recently made several trips to Budapest representing Lauer's company. He belonged to a distinguished Swedish family of diplomats, bankers, and admirals and would have no difficulty gaining the approval of the Swedish Foreign Ministry. In fact, Wallenberg had already volunteered to go to Budapest to bring out Lauer's relatives. Difficulties in obtaining a visa and a last-minute call-up for training in Sweden's home guard had prevented him from leaving.

Lauer was certain Wallenberg would accept Olsen's proposal. Gilel Storch, head of the World Jewish Congress (Swedish section), was also searching for a Swedish gentile to head a rescue operation in Budapest. Two weeks before, Lauer had recommended Wallenberg to Professor Marcus Ehrenpreis, Sweden's chief rabbi. Wallenberg had agreed to go, but Rabbi Ehrenpreis delayed making a decision. He was put off by Wallenberg's naive enthusiasm and disturbed by his insistence that he would need large amounts of money to bribe German and Hungarian officials.

Lauer was determined that this time there should be no delay. The following evening he, Wallenberg, and Olsen met for dinner at one of the Wallenberg family's many properties, the Grand Hotel in the resort of Saltsjöbaden. When the meeting ended, at five the next morning, they had agreed that Wallenberg would go to Budapest as the Swedish Embassy's special attaché for humanitarian questions. His mission would last two or three months, he would carry diplomatic credentials from the Swedish Foreign Ministry, and he would have the financial and political backing of the American government. In essence, he would be Franklin Roosevelt's personal representative in Budapest, an American agent, the only American agent sent into an Axis country for the sole and express purpose of saving the last remnants of European Jewry.

The War Refugee Board had only been allocated a budget of a million dollars, but it had also received considerable financial backing from an American Jewish philanthropic organization, the Joint Distribution Committee. To finance Wallenberg's mission to save the 225,000 surviving Hungarian Jews, Olsen promised to deposit $100,000 into his account at the Enskilda Bank.

Two days later, on June 15, the American ambassador, Herschel Johnson, met with the Swedish foreign minister. Johnson knew that since March, Swedish diplomats in Budapest had been issuing provisional Swedish passports to Jews who could prove family or business connections with Sweden. The Swedish minister in Budapest, Ivan Danielsson, had persuaded the Hungarians to treat holders of these passports as de facto Swedish citizens. They were exempted from wearing the yellow Star of David and being collected for deportation. By the middle of June the Swedish Legation had issued seven hundred of these passports. Long lines of Jews formed in front of the Legation every morning, and Danielsson had recently requested additional staff from Stockholm to help process these passports.

"I've come to congratulate you," Johnson said to the foreign minister. "I understand that you have decided to send a special representative to Budapest to assist in humanitarian tasks and that your choice is Raoul Wallenberg. An excellent choice. I think he's perfect for the assignment."

This was the first that the foreign minister had heard about Wallenberg being chosen. Not wanting to appear surprised, he pretended that Wallenberg was indeed his choice. "Yes," he said, "sending Wallenberg to Budapest *is* under serious consideration."

Johnson's bluff had worked. The following day Wallenberg was summoned to the Foreign Ministry and offered the position of Second Secretary at the Swedish Embassy in Budapest.

Unlike the Allied governments, Wallenberg recognized from the beginning the value of time. Each day he remained in Stockholm another ten thousand Hungarian Jews went to Auschwitz. "Every day costs lives," he told Lauer on the twenty-eighth of June. "I must leave as soon as possible."

He spent his final days in Stockholm negotiating with the Foreign Ministry over the terms of his employment, amassing information about friendly contacts in Budapest, and saying farewell to his friends. Rabbi Ehrenpreis finally recognized his abilities and sincerity. He named him the official representative of the World Jewish Congress, and gave him a letter of introduction to the president of the Budapest Jewish Council. As Wallenberg turned to leave, Ehrenpreis blessed him with a saying from the Talmud: "Those who set off on a mission of humanity can be assured of God's special protection."

Wallenberg's many acquaintances in Stockholm society were amazed that he had agreed to go to Hungary at such a dangerous time. To these acquaintances he appeared an unexceptional member of the Swedish upper class, an attractive and charming young bachelor with little on his mind besides attending parties, dabbling in business, and enjoying a safe, comfortable life in a neutral country made prosperous by the war.

He appeared to have accomplished these limited goals. Women loved his curly brown hair, prominent, aristocratic nose, large, dark, passionate eyes, and wicked sense of humor. His family name admitted him to the most exclusive parties and country estates. The Wallenbergs had produced generations of statesmen, diplomats, bishops, and financiers. His father's cousins, Jacob and Marcus Wallenberg, managed the world-renowned Enskilda Bank and a network of Wallenberg companies and interests. Raoul's branch of the Wallenberg family, however, was not at all wealthy. His father, who had died of brain cancer before his birth, had been a naval officer. Raoul had been raised by his mother and his maternal grandmother, two widows who, from all appearances, gave him a great deal of love and attention.

Compared with his illustrious ancestors, Raoul Wallenberg appeared to many outsiders to be something of a disappointment: insubstantial, restless, and uncertain of his talents and interests, a dilettante. When he was eighteen his paternal grandfather, a noted Swedish diplomat, had sent him to the United States for four years to study architecture at the University of Michigan. Despite his passionate love of architecture, after finishing his degree he agreed to train for a position in the Wallenberg bank. During the following year he worked as a trainee in a trading company in South Africa and a bank in Palestine.

Wallenberg's employer in South Africa reported to his grandfather, "I have found him a splendid organizer and negotiator. He has seemingly boundless energy and vitality as well as great imaginative powers, an original mind."

After working in the bank in Palestine, Wallenberg wrote to his grandfather: "I am not made to be a banker. There is something about the profession that is too calm, cynical and cold for me. I think that my talents lie elsewhere. I want to do something more positive than sit behind a desk all day saying no to people. Ever since I was a boy I have had a passion for architecture. I can remember leaving school to visit the construction sites in Stockholm and discuss the buildings with the engineers."

Wallenberg returned to Stockholm and searched for a position with an architectural firm. He submitted plans, but none were accepted. He designed buildings, but none were started. The Depression had halted the construction projects that had fascinated him as a boy. He had one success: He won an architectural competition for his design of a public bath. The bath was never built. He changed his mind about banking and asked his relatives to find him a position. Now they refused to consider him for the family bank. "No!" said Marcus Wallenberg, Sr., Raoul's great uncle. "That boy is clearly more suited to being a politician."

Instead of politics he turned to trading. He tried to import a brand of cheap zippers from Japan; nobody bought them. He backed an invention called "Quick Cork," a cork that would pop out of wine bottles without the use of a corkscrew; the French winemakers ignored him. He speculated on coffee and attempted to corner the Swedish market for Portuguese sardines. After the war broke out in Europe he joined Kalman Lauer's import-export firm.

This was the Raoul Wallenberg familiar to most: an architect who had built nothing; an aspiring banker who was refused a position in his family's bank; a wheeler-dealer entrepreneur who had failed to make a killing; one of the "poor" Wallenbergs who had neither inherited a fortune nor made his own; an executive in a small trading company; and a pleasant, witty, young man who had not lived up to his early promise and his family's reputation.

On the eve of his departure for Budapest he invited his small circle of close friends to a farewell dinner. These friends knew a different Raoul Wallenberg, a Wallenberg who only revealed his true self and ideals slowly and cautiously to those he had known and trusted for years. They knew he was uniquely energetic, idealistic, and sensitive and that, at the proper opportunity, he would use his talents and be guided by his ideals.

These friends remembered him as a secretive, lonely little boy who disappeared for hours to memorize sections of the encyclopedia or study the financial reports of his relatives' companies. They remembered the little boy who preferred long solitary hikes to soccer and other team sports and whose friends dubbed him the "Only Child." They remembered the little boy who refused to follow the lessons in school and was considered somewhat bizarre and precocious by his teachers.

They remembered the sensitive boy who so despised hunting and killing that he broke into the kennels of a neighboring estate and released the hunting dogs the night before a hunt; the fearless boy who ran outside during thunderstorms crying, "Let's see God's fireworks," while his friends cowered under their beds; the secretly religious boy who memorized long passages from the Bible and who, while feverish with malaria in the house of an aunt in Mexico City, recited and tried to act out Christian homilies.

His friends knew he was intensely patriotic. While working as a window washer and sales clerk at the Swedish pavilion during the 1934 Chicago World's Fair he had persuaded the manager to mount spotlights on a nearby skyscraper. They bathed the otherwise plain-looking Swedish building in light and set it off from the rest of the fair. Now, on the eve of his departure for Budapest, he was honored and excited that at last he had a chance to live up to his family's reputation. "Anyone who carries the name Wallenberg," he told those at the farewell dinner, "has a duty to serve his country. At last I'm being given an opportunity to fulfill that duty."

His friends knew he could be brave and calm in the face of danger. When the World's Fair ended the twenty-one-year-old Wallenberg had started hitchhiking back to the University of Michigan. A group of young toughs who picked him up suddenly turned down a deserted dirt road, stopped, and robbed him at gunpoint. He behaved so calmly that he terrified his robbers. He wrote to his mother: "After my nice 'travel companions' had counted my money, and I could see they were pleased, I thought it was their turn to do me a favor. So I told them the least they could do was to drive me back to the main road. After discussing this among themselves for some time they agreed. They got into the front seat and threw me into the rear. . . . Oddly enough, during this whole time I wasn't at all frightened. The robbery seemed like an exciting adventure. However, I think I was so calm that they became suspicious and then frightened of me. They became afraid that I'd lured them into some kind of trap. All of a sudden they stopped the car and tossed me into a ditch."

His friends knew too that he agonized over the plight of the Jews. Viveca Lindfors, a pretty young actress who had accompanied him to a dance just after he returned from working in Palestine, remembered, "He took me up to his grandfather's office and I thought he wanted to seduce me. Instead he started telling me, almost in whispers, what was happening to the Jews in Germany. I just didn't understand it. I didn't believe him; I thought he was trying to win my sympathy."

His friends knew a secret that he had kept from almost everyone: His maternal grandmother, in whose home he was raised, was one-quarter Jewish—enough of a Jew, had she lived in Hungary, to be included in Eichmann's transports. This was one reason why he became so agitated whenever anyone mentioned the persecution of the European Jews.

Because they knew the real Wallenberg, no one at this last

dinner thought it melodramatic or out of character when, at the conclusion of the evening, he said, "I am going to leave you now for one reason: to save as many lives as possible; to rescue Jews from the claws of those murderers." The following morning he flew to Berlin.

The Swedish ambassador in Berlin had assumed that Wallenberg would want to spend the weekend in Nuremberg with his half sister Nina Lagergren, whose husband, Gunnar, was posted there at the Swedish Consulate. He had therefore reserved a berth for Wallenberg on the night sleeper leaving Berlin for Budapest on Sunday evening. Wallenberg was furious when he learned of these arrangements. How could he waste so much time on a social visit while the deportations to Auschwitz continued?

He raced to the Berlin station and jumped onto the train leaving that evening for Budapest. Soldiers and Nazi functionaries had already packed the carriages and sleeping berths, so he spent the night sitting on the floor of the crowded corridor, listening to the air raids that halted the train on sidings, and leaning against his only luggage—the two battered knapsacks he had taken on his American hitchhiking tour. Inside were his weapons: a list of secret anti-Nazis who had gained prominent positions in the Hungarian government; a list of prominent Budapest Jews who might provide him with funds; messages and funds for hundreds of relatives of Swedish Jews; the names of Swedes in Budapest who were suspected of collaborating with the fascists; and a secondhand pistol. He had bought the cheapest pistol he could find because, as he told a friend, "I don't want to waste money I could otherwise spend bribing Nazis. Besides, the gun is only to give me courage. I don't plan to use it."

Sometime during the night, while he dozed in the corridor, his southbound express passed a northbound freight train carrying two thousand Hungarian Jews to Auschwitz. The week before, the gendarmes had collected these Jews from the Budapest suburbs of Ujpest, Kispest, and Pasterzsebet and sequestered them in the Budakalász brick factory. Early on the evening of July 8, Eichmann had ordered them packed into freight cars as quickly as possible. Admiral Horthy had just made his sudden and unexpected announcement suspending all deportations at midnight, but Eichmann had succeeded in shipping these Jews to Auschwitz just before the deadline.

Wallenberg arrived in Budapest on the following morning, July 9, a day too late, the day after Eichmann had completed his "dejewification" of the Hungarian provinces.

Eichmann and Wallenberg both believed that Horthy's suspension of the deportation was temporary. Wallenberg immediately set to work increasing the number of Jews under Swedish protection. Eichmann and his SS unit remained in Budapest, waiting until German pressure forced Horthy to capitulate. In the meantime, he devised ways to evade Horthy's order. He had lost the services of the Hungarian gendarmes but he still commanded 150 German soldiers, enough to carry out a small Jewish action on its own.

There were two thousand Jews in a Gestapo detention camp in the suburb of Kistarcsa. On July 14, Eichmann ordered his soldiers to pack half of them into trains and send them to Auschwitz without alerting the Hungarian authorities. His plan was foiled at the last minute when someone tipped off the Jewish Council. The Council called Horthy's chief of cabinet and Horthy ordered the police to stop the train. It was flagged down twenty-five miles from the capital, and the deportees were returned.

Two days later Eichmann tried again. This time he summoned the Council to an 8:00 A.M. meeting at his headquarters, kept them waiting for hours, and then had his aides engage them in a meaningless discussion as to whether allowing Jews to attend the cinema would ease their "fears." Meanwhile his soldiers occupied the Kistarcsa camp, disconnected its phones, and herded twelve hundred of its Jewish prisoners into trucks. At a nearby town they were transferred to freight cars. The train set off from

the frontier at top speed. When the Council was released at 7:00
P.M. it was too late; the train was almost across the border.

The last word from these unfortunate Jews was written on a
postcard that one man addressed to his wife and managed to
push out a crack in his freight car just before the train left Hungarian territory. "It is Wednesday afternoon," he wrote. "They have
packed us in and we are traveling. God be with you, my dear
family. God be with you. I embrace you and many kisses. Father."

After the transport reached Auschwitz, Eichmann's assistant,
Dieter Wisliceny, boasted to a member of the Council: "Did
you really think that Eichmann would allow that old fool Horthy
to frustrate his wishes?"

Throughout July, German pressure on Horthy to resume the
deportations increased. Eichmann was desperate to complete the
job he had begun in Austria six years before. Hitler intervened
personally and ordered Foreign Minister Ribbentrop to warn
Horthy that further delays in solving Hungary's Jewish problem
would not be tolerated.

Eichmann remained in Budapest, making plans for a lightning
action once Horthy submitted to the Führer's will. On July 25,
Dr. Veesenmayer, the Reich's supreme representative in Hungary,
reported to Germany: "It has been agreed with Eichmann that
when the renewal of the deportations of the Budapest Jews . . .
becomes possible, these should be carried out with the utmost
dispatch, so quickly that the Jews who come into question for
migration be deported before they have time for any formalities."

While Eichmann made plans to resume his deportations Wallenberg worked to ensure that if the trains started rolling north,
they would be empty, or nearly so. Within a day of arriving in
Budapest he began setting up a special humanitarian section
within the embassy whose sole function would be to place as
many Jews as possible out of Eichmann's reach.

Wallenberg believed that one way of protecting Budapest's
Jews, while at the same time relieving overcrowding in the Yellow
Star houses, was to place as many as possible in special "Swedish

houses" flying the Swedish flag and identified as under the protection of the Swedish Legation. This was why he had agreed to meet Eichmann at the Arizona. Eichmann controlled many of the houses recently confiscated from the Jews; Wallenberg wanted them back.

Throughout the Arizona meeting Wallenberg was cordial, if not overly polite. He did not mind drinking or exchanging pleasantries with Eichmann; he too saw the encounter as a chance to probe, to discover if Eichmann had a price. Before leaving Stockholm, Wallenberg had told a friend that if he thought it would save lives he "would bribe the devil himself."

The fact that Wallenberg had offered so little for the forty houses must have reassured Eichmann. Clearly he had come to Budapest without extensive financial support. Eichmann, on the other hand, was backed by the might of Nazi Germany and was fulfilling the will of the German people. Wallenberg represented a neutral government which, like the other neutrals and the Allies, had done little to impede the Final Solution.

After the Arizona meeting Eichmann appeared to dismiss Wallenberg as a minor irritant. If, however, he could have foreseen that their future meetings would not be as cordial and inconsequential as this one, and if he could have foreseen the circumstances under which these meetings would be held, he would not have waited until November before ordering Wallenberg killed.

2

August 1944

Through the windows lining one wall of the study of the Swedish minister, Ivan Danielsson, Wallenberg could see a panorama of Budapest: to his left, the hills, palaces, forests, and towers of the ancient city of Buda; directly in front of him and across the river, the rooftops, domes, steeps, and smokestacks of Pest. The Danube divided Buda and Pest; six bridges connected them. Snub-nosed barges chugged under the bridges and around the islands in the middle of the river. To the north was Margit Island and its parks, swimming pool, polo fields, and public baths; to the south, Csepel, an island dominated by the smokestacks of the Manfred Weiss Works, one of the largest steel factories in Europe. The Weiss family had recently signed it over to the SS in exchange for their freedom.

The Corso, a spacious promenade, ran along the Pest side of the river and was lined with acacia trees, palatial hotels, and outdoor cafés. When Wallenberg visited Budapest in 1943 the Corso had seemed untouched by the war. Well-dressed Jewish and Christian couples sat together sipping coffee in the cafés. Colored lights strung above the hotel terraces reflected into the Danube, and gypsy orchestras played in the bars. Now the hotels and cafés were open, but empty. The government had drafted the Christians into the army and Jews into labor battalions. The wealthier Christian women had fled the air raids, and Jews were forbidden to patronize "places of amusement."

North of the Corso were the graceful neo-Gothic spires and cupolas of the Hungarian parliament. In all of Europe, only Britain's legislature was older, its building larger. Inside the parliament, deputies had passed laws permitting Jewish citizens to be deported to Germany for "labor service." Wide tree-lined boulevards connected parliament and the riverfront to the hotels, cinemas, and shops of Pest's modern commercial district, and to its outlying suburbs and parks. In the distance the boulevards merged with roads running south and east across the plains to the Rumanian and Russian frontiers.

From Danielsson's study Wallenberg also had a splendid view of Buda's hills, Horthy's Royal Palace, and the government ministries. Nestled in one of these hills, out of sight of the Swedish Legation, was the Hotel Majestic, Eichmann's headquarters.

The Legation was situated midway up St. Gellert's Hill, at 775 feet the highest of Buda's hills. (Saint Gellert had been a Christian martyr, whom pagans had rolled down this hill in a barrel impregnated with spikes.) From this distance Budapest appeared to be the same tranquil city that Wallenberg remembered from earlier visits. If, however, he rose from one of the comfortable easy chairs grouped around Danielsson's fireplace, walked past the radio that continuously broadcast the latest news bulletins, and, standing next to the window, looked directly down into Gyopar Street, the illusion of tranquillity vanished.

Hundreds of Jews, most of them women and children and the very old, pushed, shoved, screamed, and fought for places in the ragged lines that, ten or twelve abreast, stretched down to the bottom of St. Gellert's Hill. Many had risked their lives to join these lines. They had ripped Yellow Stars off outergarments and violated the Jewish curfew to be at the Legation by dawn. The wealthier ones had hired Christian lawyers to secure good places in line.

A pair of policemen and Wallenberg's Jewish aides tried to maintain some order, but the crowd spilled into the Legation's garden, blocked the road, and surged toward a small door in a building around the corner on Minerva Street. The door led to the offices of Wallenberg's new humanitarian department, "Section C." Those nearest the door shoved and fought to squeeze through it. They believed, with good reason, that they were fighting for their lives.

Since March, Budapest had become a nightmare for the Jews. Their houses and apartments had been seized and allocated to Christians, and now as many as 125 of them were crammed into apartment houses in which no family, no matter how large, was permitted to occupy more than two rooms. Most families lived in one. Jewish shops and enterprises, bank accounts, and any possessions of value had been confiscated. Jews were forbidden from using public hospitals or applying for public relief, traveling outside of Budapest, or taking any but the last car of a trolley. They could not walk in parks, entertain visitors, have conversations in the street, or use air raid shelters. After the Allied air raids angry mobs often drove Jews from their homes and killed them.

The uniformed storm troopers of the Arrow Cross, the Hungarian fascist party, attacked Jewish houses at random and beat up Jews, usually the elderly, on the streets. Arrow Cross slogans calling for the elimination of Jews covered walls and fences throughout the city, and the Arrow Cross newspaper accused them of everything from signaling enemy bombers to spreading disease. "The capital is more than ever overrun by bugs," said one article, "and since the Jews have been moved together in Budapest, the biggest problem of the summer seems to be how to get rid of them. Nearly one hundred percent of the Jewish apartments vacated were found to be full of bugs, and this now presents a serious problem for the Christian public."

Few Hungarian Christians protected Jews from the Arrow Cross, and many appeared to approve of the harsh new anti-Semitic laws. Newspaper editorials praised the deportations of the provincial Jews: "To remove the Jews was necessary, not only because they were the blood-suckers of the Hungarian nation, but also because they reduced the Hungarian officials and peasants to the level of coolies. Their removal was further necessary, because they were an obstacle to our final victory, on which the fate of every Hungarian depends."

Now, in August, the Budapest Jews who had survived the earlier deportations—"their removal"—were fighting for places in line in front of the Swedish Legation because, as bad as conditions were, they feared they would soon become worse.

The Jews of Budapest had finally admitted to themselves what they had long suspected: that the deportation trains' last stop was not a work camp in Germany but an extermination camp in Poland. Why else had the Germans insisted on including infants, old people, and mental defectives in the earlier deportations from the provinces? The gendarmes had even grabbed terminally ill Jewish patients from their hospital beds. None were heard from again except for several thousand who sent cards postmarked "Waldsee." Each bore the same message: "I am working, I am fine." The cards, the Jews soon learned, came from Auschwitz.

Some of the provincial Jews had been deported by mistake. They were long-standing Christian converts or under the special protection of Admiral Horthy. When the Hungarian Foreign Ministry pressed the Germans to return these special Jews, the counselor of the German Legation replied that it was out of the question because "the persons handed over are so firmly embedded in German economic life that it is impossible to effect their removal. Furthermore, the technical problems presented by their re-transport would be well-nigh insurmountable."

Before March of 1944 the Jews of Hungary believed that what had happened to the Polish Jews could not happen to them.

They were too well integrated into the Hungarian nation and Hungary was too civilized. When the provincial Jews were deported, the Jews of Budapest still believed that they were safe in the cosmopolitan, more civilized capital.

Now, in the middle of August, they knew they were not. The brutal deportations from the suburbs on July 8 and the Kistarcsa episode convinced them that they were next. The last six weeks had been a reprieve, not a pardon. The regent had announced that he was suspending, not canceling, the deportations, and in July one government minister proclaimed, "The total ridding of Hungary from the Jews is no longer a programme, it is a concluded fact. The Final Solution is only a question of time."

The time appeared at hand. On August 18, SS units paraded through Budapest with armored cars, guns, and tanks: a warning to the regent to cooperate and to the Jews that resistance was pointless.

By the twentieth of August every Jew in Budapest had heard the rumors that the brick factory in the suburb of Békásmegyer was being prepared as a staging area for the transports and that deportations would resume before the end of the month. The rumors were true. The Sztójay government had capitulated to Eichmann and had given him permission to resume his roundups on August 25. Non-Hungarian Jews residing in the capital would go first.

Jews packed their bags and placed them by the front door. At night they slept fully clothed; during the day they searched desperately for ways to escape. Some besieged Christian churches and became converts, even though recently issued baptismal certificates had not protected the provincial Jews. Others fled into the countryside or to Rumania; from there they hoped to make their way to Palestine. Without the proper travel papers or ration cards they risked starvation or arrest at the train stations.

Those with money tried to bribe the Gestapo or Hungarian officials for exit visas. Some wealthy notables escaped in this fashion; others were double-crossed and found that they had paid for their passage to Auschwitz. Some were lucky to have Christian friends willing to hide them. About a thousand Jews of great achievement—writers, artists, inventors, and musicians—had special exemptions signed by Admiral Horthy. For most, however, the best escape route began at the doors of one of the neutral legations.

Everyone in the crowd that Wallenberg could see fighting to get through the door of the Swedish Legation's Minerva Street annex wanted the same thing: a Swedish protective pass.

The passes looked official. They were printed on heavy blue and yellow paper, stamped with the distinctive Swedish crowns, and carried the bearer's picture in the upper right-hand corner. To the left of the picture was a box with the type of information found on most traditional passports: name, residence, date and place of birth, height, and hair and eye color. Below the picture and personal data was a declaration in Hungarian and German signed by Danielsson, the Swedish minister. It said:

> *The Royal Swedish Legation in Budapest confirms that the above-mentioned person will travel to Sweden in the course of repatriation as authorized by the Royal Swedish Ministry of Foreign Affairs. The name of the person in question is covered by a collective passport. Until his departure the above-mentioned person and his home are to be regarded as protected by the Royal Swedish Legation in Budapest. The validity of this document expires two weeks after arrival in Sweden. The journey to Sweden can only be undertaken on a collective passport, which is the only one to be furnished with a visa.*

Although most passes were signed by Danielsson, almost everyone in Budapest—the Jews, the Hungarian gendarmes, the SS, and Eichmann's Sondereinsatzkommando—knew that the real power behind the passes was Raoul Wallenberg.

On the day of his arrival in Budapest, Wallenberg had gone

to the offices of the Jewish Council and presented his letter of introduction from Rabbi Ehrenpreis to the chairman, Samu Stern, and the vice-chairman, Károly Wilhelm. One of the other members of the Council, Ernö Petö, was, by coincidence, the father of one of Wallenberg's boyhood friends. Even though the Council was working day and night to frustrate any resumption of the deportations, fulfill the government's demand for Jewish laborers, and provide food and medical care, Stern and Wilhelm promised to do everything possible to assist Wallenberg. Their briefing on the situation of the Budapest Jews planted the seed for the idea of issuing special Swedish protective passes. In the coming months the Council was also to provide Wallenberg with invaluable help in obtaining funds, houses, cars, and volunteer workers to issue his protective passes.

The day after meeting with the Council, while meeting with other Swedish diplomats posted to the Legation, Wallenberg first voiced the idea of distributing a protective pass. Per Anger, a young career diplomat, had showed him the provisional passport which the Legation had already issued to seven hundred Jews with close family and business ties to Sweden. This was a standard replacement passport which Swedish diplomatic missions throughout the world gave to Swedish citizens who had lost their original passports. Anger and Danielsson had already stretched standard diplomatic procedure by issuing seven hundred of these passports to Hungarian Jews.

"I think I have an idea for a new, and perhaps more effective, document," Wallenberg had told Anger and Danielsson at their first meeting. He went on to suggest a document he called a "protective pass" that would state that Sweden would admit the bearer once Hungary and Germany had made the necessary transit and exit permits available. In the meantime, the bearer and his property would be under the protection of the Swedish Legation. Since this pass would promise that the Jewish bearer would soon be leaving for Sweden, it would satisfy the Hungarian fascists. Since it would only be valid for a single and specific voyage to Sweden, it would not require the paperwork necessary to issue a duplicate Swedish passport.

As soon as Danielsson approved his plan, Wallenberg scheduled meetings with officials in the Hungarian Foreign and Interior ministries. He realized that his passes had no standing in international law. If anything, they were illegal. They violated Hungary's sovereignty by withdrawing its citizens from the "protection" of its laws. The Jews that Wallenberg planned to place under Swedish protection were not prisoners of war or Swedish citizens; they were not even wounded or ill. The passes would be legal fiction, an illusion. Throughout July and August he labored to make everyone—Jews, Hungarians, and Germans—believe in this illusion.

On August 1 he met with Admiral Horthy, explained the passes, and urged him to make his temporary suspension of the deportations permanent. Horthy was so impressed by Wallenberg's arguments that he asked him to submit a report describing the passes and detailing his suggestions and arguments for a more lenient approach to Hungary's "Jewish problem." He asked that the report be anonymously authored so that he could pass it on to the cabinet for consideration. Wallenberg's finished report went far beyond what Horthy had requested. It demanded that Christian clergymen be given more freedom to intervene on behalf of Jewish converts, that all holders of the Swedish protective passes be exempted from wearing the Star of David, and that Eichmann's SS unit be expelled.

On August 3, Wallenberg met with Lieutenant-Colonel Ferenczy, the chief of the Hungarian gendarmes and the man who had helped Eichmann arrange the deportation of the provincial Jews. At the end of their conversation Ferenczy said, "I welcome these passes and am pleased that these Jews will soon be departing for Sweden. In the meantime they can live in special houses under Swedish protection."

During his meetings with Ferenczy and Horthy and with countless other Hungarian policemen, soldiers, and bureaucrats, Wallenberg exploited their fears that they would be tried as war criminals. He threatened them with trials and pretended that he had the authority to guarantee exemptions. He acted as if the war was over and he was the victors' first Hungarian representative. He masterfully exploited the political uncertainty, the double and triple loyalties of most Hungarian officials during a summer when the Allied armies were scoring rapid victories. He was so confident and energetic, his manner so intimidating, that when he first strode into the offices of the Jewish Council, its members took him to be a senior Gestapo officer.

By the middle of August, Wallenberg had succeeded in transforming his protective passes into respected legal documents. The Hungarian Ministry of the Interior gave him permission to distribute forty-five hundred passes on condition that the holders renounce their Hungarian citizenship, acquiring the status of Swedish citizens temporarily visiting Budapest, and report every week to the government agency in charge of supervising resident aliens.

Wallenberg also persuaded the Germans to honor the passes. They had a reflexive respect for any official-looking document, and the passes seemed a cheap way of satisfying the consciences of neutral diplomats and squeamish Hungarian officials.

To distribute the passes Wallenberg created his own organization within the Swedish Legation, Section C. Within less than a month he hired a Jewish staff of forty and divided it into sections responsible for reception, registration, archives, correspondence, housing, and transport. He expanded his section into houses bordering the Legation, procured a fleet of automobiles from wealthy Jews anxious to have them under Swedish protection, and organized an efficient and equitable system for issuing the passes. He borrowed chairs, purchased scarce desks and file cabinets, had three telephone lines installed and thousands of application forms printed at a time when Allied bomb attacks were disrupting Budapest's normal commercial life. Through donations and bribery he accumulated special "Swedish houses" into which he relocated his aides and some of the Jews holding his passes.

Wallenberg paid for most of his extensive rescue operation with money entrusted to him by wealthy Jews and Jewish organizations in Budapest. After the war the American Joint Distribution Committee deposited funds in Swiss banks to compensate some of these Jews. Wallenberg himself used very little of the $100,000 that the War Refugee Board placed in his account at Stockholm's Enskilda Bank. After the war, approximately half of this money was returned to the United States.

In less than a month Wallenberg had created from scratch a thriving, efficient enterprise. One of his Jewish aides who had previously worked for another section of the Swedish Legation marveled that "within a week, Section C was so expertly run that it appeared to have been in place for at least a year." Wallenberg was finally using his talents for negotiation and organization, his abilities to persuade and lead that had been so obvious to his family and closest friends. Finally, he had the opportunity that the wealthier Wallenbergs had denied him, the opportunity to manage an important enterprise and prove himself worthy of the family name.

After being in Budapest a month he wrote his mother that "I have just spent perhaps the most interesting three or four weeks of my life. Everywhere you see tragedies of the greatest proportions. But the days and nights are so full of work that one seldom has time to react. I have set up a large office with forty émployees. We rented houses on either side of the Legation and the organization grows every day."

His new "organization" was similar in form but vastly different in purpose from the usual Wallenberg enterprise. Instead of tendering loans, financing factories, or underwriting insurance, it offered, for free, the chance to live. Deciding who should have this chance proved more complicated and fraught with moral dilemmas than selling "Quick Corks" or crates of Portuguese sardines. There were approximately 175,000 Jews in Budapest, and Wallenberg had permission to save only 4,500.

He did everything to make this heartbreaking allocation fair and to magnify the effect of the forty-five hundred passes. He rationed each family to a single pass and hoped the authorities would be reluctant to deport the relatives of a new "Swedish citizen." He gave each pass a random number to make it difficult for the police to detect counterfeit or excess passes. He insisted that the passes be allocated on a first-come-first-served basis. No one could move a friend or relative to the top of the pile of applications. He dismissed two aides he suspected of accepting bribes to process applications out of order and reported to the Swedish Foreign Ministry: "It's a problem to distribute the remainders [of the passes] in a fair and just manner between those who still have not received a pass. Big monetary offers have been made for these. There are individuals not employed by the department who have accepted big fees to attempt to get applications, and passes. They claim to be in contact with members of my staff. They have been arrested."

Nevertheless, the long lines outside the Legation were so heartbreaking that he could not resist breaking his own rules. At the end of one day he emerged from his Minerva Street office for a breath of air to find a woman collapsed against the slats of the Legation fence sobbing. She held an infant in one arm; a small boy stood next to her silently. As Wallenberg comforted her she explained that the line was so long she was afraid she would not get to the front before the curfew. She had been coming every day for a week. Wallenberg told her to wait. Fifteen minutes later he returned and handed her a pass.

By the middle of August, more than twenty thousand Jews had applied for Swedish protective passes. Judging each case individually was impossible. Wallenberg was forced to formulate rules for allocating his lifesaving documents. On August 18 he assembled his staff and told them that passes should be issued first to Jews who could prove close family relations in Sweden or business connections of many years' standing. The family relations had to be at least at the level of first cousins. The applicants citing a business connection had to be prominent within the various companies, and the volume of business with Sweden had to have reached a specified average level over the last five years. Receipts and tax forms had to be submitted to prove the volume of business. Personal letters with Swedish envelopes and postmarks were necessary to prove the family connections.

He felt he had no choice but to enforce these rules. If he gave a Swedish pass to every Jew in Budapest, the passes would be worthless. If he tried to save everyone, no one would be saved. He *had* to restrict himself to the forty-five hundred passes authorized by the Hungarian government; to number them and list their owners in a registry at the Legation; and to issue them in a careful, bureaucratic manner.

As a result of these restrictions, many of the people who received Swedish passes during the summer and early autumn of 1944 tended to belong to Budapest's wealthiest and most prominent Jewish families, those most likely to have friends abroad or a large volume of commercial transactions with Sweden. Many of those whom Wallenberg chose to be his closest aides were also members of this elite. Hugo Wohl, for example, one of his most trusted assistants, had been the director of the huge Orion Radio Company. Men like Wohl had the training and experience necessary to administer the huge relief organization he was creating.

Budapest was not yet the exciting adventure that Wallenberg had anticipated. He was busy, his work was important—but it was almost as if he was working in one of his family's banks, sitting "behind a desk all day saying no to people."

Although Wallenberg was restricted as to the number of passes *he* could issue, his example and his energy inspired the other neutral legations to issue their own protective passes. His successful negotiations with German and Hungarian officials over the Swedish passes made these other passes valuable. The authorities could not very well honor the Swedish and not the Spanish, Portuguese, International Red Cross, and Swiss protective passes.

The distribution of the Swiss passes was directed by Miklós

Krausz, a Hungarian Jew who held the position of executive secretary of the Palestine Office, the Hungarian organization charged with promoting and coordinating immigration to Palestine. After the Nazi coup Krausz and his wife took refuge in the Swiss Legation. There he formed a close friendship with the Swiss consul, Charles Lutz, while also cultivating useful relationships with those Hungarian officials and politicians who remained secret anti-Nazis.

Because of his excellent contacts within the Swiss Legation, Krausz on June 19 had succeeded in sending detailed eyewitness accounts of the extermination process at Auschwitz to Switzerland. These accounts, known as the "Auschwitz Protocols," had been smuggled out of the camp by five escapees. Their worldwide dissemination led to the neutral and Allied protests that helped to persuade Horthy to suspend deportations.

After the deportations had been halted, Krausz, through his government contacts, persuaded the Sztójay regime to agree that seventy-eight hundred Jews should receive passes entitling them to emigrate to Palestine at a future date. With the assistance of Lutz, Krausz set up an office at 29 Vadusz Street to issue these passes. This office building was officially known as the "Swiss Legation Representative of Foreign Issues"; unofficially, since its previous owner had been a well-known glass merchant, it was called the "Glass House."

Krausz staffed the Glass House with hundreds of young Zionist pioneers who had evaded the Nazi labor drafts and deportations. Like Wallenberg's Jewish aides, they were issued papers stating that they were employed by a neutral legation and were therefore under its protection. They were exempted from wearing the Yellow Star and could move freely throughout Budapest. Many of the pioneers used these privileges to further their extensive underground operations. Operating out of the protected Glass House, they rescued colleagues from the Gestapo prisons, organized escape routes, and produced thousands of counterfeit Aryan papers, official German identity cards, and protective passes. Although

Krausz came to fear that their operations would endanger the Swiss passes, he nevertheless allowed them to remain in the Glass House, where they could mount their rescue operations under Swiss protection.

Ottó Komoly, president of the Hungarian Zionist Organization, was another important Wallenberg ally. Komoly had noted that the Allied victories had weakened Hungary's support for the German war effort, and throughout the summer he had exploited the fears of important Hungarian officials in order to persuade them to resist a resumption of the deportations. He was also closely allied with the International Red Cross and had prompted it to set up a special department, "Department A," which placed Jewish children in Red Cross houses and therefore protected them from deportation. By late autumn almost six thousand children lived in these houses, which also became, like Krausz's Glass House, bases for underground operations of the young Zionist pioneers.

Wallenberg was in frequent communication with Komoly and Krausz, particularly with Krausz. Almost every day the two men conferred, coordinated their rescue operations, and shared strategy and secrets.

The other neutral powers with representatives in Budapest— Spain, Portugal, El Salvador, and the Vatican—also issued protective passes similar to Wallenberg's. They, however, usually placed even greater restrictions on who could receive their passes. The Spanish issued several hundred to the descendants of Jews driven from Spain in the sixteenth century who had preserved their Spanish language and customs. The papal nuncio extended safe-conducts to a handful of Roman Catholic Jews, and the Portuguese representative and the honorary consul of El Salvador also had modest protective programs. Dr. Waldemar Langlet, the representative of the Swedish Red Cross, distributed his own protective papers, but since these did not even have the backing of a sovereign government they were theoretically valueless. The Swedish passes, however, were the most popular and proved the most likely to be honored by the government. They had a picture, weighed more, appeared to be a more substantial document, and were backed by Wallenberg's constant and energetic lobbying.

Wallenberg's example also inspired the Jews who met him to resist regulations whose only purpose was to make their impoverishment and extermination more efficient. In his earliest reports to Iver Olsen he had charged that the Jews of Budapest were afflicted by a "total lack of courage," and noted, "The Jews are so terrified that they are simply hiding in their own houses." As the summer wore on he learned the reasons for their apparent "lack of courage" and became more sympathetic.

The curfews and travel laws isolated Jews in houses and neighborhoods for most of the day, making it difficult for them to organize or exchange information. The majority of those most likely to resist, the able-bodied men between the ages of fourteen and sixty, had been drafted into labor battalions and sent to the front. It appeared to the Jews who remained that everyone in Hungary—the Germans who had instigated the earlier deportations, the Hungarian fascists who had enthusiastically carried them out, and the Hungarian Christians who had inherited Jewish property—wanted them dead. Everyone treated these surviving Jews as if they were less than human, and soon—isolated, terrified, stripped of their possessions, and awaiting deportation—they began to believe that they were.

In August, Wallenberg reported to Sweden that "it is vital to shock the Jews out of their apathetic state, to rid them of their feeling that everyone has either forgotten or abandoned them."

At first he was most successful inspiring and shocking "out of their apathetic state" the Jews who worked in his humanitarian section. According to one, Edith Wohl:

He gave us courage. He was so courageous that he made the rest of us ashamed to be afraid. Because of him we all became more optimistic.

He also shocked us by his behavior. Here he was, an Aryan who didn't believe that Jews were something vile and despicable. He even socialized with us as if we were normal people. This was amazing.

After a while it became impossible for us to consider him to be a normal human being. We didn't ask ourselves the normal objective questions about his background. In fact, we didn't even know that he was a member of the famous Wallenberg family. Instead we came to see him as superhuman; someone who had come to Budapest to save us, a Messiah.

One of his Jewish secretaries, Zsuzsi Somogyi, thought he was "the greatest personality I had ever met." He was "a born leader who combined physical stamina with a tremendous inner spiritual strength."

Not everyone in the Swedish Legation was as uncritical. Some Jews working as clerks and drivers in other sections of the Legation who had already received the earlier provisional passports rebuked Wallenberg for handing out too many protective passes. They argued that he risked provoking the Nazis into disregarding all the Swedish documents and urged him to devote his time to arranging emigration to Sweden for those already holding passes. Wallenberg ignored their advice and criticized them for their selfishness.

Some of Wallenberg's Swedish colleagues criticized him for moving too rapidly. Iver Olsen reported to the War Refugee Board in Washington, "I am of the impression that the Swedish Foreign Ministry are somewhat disturbed over Wallenberg's activities in Budapest, and they probably feel that he 'jumped in with too big a splash.' I am sure they would prefer he had dealt with the Jewish problem along traditional diplomatic lines, which would mean not helping the Jews."

Lars Berg was the young attaché at the Legation in charge of providing protection for citizens of foreign countries at war with Hungary who were trapped in Budapest. He admired Wallenberg for his "brilliance, powers of persuasion and clarity of mind," but thought he was also too reckless. He issued too many protective passes too rapidly and thereby endangered Swedish interests and bona fide Swedish citizens. Even Swedish diplomatic passports might become worthless if Wallenberg continued unchecked.

Berg pointed out to Wallenberg that the Legation had the responsibility of protecting hundreds of Swedes and foreign nationals. "How can we effectively give this protection and how can we protect Swedish interests if every other person in Budapest is carrying Swedish papers?" he wondered.

Berg was also alarmed that some of the Swedish-protected Jews were flaunting their passes in the streets and claiming they were "Swedish." He worried what would happen when the Russian Army captured Budapest. "How will they react," he asked Wallenberg, "when they march into Budapest and find all the streets decorated with Swedish flags? How can we prove which are the genuine Swedish interests? How can we even protect the Legation itself and our own lives?"

On most occasions Wallenberg overcame his colleagues' objections easily. He appeared at the daily meetings in Danielsson's study—the same study that overlooked the lines of Jews—with his proposals for increasing the protective functions of the Legation already composed in a final draft. He argued passionately that "when there is suffering without limits, there can be no limits to the methods one should use to alleviate it." He filibustered until, exhausted by the discussion and wanting to move on to more pressing business, the other Swedes unanimously approved his proposals. Berg admitted that he was "overcome by Wallenberg's willpower and intelligence."

When all else failed, Wallenberg could remind the other diplomats of the nine-point memorandum he had negotiated with the Swedish Foreign Ministry before leaving Stockholm. Much of this unconventional agreement was incompatible with normal Swedish diplomatic practice and with Sweden's position as a neutral power. It stipulated, for example, that "the government gives Wallenberg a free hand in rescuing victims by any means he deems necessary, bribery included."

It further stipulated:

> *Wallenberg [can] contact whomever he wants in Budapest, including persons who oppose either the Germans or the Hungarian regime. A list of persons who might help him in this regard will be provided to him by the British and American embassies in Stockholm.*
>
> *If the necessity of personal consultation with Sweden arises then Wallenberg can travel home without going through the usual lengthy procedures.*
>
> *If American monetary resources prove inadequate, then a propaganda campaign can be initiated within the framework of accepted journalistic practices for raising the necessary funds.*
>
> *Wallenberg can send his own dispatches and reports by official diplomatic courier.*
>
> *Wallenberg can officially ask for an audience to see Horthy in order to obtain his intervention on behalf of the victims of persecution.*
>
> *Wallenberg is authorized on request to give asylum at the Legation to those persecuted victims who hold the proper Swedish documents.*

None of the disputes between Wallenberg and the other diplomats were acrimonious or protracted. Berg admitted that their resistance to Wallenberg's passes "was weakened by the fact that we all knew of Wallenberg's accomplishments; and by the fact that we knew how many people he was saving every day who might otherwise have been doomed to death."

By the middle of August it appeared that Jews without protective passes were indeed doomed to deportation and death. The Sztójay government agreed to resume deporting Jews to Germany on August 25 and announced plans to separate protected Jews from the others by moving them into special Yellow Star houses on Pozsonyi Road.

Meanwhile, Eichmann threatened that he "would use the SS in order to carry out the deportations" if the Hungarian gendarmes refused to do the job. The Jewish Council learned that he had given the chief of the gendarmes, Lieutenant-Colonel Ferenczy, a map in which all areas from which Jews were to be deported had been underlined in red. Jews noticed more German lorries in Budapest and, as if to give weight to Eichmann's threat, German Army and SS units paraded through the city. The regent's son, Miklós Horthy, Jr., told a member of the Jewish Council that Budapest was totally unprotected by Hungarian troops and that Eichmann appeared to have a free hand. As the August 24 deadline approached, the nonprotected Jewish masses panicked and besieged the neutral legations in even greater numbers.

Wallenberg increased the hours of the Minerva Street office and increased his staff to a hundred employees. "We have so much to do," he wrote his mother, "that I've been working almost continuously day and night."

He spent his days pleading with Hungarian officials to withstand Eichmann's demands and threatening them with war crimes trials if they refused. At night he returned to Section C and helped his staff process protective pass applications before collapsing for a few hours' sleep on the floor. He was so busy that he forgot, until the last minute, his thirty-second birthday. When his staff found out, they scoured Budapest for presents. In the afternoon he returned to his office to find that his aides had heaped his desk with flowers, a calendar, a writing portfolio, and a bottle of champagne.

Moments after the short celebration he returned to work. He was obsessed by the knowledge that the more passes he issued, the fewer Jews would be shoved into Eichmann's freight cars. If he worked hard, people lived; if he was lazy, they died.

Since arriving in Budapest he had learned that every day in

June, days which he had spent negotiating over the conditions of this employment with the Swedish Foreign Ministry, as many as twelve thousand Hungarian Jews had been gassed at Auschwitz. Among them had been Kalman Lauer's relatives. "Please be so good as to inform Dr. Lauer and his wife," he was forced to write to his mother a week after arriving in Budapest, "that I have unfortunately found out that his parents-in-law and also a small child belonging to his family are already dead. That is to say that they have been transported abroad where they will not live for very long."

Wallenberg had learned in six weeks what the Allies had ignored for six years: that in the mathematics of the Final Solution, there was a direct, undeniable, and staggering relationship between time and lives.

On August 21, four days before the scheduled resumption of deportations, the representatives of the neutral legations met at the urging of Wallenberg and the Budapest Jewish Council and drafted a note of protest to the Hungarian government. The Swedish minister, Danielsson, delivered the note in person to the deputy prime minister, Reményi-Schneller, who passed it on to Admiral Horthy. It was the strongest official protest yet made by the neutrals:

> The undersigned representatives of the neutral powers accredited in Budapest have learned with painful surprise that the deportation of all the Jews of Hungary is to be started soon. We also know, and from an absolutely reliable source, what deportation means in most cases, even when it is masked as labor service abroad. . . .
>
> The representatives of the neutral powers herewith request the Hungarian government to forbid these cruelties which ought never to have started. They hope that Hungary will return to its humane and chivalrous traditions, which, until now, have guaranteed its place among civilized nations.

Two days after receiving this note Horthy learned that Rumania, Hungary's southern neighbor and a member of the Axis, had suddenly and unexpectedly surrendered to the Russians and declared war on Hungary and Germany. The Rumanian defection left Hungary's southern border open to the advancing Russian Army and convinced Horthy and other influential Hungarian politicians that the war was lost. They decided to abandon Germany and make a quick peace with the Allies. Horthy's first step was to cancel the roundup and deportation of Budapest's Jews. He had been impressed by the fervor of the neutrals' protests and by the earlier threats of retribution from the Allies.

Many other Hungarians also suddenly changed their minds about the Jews. Lieutenant-Colonel Ferenczy now confided to the Jewish Council that he had been a secret friend of the Jews (even while deporting them) and that he was opposed to further transports. On the evening of August 23, it was Ferenczy himself whom Horthy sent to inform Eichmann of his decision not to resume deportations.

"I have received orders that the Hungarian government will not agree to the deportations," Ferenczy told Eichmann. "If need be the government is prepared to back up its decisions with armed force."

Eichmann flew into a rage, swearing at Ferenczy and threatening him with arrest and torture. When he failed to intimidate him, he cabled Berlin for instructions. On August 24, Himmler replied that further deportations from Hungary were forbidden because of the Rumanian situation. The Führer had decided it was more important to keep Hungary in the Axis and protect Germany's southern flank than to allow Eichmann to complete the Final Solution.

At the end of August, Horthy replaced the pro-Nazi Sztójay regime with one headed by the more moderate General Géza Lakatos. Most of the officials who had served as virtual Nazi agents since the March coup were replaced by neutral or anti-Nazi ministers. The Lakatos government publicly announced that it would continue the fight against the Soviet Union. Privately, however, Horthy had ordered Lakatos to restore Hungarian sovereignty and "liquidate the war in an honorable fashion and put an end to the inhuman, foolish, cruel persecution of the Jews."

Eichmann was so shocked by these developments that on August 24 he asked Berlin to recall his SS unit to Germany because "they had become superfluous." On the same day Horthy also demanded that the German plenipotentiary, Edmund Veesenmayer, withdraw Eichmann's troops. Wallenberg had urged Horthy to make this move during their meeting on August 1.

Eichmann left Budapest but remained in Hungary. He gave his officers home leave, but most chose to stay in the Hungarian countryside as "observers." The Master himself spent most of the next forty-five days in the castle of Velem near the Austrian border as the guest of his former collaborator, the former minister of Jewish affairs, László Endre.

During his stay in Velem, Eichmann attempted unsuccessfully to persuade Himmler to change his mind. Himmler tried to pacify him with the award of an Iron Cross, second class. Eichmann refused to capitulate. He stayed on in Hungary, waiting for another chance to make the Final Solution final.

He did not wait long. Late in September the Reich Security Office in Berlin advised the members of Eichmann's "dissolved" SS unit to remain in Hungary for another two weeks, "in anticipation of a political change."

3

September 1–October 15, 1944

When he was certain no one had followed him, Wallenberg ducked off Veresmarty Square and into Gerbaud's coffeehouse. He parted the red velvet curtains hanging over the doorway and studied the main room. Waiters in black tie balanced pots of coffee on silver trays; stout blond women in starched aprons rolled pastry carts of strudels, poppy seed buns, and cream cakes between tables. Until several months ago, Budapest's Christian aristocracy and Jewish merchant class had jammed these tables at midmorning to conclude deals, make plans for the evening, and enjoy the tastes and aromas of coffee and cinnamon. This morning many of the tables were empty, and the odor of cheap tobacco overpowered the room.

When Wallenberg was satisfied that no one had noted his arrival, he slipped past the racks of newspapers, past the huge coffee urns, and pushed through some curtains into a small, wood-paneled room at the rear of the café. A thin man in his late twenties sat alone in a booth smoking.

Boris Teicholz was a Polish Jew who had once managed a successful import-export firm. He had entered Hungary in 1942 when the Jewish partisans he commanded on the Polish-Hungarian border were betrayed by anti-Semitic Polish underground fighters. He was captured, brought to Budapest, and then escaped to form an underground group with the code name of "Glick." He now commanded three hundred Jewish partisans. His soldiers smuggled Jews into Rumania, built secret bunkers in which Jews could survive a final fascist pogrom, and stole and forged baptismal certificates, Hungarian and German passports, and neutral protective passes. Teicholz preferred counterfeiting Swedish passes because, he said, "The value of the passes depended on how much the Hungarian and Germans respected the neutral countries and their local diplomats. Since Wallenberg was so respected and persuasive his passes were worth the most."

To distribute the counterfeit passes Teicholz dressed his blond Jewish fighters in the green uniforms of the Arrow Cross, the Hungarian fascist party. These bogus storm troopers then burst into the Jewish soup kitchens and raced up and down the rough wooden tables thrusting passes into the hands of every diner. They gave the passes to anyone who wanted them, to Jews who had never done business with Sweden, to poor Jews who had never traveled outside Budapest, and to uneducated Jews who did not know where Stockholm was. They redressed the basic injustice of the protective passes.

Wallenberg secretly approved of Teicholz's operation. He would have been the first to admit that his passes were undemocratic. Like most of the special exemptions that enabled Jews to escape the Holocaust, they favored wealthy, educated Jews over those too poor to have "significant business connections with Sweden" or "close members of the immediate family living in Sweden." There seemed no way to escape this dilemma. The wealthy, well-connected Jews could hardly be blamed for trying to save themselves and their families, and Wallenberg could not accept the idea that it was better to save no one since to save a few was "undemocratic."

Wallenberg knew that under current conditions it was impossible to increase the number of legitimate passes. His colleagues in the Legation were already complaining that too many passes had been issued too rapidly. The Hungarian officials insisted that he issue no more than forty-five hundred and that these go only to Jews with provable Swedish connections. The bogus passes enabled poorer Jews to gain protection and expanded his program. Nevertheless, he wanted to persuade those who printed and distributed them to exercise some restraint; otherwise the entire system might collapse. This was why he had persuaded his friends on the Jewish Council to arrange this meeting with Teicholz.

Neither man wanted to be seen with the other. Teicholz believed that the Gestapo shadowed Wallenberg and routinely investigated and interrogated all his contacts. Wallenberg worried that the Hungarians would finally have a pretext for expelling him if he was observed with Teicholz. To avoid being compromised they had met earlier that morning on a prearranged street corner and agreed to hold their conversation in Gerbaud's back room.

Despite these precautions Wallenberg was nervous. He gulped his coffee and kept glancing at the curtains separating them from the rest of the restaurant. Both men wanted to keep their conversation as brief as possible.

"I know you're counterfeiting," Wallenberg said.

"Yes," Teicholz admitted. He waited for an order to stop, perhaps a threat.

"I don't care," Wallenberg said finally.

"What?"

"I said I don't care. If you swear to me you're not selling the passes, I'll try to cover you. I'll also talk to Lutz [the Swiss consul] and the nuncio [the papal representative] and persuade them not to complain about your activities."

"You don't have to worry about us selling them," Teicholz said. "We give them free to anyone who wants one."

"All right, I believe you. If the police call to check on counterfeits, I'll try to confuse them; only don't print so many at one time or you'll overwhelm us."

Teicholz agreed. As soon as he left Gerbaud's he told his lieutenants to print fifteen thousand Swiss passes.

By the middle of September it appeared to Wallenberg that soon every Jew in Budapest would carry some kind of real or counterfeit protective document. The threat of deportation had receded and his mission seemed to be almost over.

At the beginning of the month the Germans had reluctantly signed an agreement with the Lakatos government stipulating that no Jews could be transported out of the country and that complete control over Jewish affairs was to be returned to the Hungarian government. In return for these concessions, Lakatos agreed to transfer the remaining Budapest Jews to camps in the provinces. However, these camps would first have to be inspected by a representative of the International Red Cross and certified as being "fit for accommodations at European standards."

Jewish leaders such as Ottó Komoly and neutral diplomats, Wallenberg included, protested vehemently against sending the Jews to rural camps. They pointed out that Eichmann and most of his aides were still in the Hungarian provinces and might spirit the Jews across the frontier as they had in the case of Kistarcsa. They also feared that the Luftwaffe might bomb the camps with unmarked planes, as had happened in Poland, or that a vengeful German Army might massacre these Jews as it retreated from Hungary.

Admiral Horthy finally reassured the Jewish Council that he would frustrate any attempt to send Budapest's Jews into the countryside. Meanwhile, representatives of the Red Cross, after traveling throughout the provinces, conveniently announced that they could not find a single site for a camp that met "European standards."

Throughout September the Lakatos government continued its clandestine attempts to negotiate an armistice with the Allies. Horthy insisted that the armistice be an "honorable one" and therefore tried to force the Germans into giving him an honorable pretext for withdrawing from the war. He demanded that Germany transfer five divisions from the western front to the Hungarian-Rumanian border. He expected them to refuse and give him the pretext he was seeking. To his surprise, the Germans sent the divisions to Hungary but quartered them in the suburbs of Budapest. The Germans had learned from the Hungary's pro-Nazi minister of finance, Reményi-Schneller, that Horthy planned to betray them.

At the end of September, Horthy sent special envoys to Moscow to settle the details of Hungary's surrender. Finally, at the beginning of October, with the Russian Army only fifty miles south of Budapest, he accepted the Russian terms and agreed to withdraw from the war on October 18. He planned to rely on loyal Hungarian military units stationed near Budapest and the forces of the growing Christian and Jewish resistance movements to foil the German-inspired coup he expected to follow his announcement. As added protection he decided to arm the Jewish labor battalions.

Throughout the first week of October, Germany's intention to use force to keep Hungary in the war became obvious. Ferenc Szálasi, a fanatical anti-Semitic Hungarian politician who had led the recently outlawed Arrow Cross party, took up residence in Gestapo headquarters and traveled everywhere with a squad of SS soldiers. At the same time the Germans openly trained and armed Szálasi's young Arrow Cross storm troopers. On the morning of October 10 the Germans took their first overt step to foil Horthy's plan by kidnapping General Szilárd Bakay, commander of the Hungarian Army Corps stationed in Budapest. Afraid that the Germans planned to stage their coup before he could act, Horthy decided to accelerate the timetable and announce his armistice three days earlier, on October 15.

Like almost everyone in Budapest, Wallenberg knew that Horthy was negotiating an armistice, and like everyone, he believed that if he failed, the Russians would capture the city by November. It seemed to him that for the Jews, the worst was over. He had recently succeeded in persuading the Lakatos government to reopen the synagogues, release Jewish detainees from Gestapo prisons, and permit Jews to be outdoors between 8:00 A.M. and 8:00 P.M. There seemed to be nothing more he could do.

On September 12 he sent the Swedish Foreign Ministry a report entitled "The Gradual Phasing Out of the Jewish Department." It said, ". . . because of the prevailing political situation it is further planned that all the reception of individuals and applications [for protective passes] will stop on the seventeenth of September and that the staff will be let go in stages. However, the distribution of the passes will continue because of the danger of a sudden pogrom when the Germans retreat from Budapest."

Several days after he filed this report, an event occurred which confirmed his fears of a vicious last-minute pogrom. In retaliation for an Allied bombing raid in which Germans were killed, the SS beat and tortured the Jewish inhabitants of two Yellow Star houses. "The Germans have threatened to take the matter of the Jews into their own hands," he reported afterward. "So far the Hungarians have sabotaged the German plan to remove the Jews to the provinces . . . but the SS battalions are still here."

The Jews also worried about a last-minute pogrom and continued to besiege Section C, causing Wallenberg to postpone his plans to phase out this department. "The numbers of rescue applications cannot be described," he reported on September 20, "and eight thousand applications have still not been examined." To process these applications he increased his staff to 250, and placed them on day and night shifts. He moved the administrative section across the Danube to a ten-room house in Pest on Tigris Street.

At the end of the month he could claim that "the situation has improved since the last report since five hundred Jews have been released from internment camps in Kistarcsa and Budapest." Nevertheless, he continued to issue passes in the hope that they would protect the Jews from a sudden pogrom. He was encouraged in this hope by the chancellor of the German Legation, who, he said, "has also informed me that the Jews with passes will receive a special treatment from the German side if the Germans were to initiate even harsher regulations."

"I will do what I can to return home soon," he wrote to Kalman Lauer at the end of September. "However, it is not easy to close down a giant operation such as this one. . . . I will certainly try to return at least a few days before the Russians march in."

During what he thought were his final days in Budapest he launched his most grandiose scheme to date—a scheme that, if it succeeded, would save thousands of Jewish men in the labor battalions from certain death. Fifty thousand Jews served in unarmed labor battalions attached to the Hungarian Army. They wore tattered summer clothes and wooden clogs and worked sixteen hours a day clearing minefields, digging trenches, constructing earthworks, and carrying supplies. They were employed without regard for their safety or health and treated with less compassion than the army's horses and mules. Wallenberg feared that many would die from exposure as it became colder. The survivors would probably be slaughtered by the SS or fascists in the Hungarian Army as the Russians neared Budapest.

In mid-September he persuaded the Lakatos government to separate all the Jewish laborers from the battalions who carried Swedish and other neutral provisional passes, or whose families carried these papers, and return them to Budapest. There, they would continue to work, but only as part of a newly formed "Swedish (or Swiss) Brigade" and only on fortifications inside the city limits. Wallenberg quartered his Swedish Brigade in houses and synagogues marked by a Swedish flag or a plaque bearing the distinctive three crowns of the Swedish coat of arms.

As the Swedish-protected laborers returned in greater numbers, Wallenberg sought permission to enlarge the Swedish brigades by including in them members of the laborer's family. He also made plans to unite the Swiss, Swedish, and Red Cross brigades into a gigantic international work battalion in order to reunite families and create large protected organizations that could withstand any sudden pogrom.

It would have been impossible for him not to have been aware of Horthy's plan to arm the Jewish laborers and use them to frustrate any German-inspired coup. This plan was well known to the Jewish Council. Wallenberg had the Council's total confidence and regularly met and communicated with its members.

Admiral Horthy had already made the Russians suspicious of Western influence in Hungary by trying to negotiate an exclusive armistice with Britain and the United States. Now, if Wallenberg's plan for an international work battalion was successful, when the Russians occupied Budapest, either because of a military victory or Horthy's armistice, they would find thousands of Jewish men of military age, possibly armed, organized into paramilitary units called the Swedish Brigade, carrying Swedish passes, quartered in houses flying the Swedish flag, and commanded by an allegedly neutral diplomat, Raoul Wallenberg, who had received financial backing from the United States.

The Jewish laborers saved by Wallenberg's scheme knew or cared little about the possible political problems their rescue might cause. Suddenly they found themselves well fed and housed, permitted to rejoin their families, and free from the fear of being massacred.

László Ernster, a former medical student, had been drafted into one of the work battalions in 1943. Since then he had been forbidden to communicate with his family and had only learned that his wife had obtained a Swedish pass when they happened to share the same streetcar while he was being taken to build fortifications in a Budapest suburb. Because of this chance encounter he was one of the first protected laborers to claim his "Swedish citizenship" and be returned to Budapest in September under Wallenberg's scheme. Many men in the battalions, because they had not talked with their families in months, had no way of knowing whether or not they were honorary Swiss or Swedes.

The government quartered Ernster and eight other Jews holding Swedish passes in the Arener Street synagogue. Wallenberg had recently persuaded the government to reopen the synagogue, and it was under his protection. The Christian army captain placed in command of this first Swedish work brigade was pleased to have been withdrawn from the front and he greeted the Jews by offering them a drink and telling them, "Now that you are members of the Swedish Company you can go home and report back tomorrow. Dismissed." The men were ecstatic. For the first time in months they would see their wives and children.

By the end of September this Swedish company had grown to forty men. Every morning they checked into the Arener Street synagogue, where they chatted, played games, and joked with their often-inebriated captain. Every day at noon the captain sent them home. They did not have to work, or wear the Star of David, because, according to Ernster, "we were 'Swedes.'" Their only concession to regulations was to wear a yellow armband while "on duty."

"We all quickly forgot our past sufferings," Ernster said, "and for the first time in months we felt like human beings again." During the first two weeks of October many other Budapest Jews also concluded that the worst was over. They defiantly ripped off their Yellow Star badges and began making plans for the future. For the first time since March, Jews laughed and smiled in public.

On October 14 everything changed. Ernster arrived at the Arener Street synagogue to find three hundred unknown Jewish laborers crowded onto benches and sprawled on the floor. Unfamiliar, hostile soldiers now guarded the door and refused to let anyone leave or contact his family. Everyone was forced to spend the night at the synagogue. The following morning Ernster woke to find that the hostile soldiers had been replaced by young teenage toughs dressed in green shirts and wearing a red and white armband of crossed arrows, the Arrow Cross.

Throughout Budapest similar scenes were enacted at the "protected" houses and synagogues of the Jewish labor brigades. The Germans and their Arrow Cross allies, having learned of Horthy's plan to declare his armistice on October 15, had taken steps to isolate the Jewish brigades and prevent them from being armed.

The Christian captain attempted to escape from the synagogue and notify Wallenberg. He was caught by the Arrow Cross and returned at bayonet point. While the guards were distracted, a Jewish laborer slipped out of the synagogue and telephoned the Swedish Legation.

Wallenberg jumped into his Packard and raced to the synagogue. Many of the Jews of the Swedish Brigade had never seen him. According to Ernster, he appeared "pale but ferocious. He intimidated the Arrow Cross boys with a series of sharp questions and several minutes later they disappeared. At such moments, we thought he was a magician, the lord of our fate."

"Be quiet and stay here—don't be seen on the streets," Wallenberg ordered his "Swedish" laborers before leaving the synagogue. "You'll receive orders from me sometime this evening." Wallenberg himself was unsure of the political situation. Horthy had not announced an armistice, yet the Arrow Cross had surrounded the labor brigades and appeared in control of the streets.

The Swedish Brigade obeyed Wallenberg's orders and remained in the synagogue, huddled around a radio. At 1:00 P.M. the regular program was interrupted "for a special proclamation from the regent." In a prerecorded announcement Horthy informed his people that he had concluded a separate armistice with the Soviet Union.

He was withdrawing from the war because "Hungary was forced into war against the Allies by German pressure which weighed upon us owing to our geographical situation"; because "Today it is obvious to any sober-minded person that the German Reich has lost the war"; and because "under cover of the German occupation the Gestapo tackled the Jewish question in a manner incompatible with the dictates of humanity."

He concluded by saying: "I have received reliable information that troops of neo-German tendency intend to raise their own men to power by using force to effect a political upheaval and the overthrow of the legal Hungarian government. . . . . Accordingly, the troops loyal to their oath and now following an Order of the Day now issued simultaneously, must obey the commanders appointed by me. I appeal to every honest Hungarian to follow me on this path, beset by sacrifices, that will lead to Hungary's salvation."

"Praise God," thought Ernster after hearing the announcement, "now we can leave the synagogue and again rejoin our wives and children. Now everyone who has survived this hell can begin a new life."

But when he tried to leave he discovered that the Arrow Cross guards had returned. They pointed their rifles at his chest and forced him back through the door. "That old fool Horthy may have capitulated," said one, "but we haven't."

At three in the morning the synagogue's radio fell silent. A Jew rushed in from the street and shouted that the Arrow Cross had just captured the broadcasting center. Minutes later the radio started playing German marches. The friendly Hungarian captain became drunk. For László Ernster, for the Jews of Budapest, and for Raoul Wallenberg, the real "hell" was about to begin.

PART TWO

GUERILLA

4

October 15, 1944

By the evening of October 15, Wallenberg and all of Budapest knew that Horthy had lost. Ferenc Szálasi, a retired army major and the leader of the pro-Nazi Arrow Cross party, had become Hungary's new leader. Horthy's crucial mistake had been accelerating the date of the armistice. This sudden shift had caught his generals by surprise, giving them no time to move loyal troops into the capital, mobilize the workers, arm the Jewish labor brigades, or fortify key buildings against Szálasi's expected coup.

In Budapest, pro-German Hungarian officers easily took control of the army and arrested or executed officers loyal to Horthy. Arrow Cross storm troopers, assisted by German soldiers and tanks, occupied the radio station, police headquarters, government ministries, and military command centers. German tanks surrounded the Royal Palace and the German plenipotentiary, Dr. Veesenmayer, informed Horthy that the SS had kidnapped his son. His life would be spared only if Horthy abdicated and nominated Szálasi as prime minister. Horthy accepted these terms and the Arrow Cross became the legitimate government.

The Arrow Cross was the most extreme, violent, and anti-Semitic of all the Hungarian fascist movements. It had begun in the mid-1930s as an admitted copy of the Nazi party and offered the same ideology of social reform, fanatic nationalism, and a "radical solution to the Jewish problem." Its members believed in the superiority of the Magyar race and culture, dressed in green shirts, wore armbands, and waved flags bearing crossed arrows.

Like Hitler, Szálasi had once been imprisoned for his right-wing views and unrestrained political agitation. Unlike Hitler, he had been a pathetic failure. In 1939, at the height of its power, the Arrow Cross had only won sixteen percent of the vote. Since then it had rapidly lost strength. Fearful of an Arrow Cross coup, Hungary's wartime governments had drafted its members into special army units that were immediately sent to the front, where they suffered substantial losses.

In the weeks preceding October 15, Szálasi had secretly recruited thousands of new Arrow Cross members. Most were old men, the war wounded, and illiterate teenage boys from Budapest's slums. Leaders listed each new recruit's name in a register and gave each an armband and a loaded automatic rifle. The armband was a license to steal from the Jews; the rifle, a means of fulfilling Szálasi's promise to "decisively solve Hungary's Jewish problem."

The young Arrow Cross recruits had been weaned on crude anti-Semitic propaganda that depicted all Jews as subhuman; to kill a Jew was to swat a fly. They believed that Jewish spies and provocateurs signaled the Allied bombers with bedsheets and were responsible for the defeats suffered by the Hungarian armies on the eastern front. When a Hungarian soldier died in battle or an Allied plane destroyed a house or killed a relative, it was the fault of the Jews.

During the Middle Ages, Hungarian peasants, like many Europeans, accused the Jews of poisoning wells and causing the Black Death. Even in the twentieth century Hungarian Christians accused Jews of kidnapping Christian children, slitting their throats, draining their blood, and offering them as a Passover sacrifice.

It made no difference that no Jew had ever been caught butchering a Christian child, poisoning a well, or flapping a bedsheet; nor that the Soviet Army despised Jews almost as much as the Hungarian. None of this mattered—the Jews were guilty.

As soon as Szálasi announced his victory his followers launched a campaign of terror which most resembled the bloodthirsty, face-to-face, personal terror of the anti-Semitic pogroms of the Middle Ages—the random raping and pillaging of the Asiatic barbarians who had swept across the Magyar plains during the Dark Ages. It was so brutal, passionate, and anarchistic—so different from the Germans' cool, methodical, "civilized" methods of, in Eichmann's words, "granting the Jews a mercy death"— that even some of the SS officers stationed in Budapest lodged protests with the Hungarians.

During the first twelve hours of Szálasi's rule, Arrow Cross "soldiers" murdered more than three hundred Jews. They killed elderly Jews in "unprotected" Yellow Star houses, broke into protected Swedish and Swiss and Red Cross houses, ripped up protective passes, and shot anyone who protested. In a village twenty miles west of Budapest they murdered 160 Jewish doctors and technicians who had been drafted into a special medical labor battalion. They rounded up fifty Jewish laborers in the northern suburb of Obuda and marched them onto the Margit and Chain bridges, opened fire, and tossed their bodies into the Danube. In Pest a handful of Jewish laborers stole arms and attempted to resist. The Arrow Cross easily subdued them and then dragged women and children out of nearby Yellow Star houses and shot them in reprisal.

On October 15 and 16 the Budapest voluntary ambulance service received over 150 calls to collect Jewish laborers with bullet wounds, dead Jewish children, and Jews who had committed suicide. Except for these courageous ambulancemen and a few compassionate policemen who tried to protect Jews from the Arrow Cross, most of Budapest's Christians ignored the savage pogroms. Many appeared to agree with Chief of Gendarmes Ferenczy who, after betraying Horthy and Lakatos and embracing the Arrow Cross putsch, declared, "At last the Jews are getting what they asked for!"

Wallenberg was stunned by the speed and ferocity of the Arrow Cross attacks. His entire Jewish staff went into hiding, taking with them the keys to his file cabinets and offices. The Arrow Cross arrested his driver, Vilmos Langfelder, confiscated his car, and occupied his principal office in Üllöi Road.

The day after the coup, Wallenberg borrowed a woman's bicycle and pedaled across Budapest, searching out his staff. He gave them protective passes and Swedish Legation identity cards to replace those lost or destroyed and persuaded them to return to work.

During these trips he also reclaimed his car and hired a new driver, Sándor Ardai. "All right, your first destination is the Arrow Cross headquarters," he told Ardai. "I'm going to retrieve my former driver."

Ardai was petrified. Although he was familiar with the stories about Wallenberg's courage and determination, in person Wallenberg struck him as being "dreaming and weak."

As he watched Wallenberg bound up the steps of the Arrow Cross headquarters, alone and unarmed, he thought, "This won't go well. How can the Arrow Cross release a man just because he asks them to?" A few minutes later Wallenberg and Langfelder walked down the steps.

Next Wallenberg ordered Ardai to drive to his Üllöi Road office. As soon as they arrived he marched inside and in forceful and impeccable German ordered the Arrow Cross soldiers occupying it to leave and threatened to notify the new minister of foreign affairs, Gábor Kemény, that they had violated his diplomatic rights. As he sat down at his desk the soldiers slunk away. "We all wondered if there would be any reprisals," said one of his aides, "but to our surprise, nothing happened."

Once Wallenberg had reassembled his staff and office he fought back.

He persuaded the neutral diplomats to send the Szálasi government a letter protesting the atrocities and threatening to break diplomatic relations unless they ceased.

He recruited Tom Veres, a young Jew who had just escaped from a labor brigade, to be his official photographer. "I want you to accompany me everywhere and take pictures," he told Veres. "I want a complete documentary record of the Arrow Cross atrocities." Veres was impressed by Wallenberg's decisiveness. A few hours later Wallenberg had supplied him with a Legation identity card and he was shooting his first pictures.

By the evening of the sixteenth, Wallenberg was issuing protective passes and other documents which he hoped would restrain the Arrow Cross. He wrote two-week vacation passes for his Swedish Labor Brigade, embossed them with the official Swedish seal, and delivered them personally to the Arener Street synagogue. In truth there was no such thing as a "vacation pass" for slave laborers. Nevertheless, they fooled the Arrow Cross guards and the men of the Swedish Brigade were permitted to leave the synagogue and rejoin their families.

He instructed his staff to issue protective passes to everyone who had applied for them prior to the Szálasi coup and to hand them out without regard for the qualifications of the recipients. The government had forbidden Jews to go outdoors, so he and his staff, who were exempted from the curfew because they worked for the Swedish Legation, delivered these passes in person. Wallenberg also kept a stack of blank passes and a typewriter in the back seat of his car so he could issue passes on the spot to anyone menaced by the Arrow Cross.

He used this traveling office for the first time on October 17 when he visited the Dohány Street synagogue, the largest in Europe and second only in size to Temple Emanu-El in New York. The Arrow Cross had driven six thousand Jews into this synagogue on October 15. Since then they had been imprisoned there without adequate supplies of food, or water, packed so tightly together that they had no privacy, room to lie down, or even bury their dead.

Wallenberg brushed past the Arrow Cross boys guarding the door, strode down the aisle of the synagogue, and climbed onto the altar. "Does anyone here have a Swedish protective pass?" he shouted at the crowd.

A number of people answered that they did.

"All right, then, everyone with a pass report to me at once." Hundreds surged toward the altar waving passes in the air. Others shouted that they had lost passes or had them ripped up by the Arrow Cross. Many had never owned one but realized that he was offering them a chance to escape.

Wallenberg formed the Jews who claimed Swedish protection into columns and marched them out of the synagogue. "These are all Swedish citizens," he told the Arrow Cross guards. "You have no right to detain them."

The guards examined the passes and were impressed by the official stamps and seals, the glossy picture, the Swedish crowns, and the signature of the Swedish minister. They were also intimidated by Wallenberg's self-assured manner, and the way he barked commands in German. They stepped aside and Wallenberg marched his column of "Swedes" out of the synagogue. When he reached his car he typed the names of those without passes onto blank passes and distributed them.

The following day he learned that Eichmann had returned to Budapest and that Szálasi had decided to invalidate all the international protective passes. The two events were related.

"As you can see, I am back," Eichmann told the Jewish leaders he had summoned to his headquarters at the Majestic Hotel on October 17. "My arm is still long enough to reach you."

One of the leaders noticed that as he talked "his face was beaming with pleasure."

"The Hungarians thought that the events in Rumania and Bulgaria [their withdrawal from the Axis] would be repeated here," Eichmann continued. "They were wrong. They forgot that Hungary still lies in the shadow of the Reich. *This* government

will work according to *our* orders. I have already been in touch
with Minister Kovarcz [the Arrow Cross minister charged with
the "total mobilization of the nation"] and he has agreed that
the Jews of Budapest shall be deported, this time on foot. We
need our trains for other purposes."

He paused, smiled, and rubbed his hands together. The Jewish
leaders were speechless. "Now we are going to work efficiently
and quickly. Right?"

Eichmann knew he would have to work "efficiently and
quickly" in order to complete the deportations before the Soviet
Army reached Budapest. On the following morning, October 18,
he met with the Arrow Cross minister of the interior, Gábor
Vajna. Eichmann was pleased to discover that the new government was unequivocally committed to "solving" the Jewish problem. He and Vajna agreed to a secret protocol that, when fully
implemented, would complete the job Eichmann had begun in
Austria six years before.

They agreed that: (1) the Hungarian government would send
fifty thousand Jews to the Third Reich to replace the "worn
out" slave laborers presently working in German factories. These
Jews would be forced to march from Budapest to the Austrian
border. The Hungarian security forces—gendarmes, police, army,
and Arrow Cross—would be responsible for rounding up the
Jews and guarding them during the march. Eichmann's SS unit
would also escort them, advise the Hungarians, and then take
complete control of the Jews once they crossed the frontier; (2)
the Jews left behind would be driven into four concentration
camps outside Budapest and made to dig trenches and build
defensive fortifications; (3) Jews too feeble to work would be
herded into a ghetto the Hungarians would construct in central
Budapest; and (4) Jews holding protective passports would not
be given any preferential treatment and would be included in
the march.

Veesenmayer cabled Ribbentrop in Berlin that after the first
successful foot march, Eichmann planned to demand additional

batches of fifty thousand Jews until Hungary had been cleansed. Veesenmayer concluded: "A final settlement of the Jewish question can now be expected."

Meanwhile, Vajna made a statement "clarifying" the government's Jewish policy which reflected Eichmann's influence. "I declare that we shall solve the Jewish question," he said. "This solution—even if it be ruthless—shall be such as the Jews deserve because of their previous and present conduct. In order to wind up this Jewish question separate detailed regulations will soon be published and carried out. . . ."

He then "emphatically warned" the Jews and neutral diplomats such as Wallenberg ("those serving the Jews' interests") that "all the organs of state power are vigilantly watching their conduct. The regulations issued and those still to be issued will be executed with particular severity because of the war. In this respect I recognize no Jews belonging to the Roman Catholic, Lutheran, or Israelite denominations, only those of the Jewish race. I recognize no letter of safe conduct of any kind, or foreign passport which a Jew of Hungarian nationality may have received from whatever source or person [i.e., Wallenberg]. Let not a single person of Jewish race believe then that with the help of aliens [i.e., Wallenberg] he can circumvent the lawful measures of the Hungarian state."

Vajna did make one concession. Because the Arrow Cross government hoped to be recognized by the neutral countries, he attempted to instill some discipline in its storm troopers. "Let nobody be an arbitrary or self-appointed judge of the Jews," he warned them, "because the solution of this question is the task of the state and this question—everyone may rest assured—we shall solve." Immediately after making this statement he declared a state of martial law but added that its severe punishments for violating public order would not be applicable "in cases of atrocities against Jews."

In the days following Vajna's announcement, while Eichmann made preparations to march fifty thousand Jews to their death,

Wallenberg tried to persuade the Arrow Cross government to reverse this policy and recognize the protective passes and the extraterritorial rights of the Swedish houses and offices. He knew that if he failed, he could not even hope to protect the Jews holding the legitimate passes, much less those who had pinned their hopes on the counterfeits. Just when it seemed that he *would* fail he gained the assistance of an unexpected and powerful ally.

5

October 15–November 8, 1944

Karl Müller had spent October 15 listening to his radio. Like every other Jew in Budapest he had experienced within a few hours the exhilaration of a condemned man gaining a last-minute reprieve and then the agony of having the reprieve withdrawn. Throughout the evening of the fifteenth he remained by his radio praying for a miracle, praying that Horthy would rally his forces, defeat Szálasi, and carry out the armistice.

In gratitude for Müller's bravery during World War One, Horthy had granted him an exemption from all anti-Semitic decrees. Because of this exemption he was able to continue managing his successful publishing house and also to undertake special missions for Raoul Wallenberg. When Wallenberg needed someone to deliver a secret message or bribe to one of the government ministers he often called upon Müller.

Müller put on his World War One captain's uniform and walked past the police guards without being challenged. None could imagine that a Jew would be cheeky enough to strut around in a uniform, or that a Jew could have won so many medals. But tonight Müller was afraid that under Szálasi even his medals would not save him from sharing the fate of other Jews. Instead of helping Wallenberg, he himself might need Wallenberg's help. Shortly after midnight his doorbell rang. He switched off his radio and, because his family and servants had retired, opened the door himself. Standing alone on the doorstep was Baroness Elisabeth Kemény. Müller had just heard that her husband, Baron Gábor Kemény, was to be Szálasi's foreign minister.

Müller had met the baroness during the summer of 1943 at the castle of his World War One commandant and friend, Field Marshal Algya Papp. Before dinner Papp had drawn him aside and, pointing out a stunning blond woman in her early twenties, had said, "I have a favor to ask. You are going to be seated next to that woman at dinner, and I want you to be particularly kind to her. My other guests avoid her because she has recently married Baron Gábor Kemény, one of Szálasi's closest associates."

Müller found his dinner companion to be delightful company. Her maiden name had been Baroness Elisabeth Fuchs; she was a daughter of an Austrian baron and an Italian countess. She was intelligent, well educated, widely traveled, spoke seven languages fluently, and had come to Hungary from her home in Italy several months before to attend the marriage of a Hungarian countess with whom she had attended boarding school in England. Her dinner partner at the marriage had been young Gábor Kemény, a member of the aristocratic Siebenvirgen family. Her mother, who had accompanied her as a chaperone, was impressed by the baron's pedigree and had encouraged their romance. At present, she told Müller, they had been married for only two weeks.

Müller asked a few discrete questions about her husband's political activities, and to his amazement discovered that she had no idea that she had just married one of Hungary's most prominent fascists.

Müller spent most of the next four months traveling abroad on behalf of his publishing house. When he returned to Budapest late in the autumn of 1943, his wife reported that Baroness

Kemény had stopped by on numerous occasions, trying to see him. He immediately called her and invited her to his office on the following morning.

When they met she told him that her marriage had been a dreadful mistake. Her husband was a fool and his family impoverished. Her two sisters, both of them nuns, had given her a handsome dowry which her husband had immediately squandered. Still, she could not divorce him. She was a devout Catholic and the Pope himself had sent a telegram on their wedding day, blessing their union. She would stay with her husband but needed to work in order to support him.

Müller hired her, and during the next eighteen months she proved to be his most talented and reliable employee. Now she was also the wife of the man who would help Eichmann rid Hungary of Jews.

Müller begged her to come inside. She refused and remained standing on the doorstep. "I have come to tell you one thing," she said. "I am going to save you and your friends. With the help of God and the Blessed Virgin I will save you all. Good night."

When he arrived at his offices the following morning, his doorkeeper informed him that the baroness had arrived an hour before and was working in her office. He went upstairs and found her bent over her desk, writing feverishly. "Good morning, Your Excellency," he said sarcastically.

She ignored him and continued working. He walked to the desk and peered over her shoulder. She was writing her own safety passes. Each said, "The bearer of this document is under my personal protection. Signed: Baroness Gábor Kemény."

She looked up and said, "I must talk to you. Now. Urgently. In strict confidence."

When they were alone in his office, she said, "You of all people must believe that I have no sympathy for this miserable government. I want you to arrange a meeting with Wallenberg. He'll believe you. Tell him about me; tell him you know and trust me; tell him I want to help him with all my body and soul; tell him he can use me however he wants."

Müller immediately telephoned Wallenberg. An hour later he and the baroness met in an empty apartment on the sixth floor of Müller's publishing house. They were instantly attracted to one another. After several minutes of conversation it became apparent that they shared the same background and convictions: Both belonged to civilized and aristocratic families; both had traveled widely and considered themselves "citizens of the world." The baroness made it clear that her first allegiance was to humanity, not her husband, yet she appeared reluctant to endanger him by her actions.

"You must believe me," Wallenberg told her. "This Hungarian government is doomed. The Allies have already promised to hold war crimes trials. Your husband and the other Arrow Cross leaders will be executed."

She burst into tears. "I am carrying his child," she sobbed. "Must this child be fatherless?"

"Not if you persuade your husband to honor the protective passes and soften his government's policy toward the Jews. I would vouch for him. Your child would have a father, and you would know that you had helped to rebuild a world in which justice and morality are important, the kind of world you would want your child to inherit."

On October 20, two days after this conversation, a messenger brought Wallenberg a letter from the baroness. She said she had persuaded her husband to argue for the restoration of the privileges previously accorded the protected Jews. That same day Baron Kemény brought up the Jewish question at a meeting of the Council of Ministers. He argued that recognizing Wallenberg's passes was the price the government must pay if it wished to be recognized by Sweden. Wallenberg had planted this argument with the baroness, who had passed it on to her husband.

Szálasi, who was completely ignorant of world politics, desperately wanted his regime to be recognized by neutral powers such as Sweden and Switzerland. Their recognition would prove that he headed a legitimate, civilized government, not a German puppet state. Persuaded by Kemény's arguments, he announced that, "at an appropriate time," he would issue orders modifying Gábor Vajna's Jewish decrees.

The baron rushed home to inform his wife of Szálasi's decision. To his surprise she burst into tears. "He's just saying that," she protested between sobs. "While he waits and thinks about it, the deportations will go on."

The baron was an extraordinarily simple, unsophisticated man. He had become at thirty-three the youngest foreign minister in Hungarian history only because of his insane hatred for the Jews and because Szálasi had learned that he could speak several foreign languages. He worshiped his wife and respected her superior intellect. Her tears perplexed and upset him. To cheer her up he proposed a shopping expedition.

She readily agreed. Once they were in the baron's official limousine her tears vanished. "Driver," she ordered the chauffeur, "go directly to the radio station."

The baron protested. She ignored him. When the car stopped in front of the government broadcasting center, she pulled a piece of paper from her handbag and gave it to him. "I refuse to leave this building until you order the announcer to read this proclamation over the air," she said.

The document was a list of new Jewish regulations dictated by Wallenberg earlier that day. They reversed Vajna's earlier decree and stated that the police and Arrow Cross should now respect the foreign passes. All protected Jews were again exempted from wearing the Yellow Star, and houses for these Jews owned by the neutral legations were again accorded extraterritorial rights. The baron, anxious to please his beautiful wife and desperate to keep her love, ordered the announcement read. Thousands of protected Jews were now exempted, at least in theory, from Eichmann's forthcoming death march.

On October 20, the same day that Kemény made his announcement, the Szálasi government began implementing the Vajna-Eichmann agreement by rounding up Jews to serve in labor battalions. The Arrow Cross stormed into Yellow Star houses and took every Jewish male between the ages of sixteen and sixty. Some Arrow Cross troopers respected the protective passes, some did not.

Previous labor drafts had been so harsh that only the sick, wounded, and crippled remained to fill this one. The Jews seized during this roundup were quartered out of doors, given almost no food or medical care, and forced to work sixteen hours a day building defenses on Budapest's southeastern periphery. One labor company received their first food ration after working for five days. In the following two weeks they received only three portions of soup. Their Arrow Cross guards stole their coats and shoes and tortured those who malingered or complained.

Two days after the first draft, women between eighteen and forty were ordered to register as laborers. Many were immediately seized by the Arrow Cross. By the end of October the Szálasi government had drafted thirty-five thousand additional Jews into slave labor battalions.

These new battalions suffered terrible casualties on November 2 when the Axis armies lost a crucial battle to the Soviets southeast of Budapest and retreated toward the capital in confusion. The advance guard of a Soviet armored column was finally halted only eight miles from the city.

During the retreat, the Arrow Cross "soldiers" in charge of the Jewish laborers panicked and shot and strangled any Jews who were too exhausted to keep up. They blamed the Jews for the Russian victory and marched hundreds onto the Danube bridges, shot them, and threw their bodies into the water. The slaughter became so frenzied and revolting that the government finally sent regular policemen to protect the Jewish laborers from their Arrow Cross guards.

During the first three weeks of Szálasi's reign of terror Wallenberg tried to rescue Jews with Swedish and other foreign protective passes from the labor battalions. Every morning he and Charles Lutz of the Swiss Legation went to Teleki Square, the Arrow Cross assembly point for Jewish laborers, and shouted, "Those with Swiss or Swedish passes stand to one side!" As at the Dohány Street synagogue, Wallenberg saved everyone who claimed their passes had been lost or destroyed. The tedious administrative and diplomatic tasks he had performed during his first hundred days, the endless visits and protests to government ministries, the bribes and favors, were finally paying off. Now his passes were saving hundreds of Jews a day from almost certain death in the labor battalions. Throughout this period he also continued to practice his lifesaving diplomacy and bureaucracy.

When the Szálasi government confiscated ration cards from the Jews one day and then announced the next that anyone without a ration card would be deported, Wallenberg and his staff stayed up throughout the night printing special "Swedish ration cards." Each announced that Section C of the Swedish Legation would provide the holder with sufficient food.

When Szálasi modified Kemény's radio announcement by declaring that only bearers of neutral passports, not neutral protective passes, would be treated as privileged foreigners, Wallenberg affixed to each pass a note stating that "this protective pass is now valid as a regular Swedish passport." By permitting Wallenberg himself to sign these notes, the Swedish minister, Danielsson, had in effect given him a power of attorney and an authority equal to his own.

During these first three weeks of the Szálasi regime, Wallenberg sent dozens of notes to the Hungarian Foreign Ministry protesting the Arrow Cross violence. He complained about conditions at the Dohány Street synagogue, charged that Swedish-protected Jews had been "illegally seized" for labor duty, and demanded their return as well as police protection for his Swedish-protected houses. For a junior secretary of a legation to bombard the Foreign Ministry of a sovereign state with so many diplomatic notes, particularly ones as threatening as these, was unprecedented.

Throughout this period Wallenberg also increased the number

of Swedish houses. Some he received as gifts from wealthy Jews hoping to prevent them from being "Aryanized." Others he purchased by bribing their Christian owners. A month after the Szálasi coup he controlled thirty-two buildings. Most were six stories high, housed between five and six thousand "Swedish Jews," and were located in Pest. Most Jews lived in Pest, and it appeared that the Russian Army would capture it first. To prepare for their arrival, Wallenberg printed Russian passes for his staff and Russian signs for his houses.

He also increased the size of his staff to four hundred. During his first hundred days he had tended to hire middle-aged professionals—accountants, lawyers, bankers, and businessmen—who were suited to the administrative needs of Section C. Now he sought out younger men who had escaped from labor battalions or avoided them through cunning and resourcefulness. They were more suited to the underground war he anticipated waging as the Russians neared the city. To accommodate his expanded staff he opened a new office on Jókai Street to supplement his Üllöi Road headquarters.

He drove himself and his staff mercilessly. Every idle moment, every moment he slept, was a moment in which he might otherwise be saving a life. He worked almost twenty hours every day, kept his battered rucksack in the back of his car, and slept wherever he was working—the Swedish Legation, Jókai Street, Üllöi Road, or one of the two apartments he maintained on Dezsu and Astram streets. He moved frequently to avoid Arrow Cross assassins. In comparison with his first three months of diplomacy and bureaucracy, he found the danger and lack of sleep exhilarating.

In November he wrote to his mother:

Today you will only get these very hurried lines.

Rest assured that all is well with me. Times are extraordinarily exciting. The main thing is that we are working and fighting successfully.

At the moment we are sitting by candlelight and trying

to finish preparing the mail bag for the diplomatic courier.
There has been a power cut which is the last thing we needed
now that we're in this enormous muddle. If only you could
see me here! Dozens of people are standing around, all with
urgent questions, and I have no idea whom I should answer
and give advice to first.

I hope that you are well and I promise with all my heart
that next time you will get a much fuller report.

I shall close now. I greet and kiss you all.

Your Raoul

He never found time to send the "fuller report" he promised
his mother. "There simply can be no rest from our work nor
can we expect a reward for it," he told his staff at the Üllöi
Road office. "If we fail to act promptly lives will certainly be
lost; of course on the other hand you must realize that if we
are too successful our own lives will be in danger."

In Eichmann's opinion Wallenberg was already too successful.
At the beginning of November he summoned him to a meeting
at the Majestic Hotel, headquarters in Budapest for the Gestapo.

Now Eichmann took Wallenberg more seriously than he had
when they had first met at the Arizona nightclub. Wallenberg
had tricked the Hungarians into honoring his passes and had
obstructed the formation of the labor battalions. He might also
interfere with Eichmann's plan to march fifty thousand Jews to
Austria.

Others had already tried and failed to obstruct his efforts to
finish the cleansing of Hungary. Himmler himself, who was scared
by the Allies' threat to hold war crimes trials, had ordered the
gas chambers at Auschwitz dismantled and the extermination
program halted. Eichmann had surmounted this obstacle by
claiming that the deported Hungarian Jews would work building
the "East Wall" that would protect Vienna from the Russians.

He knew, however, that few if any Jews would survive the march or the first few months of labor.

Allied bombers had already interfered with his plan to ship the Jews to Vienna in freight cars. The important Györ junction and other vital sections of the Budapest–Vienna line lay in ruins. He had overcome this difficulty by persuading the Hungarians to agree to a foot march and had already held several meetings with the Hungarian officials to plan the route of the march. They had decided that Jewish labor servicemen who had been drafted before October 15 and were working in the provinces, would march along byroads south of the Györ–Hegyeshalom line; Jewish men and women from Budapest would march on the Györ–Hegyeshalom road; and labor service companies withdrawn from the northern and eastern theaters of war would march westward over roads north of the Györ–Hegyeshalom line.

Now Eichmann had learned that Wallenberg was trying to obstruct his march by lobbying with the Szálasi government to cancel or postpone it, or at the very least to exclude from it Jews holding protective passes.

As soon as Wallenberg walked into his office Eichmann tried to throw him off balance. "Why did you go to Palestine in nineteen thirty-seven?" he shouted.

Wallenberg answered in measured tones. "Because it interested me. I believe that the Jews should have a state of their own, don't you?"

"I know all about you!" Eichmann screamed. "You're a Jew-lover who's received all his dirty dollars from Roosevelt. We know that the Americans have put you in Budapest and we know that your relative, Jacob Wallenberg, is also a Jew-lover and an enemy of the Reich. We have proof that he has been conspiring with Gordeler [Carl Gordeler was a former mayor of Leipzig who had been one of the leaders of the July 20, 1944, attempt on Hitler's life]."

Wallenberg said nothing.

Eichmann continued screaming. "We have enough proof to

arrest you because of your association with Jacob Wallenberg."

Finally Wallenberg spoke. "All right. I'll admit that Jacob Wallenberg is an enemy of Nazism. So what? That's none of my concern."

Eichmann became irrational with fury. "We also know all about your so-called passports. They're all frauds. The handful of Jews who've used them to escape to Sweden are all enemies of the Reich. We know that they've helped Jews escape from Denmark."

Wallenberg refused to shout back or rebut Eichmann's charges. Instead he sent his driver down to his car to fetch a bottle of Scotch and a carton of cigarettes, which he offered to Eichmann.

According to later testimony by Eichmann's deputy, Dieter Wisliceny, "In spite of his high rank, Eichmann could never get rid of his lower middle-class habits and mentality . . . he did not trust himself [with the elite], he was afraid of making a fool of himself in a milieu alien to him." Eichmann was impressed by the Wallenberg name and pleased that Raoul Wallenberg would drink with him despite their differences; it proved they were both gentlemen. After several shots of whiskey Eichmann's entire mood changed. He smiled and became expansive. Wallenberg had sensed Eichmann's social insecurities and was successfully catering to them.

"You know, Wallenberg," he said. "I have nothing against you personally; actually I rather like you. Let me do you a favor. If you want, and of course if the price is right—say seven hundred and fifty thousand Swiss francs—I would be happy to put a train at your disposal. You could then take all your protected Jews to Sweden. What do you say?"

Wallenberg said he would consider the offer. He feared that once the protected Jews were gone Eichmann would be able to persuade Szálasi that he could deport the remaining Jews without offending the neutral powers. He and Eichmann shared more Scotch and cigarettes and then parted on friendly terms.

Several days later Eichmann screamed at a member of the International Red Cross: "I'm going to kill that Jew-dog Wallenberg."

Soon afterward a sympathetic Hungarian gendarme officer warned Wallenberg that he had received orders to murder him. Later in November a heavy truck belonging to the SS ploughed into Wallenberg's car at high speed, demolishing its front. By chance, Wallenberg was using another car at the time.

On November 9 the Hungarians began to collect Jews for Eichmann's death march. Since Eichmann had failed to eliminate or neutralize Wallenberg, he was forced to exclude the protected Jews, but only for the time being. He could always include them in the last batch.

6

November 9–22, 1944

BUDAPEST AND BÉKÁSMEGYER

At noon on November 9, gendarmes, policemen, and men and boys in green Arrow Cross shirts rang bells and pounded on the doors of the Yellow Star houses in Budapest's Fifth District, a neighborhood bordering the Danube in Pest with a high concentration of Jews. The bells and pounding fists echoed deep inside the massive six-story stone buildings. Janitors turned heavy locks, swung back thick wooden doors, and opened iron grilles. Before March they had guarded their tenants, locking their buildings at 10:00 P.M. and charging a small sum to open the doors. Now the government paid them to compile and post a list of the names and locations of all the Jews in their building. They could earn a bounty by reporting those who broke curfew or peered out their windows.

The Arrow Cross grabbed the lists of Jews, then raced through the open courtyards of these buildings and up their staircases. They burst into apartments and ordered everyone—no exceptions—to gather in the courtyards with a coat and one suitcase.

Soon, at each building, between fifty and a hundred Jews stood outside shivering in the wintry November drizzle. More than three-quarters were women: women carrying infants; sick and pregnant women whom the Arrow Cross had rejected for labor duty on October 22; women whose husbands served in the labor battalions; women who had lost their entire families.

Most of the men were younger than twelve, older than seventy, and so sick and crippled that they had been sent home from the labor battalions. The healthiest and youngest adults had been saved from earlier labor drafts by their protective passes. In some buildings the Arrow Cross respected the passes and allowed their bearers to return to their apartments; in others they ripped up passes, beat up those presenting them, and screamed that this time there were to be no exceptions.

In most buildings the Arrow Cross shoved the Jews into columns, stripped them of their warm clothing, and then searched their luggage for valuables. Paul Gidaly, a young man who had recently escaped from a labor battalion and was hiding in a Yellow Star building, watched from a second-floor window as an Arrow Cross woman yanked off his mother's wedding ring and then pulled her eyeglasses off her nose.

His mother protested. "No! Please give them back. I'm nearsighted and need them to see."

"You won't need them where you're going," the Arrow Cross woman shouted.

Moments later Gidaly watched the Arrow Cross march his mother and sister through the courtyard and into the street. Everywhere similar columns of Jews, some stripped of all possessions and with their hands over their heads, marched out of Yellow Star houses. The columns merged with one another and grew in size until they filled even the widest boulevards.

The Arrow Cross guards shot those who stumbled or fell out of line, old men who clutched their chests and doubled over with heart attacks, or anyone who tried to escape. They beat those who cried or talked. Nevertheless, people whispered to one another: "How far will we go today?" "Where will we stop?" "Where are they taking us?" "Are we going to Germany?"

Susan Tabor did not care where they were going; she was

certain it was a place of execution. She looked at her feet, at the feet of the other marchers, anything to avoid looking at the faces of the Arrow Cross boys. She did not want to remember their faces and she feared she would recognize the son of her building's superintendent. She could remember him as an infant and then as a young boy.

For five years she and her family had struggled to escape this last march. In 1939 her father, a well-to-do textile manufacturer, had gone to Paris and succeeded in getting the family visas for the Dutch East Indies. Her mother, however, refused to go without her parents, uncles, and cousins. They never used the visas. In 1940 they tried to emigrate to Brazil, Australia, and the United States. They were among the lucky few to get American visas, but before they could leave, the United States and Hungary were at war. In 1942, they purchased bogus baptismal certificates.

During the next two years the situation of Jews in Hungary seemed so secure that they mislaid the baptismal papers. After the 1944 German occupation they obtained visas for Palestine, but soon afterward the government changed its policy and forbade Jews from using Palestinian visas. Finally, in desperation, Susan cabled a Swedish youth she had met in Budapest several years earlier. She had learned about the Swedish protection program and hoped to use a letter from him to obtain Swedish protective passes. He never replied (she later learned he was at sea with the navy). At last, in August, she succeeded in buying new baptismal papers and in obtaining a Swiss protective pass. It was not as highly regarded as the Swedish, but it was something. After the Szálasi coup she hid in the house of one of her father's business associates. But upon hearing that her father had been drafted into a labor battalion she returned to her parents' Yellow Star house to comfort her mother.

Now that, after years of scheming how to escape, she had finally been caught, she found to her surprise that she no longer cared. "I was convinced I was going to die," she said later. "Once I knew this I was no longer afraid. I just waited for the worst to happen."

Katherine Szenes felt the same way. When she and her sister parted in the courtyard of their building (the Arrow Cross had honored her sister's Swedish pass), her sister had been hysterical but Katherine "had no tears left to shed." The day before she had learned that the Szálasi regime had executed her daughter Hannah.

Hannah Szenes had been one of three Palestinian Jews sent into Hungary by the British for the purpose of organizing and leading a Jewish underground movement. She was captured as soon as she arrived, tortured for three months by the Gestapo, and executed on November 17. The Gestapo had also arrested Katherine Szenes and had kept her in a cell near her daughter. While her daughter was alive she too had struggled to live. Now that her daughter was dead she felt "totally indifferent." She said later: "After my Aniko [Hannah] was murdered, this [the march] appeared to me to be a fitting solution."

Like Katherine Szenes, Susan Tabor, and Paul Gidaly's mother and sister, most of the women on the death march had survived through luck, bribery, cunning, or the kindness of Christian friends. Now, isolated from husbands, sons, and relatives, many gave up and prepared to die; some believed that they deserved to die. Susan Tabor said, "I felt totally alone, isolated. They had treated us like animals for so long that I came to believe that I was an animal. They had told us that we deserved to die so many times that I finally agreed with them."

On the first day of the roundup more than ten thousand Jews—the "Jews to be lent to the Germans to work on behalf of Hungary"—marched down tree-lined boulevards, past the cinemas they had once attended and the shops they had patronized, past the smart cafés and hotels of the Coros, and past their neighbors.

Thousands of Budapest's Christians witnessed the march. Near the approaches to the Danube bridges the Jews passed men huddled around fires, eating chestnuts and slices of hot pumpkin. On the bridges they passed peasant women from the countryside, their shawls transferred from their shoulders to their heads to protect them against the wintry drizzle. Along the boulevards the few middle-class women who had not fled the capital shoved their hands deeper into their fur muffs. Men buttoned fur collars and pulled down the brims of their hats to protect themselves from the cold winds that swept down the Danube. If most bothered to look at the marchers for any length of time they saw not people, but Jews, the equivalent of enemy soldiers—or, as the newspaper *Osszeartas* [*Solidarity*] put it, "the satellites of Anglo-American-Bolsheviks" who "from the outset have stood on the side of our enemies everywhere and . . . must be treated accordingly!"

At nightfall the columns stopped at a brickyard in the northern suburb of Békásmegyer. High walls surrounded the yard and its several drying sheds. Deep pits pockmarked the open ground between the sheds.

The Arrow Cross pushed and whipped the marchers into the brickyard, smashing with their rifle butts anyone who hesitated. In the darkness some people stumbled into the drying pits and broke their legs. The Arrow Cross shot them. Others slipped in the mud and were trampled to death. The lucky ones, among them Katherine Szenes, found a place to lie near the still-warm kiln. Others found shelter in the drying sheds. Most had to lie in the open courtyard, pelted by the freezing sleet, without food or water and terrorized by Arrow Cross boys.

Susan Tabor lay on the floor of a drying shed that was so crowded she could neither stand up nor move. No one around her slept. They cried, screamed out the names of their relatives, and relieved themselves where they lay. At midnight there was an air raid and she heard Allied planes bombing nearby factories. She begged God to let them hit the brickyard. "Are they right?" she wondered as she lay awake. "Are Jews really just animals? How could we be human and be treated this way?"

The next morning she saw an ancient Packard speed through the gates of the brickyard. A man of medium height wearing a broad-brimmed hat and a frayed raincoat jumped out and, after talking with an Arrow Cross leader, climbed onto a loading ramp.

He carried a briefcase in one hand, a megaphone in the other. He was the only Christian in the brickyard without a rifle slung over his shoulder.

Wallenberg raised the megaphone to his mouth and shouted, "I am trying to get you some food and water and to arrange for more humane treatment. I promise you that I'll return in a few hours with doctors and nurses. When I return I'll take anyone with a protective pass back to Budapest."

He paused and then turned his megaphone toward the guards and bellowed, "It is illegal to take these people and treat them like this."

When he left, the Arrow Cross led the Jews to the latrines for the first time. Several hours later a car of doctors and nurses from the Jewish hospital arrived with medicine and boxes of food supplied by the Swiss and Swedish legations. The marchers shared the food and for the first time since the roundup, recited prayers in unison. According to Susan Tabor, "He [Wallenberg] made me feel human again. For the first time I had hope. In fact, I think that everyone felt different after his first visit. He showed us that we were not animals, that someone cared about us."

Wallenberg returned on the following day leading a convoy of trucks and accompanied by Charles Lutz, the Swiss consul. Within minutes he had succeeded in transforming the brickyard into a scene of chaos. "Those holding Swedish protective passes form a line here," he shouted, pointing to one corner of the brickyard. "Those with Swiss passes over there, Red Cross there, Vatican there, and Portuguese there," he said, pointing to different spots.

The Jews ran helter-skelter around the brick factory. They changed lines and jostled one another to get a good place as Wallenberg backed his trucks into the yard. The Arrow Cross guards lost control. They too raced around, pushing the Jews into lines and examining their passes. In the confusion many Jews simply walked away or bribed individual guards to let them escape. Susan Tabor gave her Yellow Star coat to a friend, slipped away, and walked back to her house in Budapest.

Meanwhile Wallenberg bribed a police official to let him save Jews without protective passes. "I have permission to take five hundred women back to the Swedish houses in Budapest," he announced. The confusion increased as women ran to form new lines. Wallenberg walked down the lines of women, counting them off. His chauffeur wrote their names onto blank passes and listed them in the registry. Wallenberg gave the last pass to Maria Hegedus and her three-year-old daughter, Eve. Maria's best friend was in the row of women just behind her. The following day, November 10, Elly Gidaly, Katherine Szenes, and others Wallenberg had been unable to save were sorted into groups of two thousand each. Every day the Arrow Cross marched a new group out of the brickyard and onto the Vienna highway. Every day they rounded up more Jews in Budapest and brought them to the brickyard. Eichmann's death march had begun.

But because of Wallenberg's alliance with Baroness Kemény, and because of his promises to the Szálasi government of imminent Swedish diplomatic recognition, it had begun without most of the Jews under neutral protection and those holding forged protective passes. However, nine days later, on November 19, Szálasi had tired of Wallenberg's stalling. He was ready to agree to Eichmann's demand that every Jew in Budapest be deported. Those too young, sick, or old to march to Vienna could be marched into the Danube.

7

November 19–22, 1944

"I am not speaking from home because I might be overheard," Baroness Kemény told Karl Müller on the morning of November 19. "Something extremely unpleasant has happened. You must come and see me right after lunch."

Müller was relieved the baroness had called—today was the first time since the October 15 coup that she had failed to report for work—but he was upset by her message: "Something extremely unpleasant." He rushed over to her apartment early that afternoon.

He scarcely had time to greet the baroness and take off his coat when, unexpectedly, her husband returned home. He was surprised to find Müller in his apartment.

"I just happened to be passing by and wanted to make sure your wife was all right," Müller explained. "This is the first time I can remember her missing a day of work."

The baron was so excited he brushed aside Müller's explanation. "Actually it's good that I bumped into you," he said, his voice rising. "The investigators of the Interior Ministry have discovered that you and my wife are mixed up in the machinations of this Jew-loving Swede Wallenberg. You can tell Wallenberg that he won't lead me around by the nose any longer. . . ."

The baron stopped and reflected on his words. There was something uncomplimentary, if not undignified, in the image of *him* being led by the nose. He corrected himself. "That is, he just *thinks* he has led me around by the nose. I have known about his children's fairy tale of 'imminent Swedish recognition' for ages. However, I myself, Baron Kemény, wanted to prevent mass bloodshed and so I passed Wallenberg's stories as though they were reliable on to the Council of Ministers.

"For weeks I've been lying . . . lying . . . lying," he continued, his voice becoming louder with each word. "But now that's finished! Today the Council adopted my resolution. Today I will give the Swedish government an ultimatum: three days and no longer. If Stockholm doesn't recognize our government by November twenty-second then I'll hand all the Jews in Budapest over to Interior Minister Vajna."

"And what does that mean, Baron?" Müller asked.

"It means they'll all be drowned in the Danube," he screamed, "and on November twenty-second, Budapest will be 'Judenrein.' "

Müller and the baroness stared at one another, speechless. Müller wanted to escape and warn Wallenberg, but the baron continued ranting about Jews and Wallenberg. Suddenly Müller remembered that it was the baroness's birthday.

"I'm shocked, Your Excellency," he said, "shocked to hear such an outrageous threat from a descendant of Hungary's most famous duchy. Particularly today, when you should be celebrating the birthday of the mother of your future child."

The baron opened his mouth in surprise. Suddenly his whole demeanor changed. "For God's sake, Mr. Director, a thousand thanks . . . how terrible . . . how frightful of me to forget such a thing. . . . My God . . . my God . . ." he stammered. "What shall I do? . . . Poor Liesl . . . and now I have to go straight back—the Council of Ministers is still in session. I haven't even got time to . . ."

He stopped and pulled Müller aside. "What shall I do?" he asked.

"Your Excellency, I am happy to be of service," Müller said. "Just tell me what sort of birthday present you have in mind and I'll get it for you."

"Yes . . . yes . . . do that. I'll be eternally grateful. I will leave the choice in your hands. But quick, quick! Send it to me at the Ministry so that I can surprise Liesl with it tonight."

Müller agreed, and as Baron Kemény accompanied him to the door the baroness held an imaginary telephone receiver to her ear, signaling that she would call him immediately.

Suddenly the baron became serious again and told Müller, "But be sure you tell Wallenberg what I said."

Müller raced to one of Wallenberg's offices. There Klara Rothschild, previously the owner of Budapest's foremost women's clothing salon, stitched together two nightgowns in less than two hours. Müller paid for the material with money from the Swedish Legation's petty cash and sent them to the Foreign Ministry. When he returned to his own office the telephone was ringing.

"I'm coming straight over," the baroness whispered. "Make sure that the chairman of the board of our corporation [Wallenberg] is also there."

At six that same evening the baroness, Müller, and Wallenberg met in the Swedish Legation to decide how to prevent Baron Kemény from handing the Jews over to Gábor Vajna. Wallenberg had already heard of Vajna's plans from Lieutenant-Colonel Ferenczy. He knew that the protected Jews would not really be deported, but murdered along with the Budapest Jews not participating in Eichmann's death march. Ferenczy had told him: "Vajna has ordered me to eliminate all the Jews at eleven P.M. on November twenty-third by shooting them or chasing them into the Danube. He claimed that 'By morning the Jewish problem will be solved.' "

Wallenberg had immediately visited Vajna and, without revealing the source of his information, said that he believed the government was contemplating a major action against the Jews. "If the Jews are endangered, then Hungarians all over the world will pay dearly," he had threatened, "particularly Hungarians sympathetic to the Arrow Cross."

Vajna had called his bluff. "But, Mr. Secretary, there *are* no Hungarians abroad who are sympathetic to us," he had said. "And as for the others, I couldn't care less what happens to them."

Having failed to intimidate Vajna, Wallenberg now concentrated on preventing Baron Kemény from handing the protected Jews over to the Interior Ministry. While he, Müller, and the baroness discussed the kind of arguments that her husband would find persuasive, a phone call came into the Legation from the Foreign Ministry: Baron Kemény had an important message for Secretary Wallenberg and wished to deliver it personally tomorrow morning.

"I am giving you an ultimatum," Kemény told Wallenberg when they met. "Unless we are recognized by Stockholm within three days, all protected Jews will be handed over to the minister of the interior for immediate deportation."

Wallenberg tried out the arguments he had practiced with the baroness the night before. He spoke calmly and politely and showed Kemény the deference that one might expect when, under normal circumstances, a junior legation secretary was granted an audience with a foreign minister.

"Your Excellency must surely realize that satisfying your ultimatum in three days is impossible," he said. "In the first place, to be honest, at present the reports from the Swedish Legation to Stockholm on your government are not entirely complimentary. However, if the Hungarian foreign minister were to himself make a few praiseworthy humanitarian gestures I could guarantee that these reports would soon be more sympathetic. This of course could not happen within the space of just three days.

"Secondly, you must try to understand that since Sweden is not at war its press is uncensored. Recently there have been some disparaging articles about your government in the Stockholm newspapers which have turned the Swedish public against your government. I'm sure that more favorable reports from the Legation would also result in more favorable press coverage. Public opinion might then support recognition. Of course all of this would take time; it could not be accomplished in three days.

"Last of all, Your Excellency, as an experienced and exceptional diplomat, you must realize better than anyone that the question of recognition cannot be decided only in Stockholm. World affairs are presently too complicated. My government will have to give Washington, London, and Moscow an opportunity to file the protests they will inevitably make before recognition is announced. This too will take time."

After Wallenberg had finished, Kemény said that he would take his suggestions under consideration. He dismissed him without indicating if he would rescind his ultimatum. As soon as Wallenberg returned to the Legation he called Müller and asked him to visit the baroness in the afternoon in order to ascertain the baron's response.

The baron himself opened his front door for Müller. Twice in two days this meddlesome Jew had visited his home unannounced. "Tell me, Mr. Director," he said without attempting to conceal his anger, "do you plan to be a self-invited guest in my apartment every day?"

"I've only come to ask if you found your wife's birthday present suitable," Müller replied.

As it had the day before, the baron's entire demeanor changed as soon as his wife was mentioned. He slapped his forehead, thanked Müller profusely for his help, and then invited him into the dining room, where the baroness sat finishing her lunch.

The baron invited Müller to join them at the table. When he was seated, Müller said, "By the way, Your Excellency, I gave Wallenberg your message yesterday as soon as I left you."

"Yes, thank you. He came to see me today," the baron answered.

"Wallenberg was with you, Gábi?" the baroness asked indifferently. "What rubbish did he say this time?"

"No, no, no," the baron replied. "This time he was not in the wrong. In fact, his reply to my ultimatum was entirely reasonable. I shall have to give him more time."

"How much more time, Gábi?" she asked innocently.

"Well, I think until the end of the month."

"Gábi, Gábi," she said softly, "November twenty-second and November thirtieth are pretty much the same. You really haven't given up much, have you?" Müller thought she sounded "like a purring cat."

"Well, what do you think, darling?" asked the baron, helpless and indecisive as usual.

"I think . . ." She paused, pursed her lips, and pretended to concentrate. "I think at least until the New Year."

Kemény lost his temper. He smashed plates and glasses on the floor and bellowed, "Do you want to ruin me? To bring about my downfall?"

The baroness ran over and stroked his face. Disarmed by this rare show of affection, he calmed down and said, "All right. I'll give the Swedes until December fifteenth."

Müller was ecstatic. The Russians would be in Budapest before the middle of December. He asked if he could relay the news to Wallenberg.

"I shall of course notify him officially," the baron said. "But you can make him aware of my decision."

However, as Müller got up to leave, the baron changed his mind. "No. It won't do. I can't wait until December fifteenth," he said.

"I can't believe it, Your Excellency, that—that—" Müller stuttered, "that the Hungarian foreign minister would change his decision on such a matter in the space of a minute."

"No. I can't wait until the fifteenth. It will have to be December fourteenth at the latest."

Müller and the baroness struggled to smother smiles. When

Müller asked why he had made this change, the baron looked at the ceiling and said in a reverential voice, "On December fourteenth I shall be thirty-four years old, the youngest foreign minister in the world. As a birthday present I should like to have the Swedish minister hand over the letters of recognition to Prime Minister Szálasi."

Müller hurried off to tell Wallenberg the good news. They had saved the protected and unprotected Jews from the Danube, at least for a month. As long as Szálasi and Kemény believed the lie that Swedish recognition was imminent, they would not permit Vajna to mount his pogrom under the eyes of the neutral diplomats.

Outside of Budapest, however, the Jews on the death march continued to suffer. Since November 10 the Arrow Cross, with the assistance of the gendarmes and the army, had marched between two and three thousand Jews a day from the Békásmegyer brickyard to the frontier post of Hegyeshalom. The journey took seven to eight days and each day the Jews marched at least twenty miles. At the frontier they were joined by Jewish labor battalions which had been marched from provincial towns. By November 22 the Hungarian police estimated that at least twenty thousand Jews had been delivered to Eichmann's SS commando at the Austrian frontier, thirteen thousand were "in transit," and ten thousand had "disappeared."

8

November 22–29, 1944

BUDAPEST AND THE ROAD
TO HEGYESHALOM

During November Waffen-SS General Hans Jüttner drove from Vienna to Budapest along the line of Eichmann's march. He was so appalled by the condition of the Jews that upon arriving in the capital he protested to the senior SS officer in Hungary, General Otto Winkelmann. "About halfway to Budapest, or a little later, we met the front columns," Jüttner said after the war. "Further columns followed at intervals of between twenty-five or thirty kilometers. As far as I can remember, they consisted mainly of women . . . the first columns made a truly terrifying impression. . . . Between the individual columns we met stragglers who had been unable to march on and lay in the road ditch. It was at once apparent that they would never be able to march as far as the frontier. After we arrived I demanded to see the man responsible for the execution of this march. I was told that he was Obersturmbannführer Eichmann."

The condition of the marchers so appalled the Hungarian police officer, Captain Nándor Batizfalvy, that on the morning of November 22 he delivered a horrifying report on the suffering along the route to a meeting of neutral diplomats held at the Swedish Legation. Present were Wallenberg, Miklós Krausz, and a Dr.

Koerner and a Dr. Farkas from the Portuguese and Spanish legations.

Batizfalvy estimated that thirteen thousand Jews were at present on the road to Hegyeshalom and that another seventy-eight hundred had already been handed over to the Germans. He described forced marches of over twenty-six miles, people given nothing to eat for days, and piles of corpses. His report shattered the diplomats. Immediately afterward Krausz persuaded him to obtain four "open orders" from Lieutenant-Colonel Ferenczy which would permit representatives of the neutral legations to travel along the line of march dispensing food and collecting Jews holding protective passes. Batizfalvy also agreed to accompany the neutral diplomats and assist them in returning their protected Jews to Budapest.

At dusk on the evening of November 22, in the same kind of rainy, wintry weather that had persisted throughout the march, Wallenberg set out for Hegyeshalom. He was accompanied by his chauffeur, Vilmos Langfelder, Per Anger, and Johnny Moser, a young Aryan-looking Jewish aide. A caravan of three cattle trucks containing food and medicine and a car of doctors and nurses followed Wallenberg's Packard. Relief caravans from the International Red Cross and Swiss Legation left Budapest at roughly the same time.

Fifteen miles west of the city Wallenberg overtook the columns of marchers who had left Békásmegyer that morning. Caught in the headlights of his car were barefoot children, women carrying children, and old men dragging their wives. As Langfelder slowed down to avoid hitting them, some recognized Wallenberg and shouted for help. He slumped down in the back seat and pulled his hat over his eyes to conceal his tears. He knew that compared with those who had been on the road for eight days, these marchers were well off. He wanted to start his work at Hegyeshalom, among those about to be handed over to Eichmann. If he drove all night he could reach the frontier by dawn, the time when the Arrow Cross loaded the marchers into freight cars for the trip across the border. If he arrived too late, after nine o'clock, he knew that another two thousand Jews would be lost to Eichmann.

He stopped briefly at Gönyü, one of the designated evening "rest stops" for the marchers, and found a thousand Jews quartered in two abandoned barns. He bribed the guards with rum and cigarettes to allow him to go inside. He switched on his flashlight. Hundreds of people lay on filthy pallets of straw, moaning and writhing in pain. Some, too exhausted to move, were slumped in pools of filthy water. Many suffered from typhoid fever and dysentery; almost all had lice. In two days they had received a single cup of watery "soup." With the help of Langfelder, Moser, and Anger, he unloaded sacks of food and dragged them into the barns.

Wallenberg did not know it at the time but he had stumbled across the more fortunate Jews quartered at Gönyü. Nearby, the Red Cross representatives traveling to Hegyeshalom encountered a group of marchers being lodged on barges moored in the Danube. They reported: "In Gönyü we saw that a part of the deportees were driven on board the ships anchored in the Danube. Many—in their great distress—committed suicide. In the still of the night one scream was followed by the other; the doomed people were jumping into the Danube, which was covered with drifting ice. They could not stand the tortures any longer. . . . With our own eyes we saw the gendarmes driving the Jews, who arrived in pitch darkness, over the narrow gangways covered with ice, so that scores of them slipped and fell into the icy river."

Wallenberg drove on in the darkness past vineyards and farms toward Hegyeshalom. During the night he passed the other Jewish rest stops: the open sports stadium, the cattle pens, and the open fields where Arrow Cross guards had announced over loudspeakers that if anyone tried to escape they would machine-gun the entire group. He might have passed Katherine Szenes, Elly Gidaly, and her brother Paul, who had finally obtained a Swedish safe pass for his sister and, disguised as a Hungarian soldier, was now searching for her. His mother had already escaped from an earlier column.

At daybreak Wallenberg knew he was nearing Hegyeshalom. The marchers were now mostly young girls and boys; many of the older Jews had "disappeared."

He arrived at 7:00 A.M., just as the Arrow Cross was delivering a batch of Jews to Eichmann's SS at the railway station. "At Hegyeshalom," reported the Swiss diplomats traveling in Wallenberg's convoy, "we found the deportees in the worst imaginable condition. The endless labor of the foot march, the almost total lack of food, made worse by the torturing steady fear that they were being taken to the extermination chambers in Germany, have brought these pitiful deportees to such a state that all human appearances and all human dignity have completely left them. . . . Human dignity can be preserved among the poverty-stricken and the suffering, as long as there are legal rights, and this dignity is lost when one is totally deprived of one's rights and at the mercy of someone else. . . . All social conventions, results of civilization and progress, cease completely among these people."

The Hungarians had already sorted the Jews into groups of a hundred each. Some groups had already boarded the freight cars and their doors had been locked and sealed; others stood on the platform, in front of the empty cars, awaiting orders to board. German SS officers, Hungarian Arrow Cross men and gendarmes paraded down the platform inspecting the cargo.

Eichmann's deputy Dieter Wisliceny commanded the SS contingent. "The main thing is the statistics," Eichmann had told him when the march began. "Every arriving Jew must be mercilessly taken over." But Wisliceny only followed Eichmann's orders up to a point. He asked the Arrow Cross for the numbers of Jews delivered and made no attempt to list their names, sex, or age, but he did try to persuade the Hungarians to take back Jews who were pregnant, sick, and almost dead. He knew that these Jews would die anyway during their march back to Budapest. The Hungarians, however, refused to reclaim them. Shouting matches ensued as the Arrow Cross and SS argued whether a feeble Jew was to die while traveling by train to Vienna or while walking back to Budapest.

One Jew who was standing on the platform on the morning that Wallenberg arrived in Hegyeshalom said: "For me that train meant one thing—death. I was positive that if I climbed onto that train I would die. Just as I was about to get on board and everyone was crying, I saw a handsome man, as if in a dream, who was trying to take people away. And I asked, 'Who is this gentleman?' because I thought that everyone, the whole world, was against us."

Wallenberg showed his diplomatic credentials and ordered the Arrow Cross guards at the station to stand aside and allow him to remove Jews holding Swedish passes. The guards lowered their bayonets so they touched his chest and forced him back, away from the deportees. Wallenberg ran around to the other side of the station, climbed onto the roof of one of the sealed freight cars, and shouted through the air vents, "Are there any Swedish-protected Jews in there who've lost their passes?"

Voices inside shouted, "Yes!" and hands shot through the air vents. Wallenberg ran along the roof shoving blank passes into each hand. The Arrow Cross ordered him off the roof. He ignored them and continued. Finally, a volley was fired over his head and he climbed down.

He returned minutes later with a gendarme officer and a squad of Hungarian soldiers he had bribed with rum and cigarettes. Intimidated by Wallenberg's show of force, the Arrow Cross guards agreed to permit him to remove Jews with Swedish passes, Jews claiming to have lost their passes, and Jews who had been collected for deportation before they could pick up their passes at the Swedish Legation. The Arrow Cross insisted that these people must all be listed in Wallenberg's register of protected Jews.

Wallenberg opened the large leather-bound ledger book containing the names of his "Swedish Jews" and announced in a loud voice, "I have passes for the following people. . . ." He then turned to a blank page and began reciting a list of the most common Jewish surnames.

Dozens of Jews stepped forward. Some had heard their surnames; others understood the ruse and claimed to have one of the names he had read out. When they stepped forward Wallenberg asked them to repeat their full names. Meanwhile, Langfelder quickly wrote each name on a blank pass.

Wallenberg pretended to check off the names in his register. "Sorry you couldn't make it to the Legation in time," he said to one man. "So here you are, we had to bring it to you."

He paused from time to time to scold the Arrow Cross. "See, I have a pass for this man," he said, "and you took him away before I could give it to him."

When he was certain he had intimidated the guards, he shouted to the Jews, "Which of you has recently lost your Swedish pass? Raise your hand." His assistant, Johnny Moser, raced through the crowds of Jews whispering, "Raise your hands! Raise your hands!"

Hands shot up everywhere.

Wallenberg moved through the crowd, touching some of the raised hands and sending these Jews to Langfelder to pick up a pass. "Aha!" he said to one man, pretending to recognize him, "there you are—I've been looking for you."

"Are *you* caught without a pass again?" he said to another in a loud voice.

"Why, I just gave *you* a pass several days ago. Off you go, now," he said to still another. As he walked through the forest of raised hands he said again and again in a soft voice, "I want to save you all but they will only let me take a few. So please forgive me, but I must save the young ones because I want to save a nation."

He saved three hundred Jews from the three thousand gathered at Hegyeshalom on November 23. Ninety percent had never had a Swedish protective pass. Before departing he unloaded most of his food to make room for them on the trucks. He bribed the Hungarian military commander of Hegyeshalom to distribute this food to the Jews left behind. "At least they can satisfy their hunger once before leaving Hungary," he said to Anger. He was too shy to hand out the food himself and he wanted to avoid the displays of gratitude he knew would follow its distribution, so he watched from a distance as, according to Anger, "the death-pale faces of the marchers swam with tears."

He left Hegyeshalom in daylight, and for the first time he saw conditions along the highway. Every twenty miles he encountered a column of Jews he later described as "starved, sick, unfortunate people, from twelve-year-old children to seventy-four-year-old matrons . . . ragged and dirty." He passed a group of servicemen from the Bor copper mines who had not eaten in a week and were "half-naked and insane with hunger."

Elderly Jews who had hidden some money now used it to pay local farmers to haul them toward Hegyeshalom in horse-drawn carts. Those without money or the energy to continue sat in groups by the side of the road, waiting patiently for the Arrow Cross to execute them.

Everywhere Wallenberg saw the work of the Arrow Cross. Bodies swung from trees, were slumped in ditches, or, in cases where the Arrow Cross had used hand grenades, lay in heaps by the side of the road. Some people had been squashed into a red pulp by the tires of police cars and military trucks.

He drove through villages where peasants laughed at the sight of the marchers and shrieked at the Arrow Cross guards to "Kill those Jewish whores now!" In other villages sympathetic Christians rushed out to the Jews with cups of water. The Arrow Cross had posted signs everywhere warning that anyone caught feeding the marchers would be immediately executed.

Sometimes Wallenberg stopped to speak with the gendarmes who had assisted the Arrow Cross. Some confided to him that they would prefer fighting the Russians to witnessing such suffering and agony. One group of Hungarian soldiers forced into escort duty mutinied and demanded to be sent back to the front.

He stopped frequently to grab children from the arms of their dying mothers and put them on the floor of his own car. His trucks were so full he could not take any more adults back to Budapest. He stopped also to bribe the Arrow Cross and hand out passes. He knew that those who received them would need a miracle to survive. They would have to make their own way back to Budapest without food and without being killed by the guards in other columns.

He almost saved Katherine Szenes. She saw his car stop and remembered: "Occasionally a car would appear, names would be called out, and certificates waved in the air. We had the impression that attempts were being made to save people and some perhaps were rescued. We were too far in the rear to see what was happening." Later she escaped during an air raid and found refuge in the home of a sympathetic Hungarian Christian. Paul Gidaly, however, arrived in Hegyeshalom with his precious Swedish pass too late to save his sister.

At dusk Wallenberg stopped at an abandoned factory where some marchers had halted for the night. He set up a soup kitchen and walked among people dispensing medicine, rum, and the last of his food. He was in agony. "My trucks are full," he was overheard saying to an aide, "and these people don't have the strength to walk back to Budapest even if the guards permitted it. They're all going to die."

At about the same time that Wallenberg was returning to Budapest, Eichmann was also motoring along the route of his march. He admitted later (during his trial in Jerusalem) having seen "two people dead" and some "figures swaying to and fro."

When Eichmann arrived in Budapest, General Winkelmann and László Endre threw a party to honor his achievements. In three weeks he had shipped his first batch of 50,000 Jews across the border. In August, when "that old fool Horthy" had frustrated his plans, 225,000 Jews had remained alive in Hungary; now there were 175,000. He planned to finish off the rest by December.

Eichmann enjoyed the party given in his honor. "I was so happy to be in the company of prominent Hungarian government members," he said later. "Winkelmann congratulated me on the 'elegant performance' [of the march]. So did Veesenmayer. So did Endre. We even toasted it and for the first time in my life I drank mare's milk alcohol [brandy and milk]."

Eichmann's celebration was short-lived. Soon afterward, Szálasi, influenced by the protests of the neutral diplomats and accounts of atrocities along the road to Hegyeshalom, announced that he was suspending the march although Hungarian Jews would continue "to be lent to the German government as fit for work, this being for the welfare of the Hungarian nation." He also announced that in the future women could only be deported to the Reich in trains or trucks. Veesenmayer reported to Berlin that, since the overwhelming majority of Jews left in Budapest were women, "Szálasi's edict is practically equivalent to canceling deportation."

The death march was also suspended because of the protests of SS officers in Austria who had received the surviving Jewish marchers. Most were too old and feeble to work, and they could not be gassed, since Himmler had closed the remaining extermination centers. Veesenmayer reported: "The chief executive in the deployment of Jewish labor for the lower Danube region, SS Obersturmbannführer Hoess, has declared that he can only use able-bodied men, preferably under the age of forty. . . . Jews, including women, who fail to answer such requirements are at the time a heavy burden on his labor units, so that he has considered the rejection of the group reaching the border of the Reich on foot as inadequate material. . . ."

Eichmann appeared to have reached a dead end. Himmler refused to gas Hungarian Jews, the Arrow Cross refused to march women to their deaths, and the SS in Austria refused to work them to death. Only he and Wallenberg seemed to care passionately about what happened to this last remnant of European Jewry. Like Wallenberg, he was resourceful. Several days after the march was canceled he had devised a new means of reducing the Jewish population of Budapest.

November 29–December 8, 1944

BUDAPEST

"They've rounded up all the protected laborers and taken them to the Jósefváros freight station," a voice whispered over the telephone. "They're packing them into boxcars. Hurry!"

Wallenberg slammed down the phone, shouted at an aide to send his staff to Jósefváros with blank passes, and then ran out of his office. His car was missing. The Arrow Cross had stolen it again. He jumped onto a bicycle and pedaled toward the freight yards in eastern Pest.

Until now his Swedish-protected labor brigade, like the other brigades under neutral protection, had been spared the horrors of the Arrow Cross pogroms and the death march. The seventeen thousand men of the protected brigades had remained in Budapest, digging trenches and removing rubble from the air raids. They were the only large group of healthy, able-bodied Jews left in the capital.

Eichmann wanted them. Two days earlier, on November 27, he had persuaded the Interior and Defense ministries to sign an agreement "loaning" these seventeen thousand Jews to the Reich for the purpose of building earthworks outside Vienna. To transport them to Austria, Eichmann had again done the impossible: obtained trains from the badly pressed army transport center in Vienna. His aides were stunned; it was another of the Master's miracles. He put his own SS unit in charge of the actual deportations and ordered the less reliable Hungarians to assist them. Repairs had been made and the rail line between Budapest and Hegyeshalom was reopened.

Wallenberg dashed up the steps of Jósefváros Station to find his way blocked by two Arrow Cross guards. He screamed curses and orders at them in German. Neither spoke German, and fearful that he was a Nazi official, they lowered their bayonets. He ran through the station's warehouse and onto the loading platforms.

The scene on the platforms was similar to that at Hegyeshalom. Thousands of Jews stood in columns in front of empty freight cars. Several cars had already been loaded and sealed. However, unlike at Hegyeshalom, this time the SS, not the Arrow Cross, was in charge.

The young SS transport officer in charge drew his revolver and pointed it at Wallenberg's stomach. Wallenberg jumped up and down, swearing and screaming in German at the top of his lungs: "This is an outrage! An outrage! How dare you threaten a diplomatic representative of the kingdom of Sweden?"

The SS officer reholstered his gun. He was unnerved by the authority and fluency of Wallenberg's German.

Wallenberg continued screaming and jumping. "And this too is an outrage," he yelled, gesturing toward the Jews. "I have it on good authority that among those arrested by you for deportation are Jews protected by the king of Sweden. How dare you rob them of their freedom? Release them at once!"

The officer hesitated. The loading was suspended as the Jews and the guards watched, transfixed by the spectacle.

"At once or I'll lodge a formal diplomatic protest with your superiors!" Wallenberg shouted.

The German capitulated.

Wallenberg strode down the platform bellowing, "Anyone

holding a Swedish protective pass fall out of line and follow me." Dozens of men obeyed him.

He stopped at one of the sealed freight cars. "Open it!" he ordered a guard. "There may be men inside holding Swedish passes."

As the door opened the SS officer ran over and said, "Anyone with a Swedish pass can come out, but if anyone tries to bluff I'll shoot him on the spot."

Inside the car was a young Jewish medical student who had a counterfeit Swedish pass. He now underwent, he said later, "the most difficult decision of my life." Finally, reasoning that to stay in the freight car meant certain death, he climbed out and joined the dozens of men lined up in front of Wallenberg.

Wallenberg's aides had arrived from Üllői Road with the registry of protected Jews. Wallenberg himself sat at a table comparing the passes with those in the registry. The SS officer looked over his shoulder from time to time to make certain he was not accepting forgeries.

"It's a fake," the medical student whispered as he handed Wallenberg his pass.

Wallenberg quickly said in a loud voice, "Ah! You again. I certainly don't need to check *your* pass. I remember giving it to you personally just the other day."

Wallenberg was disappointed in the turnout. Only about fifty men among the thousands at Jósefváros carried legitimate Swedish passes. It was not enough. "There must be hundreds of men whose passes were stolen by your people when they were collected," he said to the SS officer. "I'll take *them* with me as well." Now thoroughly intimidated and confused, the officer did not dare object.

Wallenberg shouted to the remaining Jews, "Which of you has documents in Hungarian proving that you once held a valid Swedish pass?"

Many of the men quickly understood the ruse. At first one by one, and then by the hundreds, they dug into their pockets and pulled out any piece of paper printed in Hungarian that appeared to be remotely official.

"Present these documents to me at once!" Wallenberg commanded. About 250 men jumped out of freight cars and, waving bits of dirty crumpled papers, lined up in front of Wallenberg.

He solemnly examined their post office receipts, vaccination certificates, ration cards, tax forms, and bills of lading. "Yes, that shows you had a pass. . . . Yes, obviously you had one, too. . . . You too . . ." he exclaimed as he pretended to scrutinize each scrap of paper. He had gambled that, like himself, the SS officer could not read a word of Hungarian.

One of the men in line had no paper at all. "Once I was in Uppsala, at the university," he said quickly in German.

"He has no pass, no paper," said the SS officer.

"Name a street in Uppsala," Wallenberg demanded before the man could be pulled from the line.

The man mumbled a Swedish street name.

"That's right!" he exclaimed. "It's obvious that this man is under Swedish protection. Next!"

This man and about three hundred others survived. Wallenberg's aides hastily gave them new passes and loaded them into trucks along with those holding legitimate passes. Wallenberg drove away from Jósefváros Station with three hundred Jews.

As soon as he had deposited these Jews at Swedish-protected houses he bought a bouquet of flowers and hurried to the Deli railroad station in Buda. He had just learned that Baroness Kemény was being exiled to her family's home in northern Italy. The day before, the police had reported to Interior Minister Vajna that she had become one of Wallenberg's most useful and active agents. Vajna had immediately ordered her arrested, but Szálasi had intervened. She could escape arrest, he told Baron Kemény, but only if she left Budapest within twenty-four hours.

By the end of November, Deli Station had become the first stop on one of the principal escape routes to the west. Soldiers and civilians lived in the station for days, sleeping on suitcases and duffel bags, sprawled in heaps, waiting for tracks to be repaired and for trains to run again. When a train was announced the station resembled an anthill. People leaped up, fought to separate their baggage from the piles, rushed onto the platform, and attempted to push onto one or two darkened carriages.

A special compartment had been reserved for the baroness. Because she was the wife of the foreign minister, representatives from each embassy and legation had turned out to bid her farewell. The baron had told them that she was taking a "recreational trip" to the Italian Alps.

Wallenberg stood in line with the other diplomats and shook the baroness's hand with the customary formality. However, as the other diplomats and her husband turned to leave, he slipped over to the door of her sleeping compartment and handed her a bouquet of flowers that one of his aides had been hiding. She burst into tears. "I must save the life of my unborn child," she sobbed. "That's my only excuse for abandoning you."

In the six weeks they had known one another, Wallenberg and the baroness had become extremely fond of each other. It is not clear whether or not they had become lovers, although according to Elisabet Szel, the wife of one of Wallenberg's drivers, they had become "extremely close."

The morning after the baroness's departure Wallenberg returned to Jósefváros Station. He had learned that the SS planned to deport another batch of protected Jewish laborers. However, when Eichmann had learned of the events of the previous day he had replaced the young SS transport officer with one of his most senior and trusted aides, Captain Theodor Dannecker, the man responsible for shipping French Jews to the extermination camps. The moment Dannecker saw Wallenberg he drew his pistol and, ignoring his protests, chased him from the station.

Wallenberg drove directly to the German Legation to protest this violation of his diplomatic immunity to SS Brigadierführer Grell. After listening to Wallenberg's description of his encounter with Dannecker, Grell said, "My advice to you, Mr. Secretary, is to worry more about the real Swedes living in Budapest. These Jews aren't Swedes. However, if you insist on becoming involved in things that don't concern you, then I cannot, unfortunately, protect you from the consequences."

"Several weeks ago a German military truck demolished one of my official cars," Wallenberg said. "Since then other of my cars have been the victims of similar 'accidents.' Is this what you mean by 'the consequences'?"

"I suggest that you return to peaceful Sweden, Mr. Secretary," Grell replied. "There, the military vehicles are in less of a hurry. They can take more care not to endanger pleasure trippers such as yourself. I would advise you to take my advice. Good day."

Wallenberg was defeated. In the following week Eichmann deported seventeen thousand men of the international labor brigades from Jósefváros Station. Wallenberg had saved only three hundred. However, because of transportation difficulties most of these Jews never reached the Reich. They were interned instead in concentration camps near the western Hungarian villages of Fertörákos and Balfnad Koszeg. Most died of typhus or starvation, or were tortured to death by their Arrow Cross guards. After the war mass graves were found near the camps.

Wallenberg's failure to save most of the labor servicemen threw him into a deep depression. Several days after this setback he was visited by Marton Vörös, a Hungarian who ran the small office maintained by the Swedish Red Cross in the city of Pécs. Vörös found Wallenberg in a dark room in his Phoenix Street office, slumped behind his desk and looking "tired and sad." His eyes were puffy and ringed with dark circles, and the black stubble on his chin—he had not shaved in days—accentuated his pale complexion. He appeared to be in a trance and did not seem to notice that Vörös had entered the room.

Vörös introduced himself by showing Wallenberg his Swedish protective pass and reminding him that he had signed it personally. He then explained that he was searching for the head of the Swedish Red Cross in Budapest, Dr. Langlet. Could Wallenberg help locate him?

Wallenberg finally came to life. "Oh, yes, I see. So that's what you want," he mumbled. He got up, put his arm around Vörös's shoulder, escorted him over to the window, and pointed down to the street.

"Every minute," he said in a low voice, "there is something to see down there." His eyes scanned the street as he spoke. "And if not there, somewhere else. Even while we speak, somewhere, someone else is being murdered by the Arrow Cross."

To distract him Vörös began to report on the situation in Pécs. He said that the handful of Jewish survivors had protective passes from the Swedish Red Cross. They had unreasonable expectations that the Red Cross could save them. Was it better to encourage these expectations? Or to make them see things more realistically?

"If people have such great expectations then it can only help them. From their faith and confidence they'll gain the strength to resist. If they believe the passes are legitimate and powerful then they may convince others, even the police, that they're powerful. The confidence and faith of the Jews here has given us all strength. It gives me strength. Anyway, reality doesn't matter any longer, illusion does. It's our job to create this illusion."

Vörös appeared not to understand.

"Look," Wallenberg continued, dropping his voice to a whisper, "when I came to Hungary all I had was a knapsack—that was the reality; but my most powerful weapon was my imagination and that could not fit into any knapsack."

Vörös brought the conversation back to his search for Langlet. Wallenberg suggested that he ask Per Anger at the Swedish Legation and that he inquire at the headquarters of the International Red Cross on Benczur Street. "It's possible that you'll find nothing," he said. "There may be nobody at any of these addresses. Laws no longer exist here; anything can happen. Sometimes one can't get from one street to the next . . ."

Wallenberg stopped in mid-sentence. At the end of Phoenix Street a group of Jews was being taken somewhere by a patrol of gendarmes. Wallenberg turned away, returned to his desk, and sank into his chair without saying another word. His eyes glazed over. It seemed to Vörös that he had fallen into a trance. A full minute later he noticed Vörös standing by his desk. "What did you say just now?" he asked.

"Nothing," replied Vörös, more confused than ever. "I didn't say a thing."

"Well, maybe we should send someone from this department to help you in Pécs," Wallenberg said, recovering. "It would have to be . . ."

He stopped again in the middle of a sentence, interrupted this time by the clattering of soldiers' boots on the cobblestones below. He jumped up and hurried to the window. An SS detachment was marching by and as they passed underneath they began singing in cadence with their marching.

Vörös noticed that instead of looking at the soldiers, Wallenberg was again staring into space, hypnotized by the marching and singing. Vörös started toward the door to leave. At the last minute he changed his mind and decided to say something. When he turned around, Wallenberg had vanished. Finally he saw him sitting hunched over in a chair in the darkest corner of the office. He looked over at Vörös and said, "Someone who no longer has the possibility . . ." He left the sentence unfinished and Vörös departed.

Several days later Vörös returned to the Phoenix Street office. Everything was different. Wallenberg had just succeeded in saving some Jews from the Arrow Cross death squads. Aides were busily writing out passes and Wallenberg was animated and happy.

After the departure of the labor servicemen, most of the Jews remaining in Budapest fell into two categories: Jews under international protection and unprotected Jews. Most of the latter were those who, because of poor health, because they were too young or too old, or because they were poor and without influence, had failed to obtain protective passes. Szálasi's decree that women must be deported in vehicles had saved many from joining Eichmann's march.

By the end of the first week of December, Eichmann and his Arrow Cross allies had successfully segregated these two classes of Jews from one another as well as from the rest of Budapest. On November 18 the government had informed the Jewish Council that all unprotected Jews would soon be concentrated into a ghetto—a one-tenth-of-a-square-mile area in Pest's Seventh District, which already contained numerous Yellow Star houses. Jews currently living in Yellow Star houses outside the ghetto would move into it and turn over their houses to Christian families living within the area designated as the ghetto.

This transfer of populations occurred at the end of November and the beginning of December. Jews moving into the ghetto were forced to leave behind most of their furniture and belongings. Jews could take into the ghetto only what they could carry in their hands or on their backs, and Arrow Cross gangs stripped them of even these possessions as they moved.

By December 7, seventy thousand unprotected, impoverished, starving Jews had been jammed into the central ghetto's 243 serviceable houses. An average of two hundred and ninety Jews lived in each house, an average of fourteen to a room. As in the case of the Warsaw ghetto, a tall wooden fence, built at Jewish expense and by Jewish labor, encircled the ghetto. And as in Warsaw, the fence had only four gates, each situated at one of the ordinal points on the compass and each guarded by a contingent of Arrow Cross and regular policemen. Jews were permitted to walk the streets of the ghetto only two hours a day. Any Jews found in the streets outside the ghetto were arrested and brought inside.

On December 10 Eichmann ordered the ghetto to be officially "sealed." Jews could enter the ghetto, but not leave it. Once inside they were at the mercy of Eichmann and the Arrow Cross.

The concentration of Jews into a central ghetto made Eichmann's task simpler and gave him two options. If he could obtain enough trucks or railway cars he could quickly round up the Jews for deportation; on the other hand, if it appeared that the Russians would capture Budapest first, he could order the ghetto bombed from the air or destroyed by German tanks. This had been done in Warsaw.

Six days after Eichmann sealed the ghetto, Gábor Vajna visited Berlin to discuss the status of the Hungarian Jews with Himmler's deputies. Vajna later testified that it was agreed at this time that "all surviving Jews should be 'taken away' by the most forceful methods. I was to arrange details in Budapest with Winkelmann and Eichmann."

By mid-December the only Jews left outside the central ghetto were the approximately fifteen thousand in hiding, the thirty-three thousand protected Jews living in their own "International Ghetto," and the six thousand children housed in Red Cross shelters. Some of the children had been placed in the shelters by parents seeking to protect them from the Arrow Cross, others were orphans, and each shelter held as many as five hundred children. As the Russians neared Budapest, and as the air raids increased and the shelling worsened, many of the Hungarian employees of these shelters fled to the west.

An International Red Cross representative reported that in one home, "Children of two to fourteen years, famished, ragged, emaciated to mere skeletons, frightened to death by the droning and detonation of bombs, had crept into corners; their bodies were eaten by filth and scabies, their rags were infested with lice. Huddled up in fear and infinite misery, they made inarticulate sounds. They had not eaten for days, and for many days there had been nobody to look after them. Nobody knows where their nurses had gone and when it was that they ran away."

The protected Jews in the so-called International Ghetto were scarcely better off. On November 15, the Szálasi government had ordered all Jews holding Swiss, International Red Cross,

Spanish, Portuguese, and Swedish protective passes to move into the Yellow Star buildings on or near Pozsonyi Road, Pannonia, and Tátra streets in Pest's St. Istvan District. There they were to be segregated into houses depending on the nationality of their protective passes.

During the three days following Szálasi's announcement Pest's streets were clogged by protected Jews moving their belongings in hand carts toward the International Ghetto. The Arrow Cross terrorized stragglers, stole their possessions, shot them at random, and carried some off to their Andrássy Street headquarters where, after being tortured, they were sent to join the death march. All unprotected Jews who had formerly occupied the Yellow Star houses in the International Ghetto were taken to Békásmegyer and made to join the march.

Szálasi had created this International Ghetto in order to facilitate the deportation of the unprotected Jews and to facilitate the repatriation of the protected Jews to whatever country claimed them. "Their departure," he announced, "is to be made the subject of the development of diplomatic relations between Hungary and the representative neutral states and the settling of transportation problems between these states and Germany."

When the population transfer of Jews into and out of the International Ghetto was completed there should have been, according to government figures: 4,500 "Swedish" Jews, 7,800 "Swiss," 700 "Portuguese," 100 "Spanish," and 250 under the protection of the Vatican—all crammed into houses that, until a week before, had held only 4,000 nonprotected Jews. Because of the large numbers of counterfeit protective passes the real population of the International Ghetto approached 35,000.

The Swiss houses were the most crowded. The Swiss had inadvertently made their passes the easiest to copy. They had also failed to exert the kind of administrative controls practiced by Wallenberg. As a result, about ten thousand Jews holding bogus Swiss passes tried to cram themselves into the Swiss houses along with the seventy-eight hundred holding legitimate passes.

This overcrowding produced chaos. According to Charles Lutz, "All the protected houses in the St. Istvan (District V) are over-crowded to such an extent that part of the people accommodated in them are obliged to live in the staircases, corridors, and cellars. In case of an air raid the lodgers of the house cannot, of course, use the shelters which are already overcrowded. It was reported on November 24, from the house at 54 Pozsonyi Road, that the number of people living there amounts to eighteen hundred. Communication on the stairs is impossible as even they are crowded with sitting or sleeping people. For five days the inhabitants had no food at all, and very little afterward. As Jews are forbidden to go out into the streets, it is impossible to provide food for these houses. . . ."

The government replied to Lutz's protests and requests for more houses by raiding the existing Swiss houses and dragging away thousands of people at random, regardless of whether their passes were genuine or bogus. Some of these Jews were put on the deportation trains leaving from Jósefváros Station; others were dumped into the Central Ghetto.

The thirteen thousand Jews quartered in the thirty-two Swedish houses fared somewhat better. Wallenberg had set up a network of hospitals, soup kitchens, and children's nurseries and, because of his contacts in the police force and government, was more successful at protecting his Jews from Arrow Cross raids.

Wallenberg had in fact issued more than double the forty-five hundred passes permitted him by the government. Many residents of the Swedish houses also held counterfeit passes, but he made no effort to evict them. Upon learning that the government had ordered a census of all the international houses he bribed the Arrow Cross census takers with Swedish protective passes. In return they permitted his Jewish aides to conduct the census in the Swedish houses. The aides reported that forty-five hundred Jews were in residence. Meanwhile the government continued its almost daily raids on the Swiss houses.

At the end of the first week in December the status of all

the protected Jews had again become precarious. Gábor Kemény informed Wallenberg that he would not extend his deadline. Unless Sweden recognized his government before his December 14 birthday, he would cancel the privileges of the protected Jews and fulfill his threat to "give them" to the brutal Vajna. They would then suffer the same fate that Eichmann planned for the Jews of the Central Ghetto. Wallenberg knew that Sweden would never recognize the Szálasi government. His only hope was that the Russians would capture Budapest before the baron's birthday.

On the morning of December 8 the Russian Army launched a new offensive aimed at encircling Budapest. For the first time Russian artillery shells landed in the middle of the city and artillery barrages were added to the sufferings of Jews in both ghettos.

The Swedish minister, fearing that Budapest would soon be surrounded and cut off, hurriedly assembled a last diplomatic pouch on the evening of December 8. Wallenberg added to it an official report and letters addressed to Kalman Lauer and his mother.

His report was pessimistic. It said, "In general, the Jews have been plundered to a great extent of everything they once owned. . . . The food situation will shortly become disastrous. The Arrow Cross men carry off a great number of Jews to their own premises, where they maltreat and torture them. Then they drive them to assembly points and deport them."

In his letter to Kalman Lauer he admitted that he was already busy making plans for the inevitable Russian occupation and said, "Before coming home I plan to start a foundation that will help the Jews regain their property." He ended his letter, "On the whole I am in good spirits and enjoying the struggle."

At the beginning of November, Wallenberg had confided in his five most trusted aides that he had been sent to Budapest by the American War Refugee Board as well as the World Jewish Congress and that the American government and private American Jewish philanthropies had provided some of his funds. When the war was over, he said, more money would certainly be available for relief work. He planned to use it to found a humanitarian organization that would assist homeless and impoverished Jews. He asked these selected aides to think about the structure of this future organization. He gave no indication of worrying that the Russians might have their *own* plans for postwar Hungary, nor that he thought they might object to what he later decided to call the "Wallenberg Institute for Support and Reconstruction." Also on December 8 Wallenberg wrote to his mother:

I really don't know how I can repay my debt to you [for her letters]. Another courier is leaving today and again I'm afraid I can only send you a few hurried lines.

The situation here is very exciting and full of adventure although I am terribly overloaded with work. Gangs of bandits prowl Budapest beating up people and shooting them. Already forty members of my staff alone have been beaten up and mistreated. Nevertheless, we are all in fairly good humor and happy to be waging this battle. . . .

We can hear the thundering cannons of the approaching Russian Army night and day and diplomatic activity has also become very lively since the arrival of the Szálasi regime. I represent the Legation to this government almost single-handedly. To date I have seen the foreign minister ten times, the deputy prime minister twice, the interior minister twice, and the finance minister once, etc.

I was fairly friendly with the foreign minister's wife but unfortunately she has recently gone to Merano.

The need for food in Budapest is tremendous but we have managed to lay away good stores. I have the suspicion that it will not be easy for me to return home directly after the occupation so I don't think you should expect me in Stockholm until Easter. But that's all speculation. Nobody really knows what the occupation will be like. In any case, I shall try to come home as soon as I can.

In the present situation one cannot really make plans. Be-

fore I was convinced that I would be home by Christmas. Now I find myself wishing you Merry Christmas and Happy New Year by letter. Let's hope that peace is not long off.

Dearest mother, I am sending you two photos with this letter. They have just been developed and show me at my desk surrounded by my co-workers and employees.

I have so much work to do that time has passed very quickly. I am often invited out for dinners of roast suckling pig and other Hungarian specialties.

Dearest mother, I shall have to say goodbye for now. We must send the bag. I embrace and kiss you and the whole family with all my heart and soul.

Your Raoul

P.S. Many kisses for Nina and her little girl.

P.S.S. It is possible that I shall be here for a long time.

On December 9, the day after the Swedish Legation sent out its last diplomatic pouch, the Soviet Army suddenly and unexpectedly broke through the defenses north of Budapest and reached the Danube twenty miles away at the town of Vac. Many German and Hungarian units were cut off and forced to surrender. The Russians now controlled the roads and railroads to the north, south, and east; only those to the west remained open.

Several days later, the parliament and most of the Arrow Cross government, including Baron Kemény, fled west to Sopron, a town near the Austrian frontier. Gábor Vajna and Adolf Eichmann stayed behind.

10

December 8, 1944–January 7, 1945

Wallenberg arrived at the doorstep of his Buda apartment at the same time as Eichmann and an aide. Eichmann had dressed in a civilian suit to have dinner with the Swedish first secretary. This was to be a social occasion: the son of an accountant, a former traveling salesman, dining with a member of one of Sweden's most aristocratic families.

Wallenberg had forgotten he had invited Eichmann to dinner.

He had invited him after remembering how Eichmann had softened and become more reasonable when Wallenberg had offered to share a drink during their previous meeting. If he invited Eichmann to dinner, perhaps he could persuade him to spare the surviving Jews.

Wallenberg pretended that nothing was wrong. He greeted Eichmann and ushered him into his apartment. After handing him and his aide a drink he excused himself and went into another room to telephone Lars Berg. "I've got Eichmann here," he whispered, "and I've forgotten that I invited him to dinner. Can you set up something this quickly?"

Berg said he could. He and another Swedish diplomat, Göte Carlsson, lived nearby in the mansion of a wealthy Hungarian count who had been accused of having Jewish blood. The count and his family had fled, entrusting their houses, their servants, and their priceless antiques to Berg. In spite of rationing, the count's cook, Magda, was somehow still able to produce the huge amounts of food she had once prepared for the count's family. Berg and Carlsson suspected she fed her entire family from the leftovers, but tonight her profligacy would come in handy.

Wallenberg returned to Eichmann. "We are going to dine tonight at the home of two of my colleagues," he said. "I think you'll enjoy seeing their house." When they had finished their drinks he walked them over to Berg's house.

The dinner was one of Magda's best. They ate off the count's fine china, cut the meat with his silver knives, and drank rare wines from his cellar. Wallenberg steered the conversation away from the war and Eichmann relaxed.

After dinner they retired to the huge sitting room for coffee and brandy. Wallenberg seated everyone with great care. He guided Eichmann to a comfortable stuffed chair facing the curtains that the servants had drawn to cover the room's large east-facing windows. Once Eichmann was cradling a brandy snifter Carlsson, on Wallenberg's instructions, pulled open the curtains. Wallenberg extinguished the lights.

The eastern horizon blazed with the exploding shells of a Soviet artillery barrage. Without the thick curtains as mufflers, the heavy thumps of the guns were easily audible. Red bursts of light from the nearest shells flashed again and again. They bathed the room in light and then pitched it into darkness, as if a red neon light was flickering outside the window. The portraits of the count's family, Eichmann holding his brandy, and Wallenberg, standing next to the window like a teacher at a blackboard, appeared, disappeared, and then appeared again for several seconds during a long barrage.

At first Wallenberg pretended to ignore the spectacular show outside the window and, with the cannon fire flashing on his face, launched into a theoretical discussion of the principles of Nazism. He spoke dispassionately, as if delivering a lesson in simple logic to a class of dim-witted schoolboys. "Nazism is not really a bona fide ideology," he said at one point. "It's just the political incarnation of a single basic human emotion, hate. How can it last?"

Eichmann was shocked that anyone could criticize his religion so openly. He answered with propaganda phrases and unconnected fragments of thought about the "Jewish-Bolshevik menace."

Wallenberg pointed out the window. "Look how close the Bolsheviks are," he said, his voice rising, his earlier control vanishing. "Your war is almost over. Nazism is doomed, finished, and so are those who cling to this hatred until the last minute. It's the end of the Nazis, the end of Hitler, the end of Eichmann."

"All right, I agree with you," Eichmann said calmly. "I'll admit it. I've never believed in all of Hitler's ideology, but it has, after all, given me a great deal of power and wealth. You're right—soon, very soon, this comfortable life will end. No more airplanes bringing women and wine from France. The Russians will take my horses, my dogs, and my palace in Budapest. They'll probably shoot me on the spot. For me there's no escape, no liberation. There are, however, some consolations. If I continue to eliminate our enemies until the end it may delay, if only for a few days, our defeat. And then, when I finally do walk to the gallows, at least I'll know I've completed my mission."

As soon as Eichmann finished he got up to leave. As he shook Wallenberg's hand he said loudly, "I want to thank you for an exceptionally charming and interesting evening." He then lowered his voice and said, "Now, don't think we're friends; we're not. I plan to do everything to keep you from saving your Jews. Your diplomatic passport won't protect you from everything. Even a neutral diplomat can meet with an accident."

On December 22, several days after this dinner and before Eichmann could make good on his threat to kill Wallenberg or destroy the ghetto, the Soviet Army broke through the Balaton–Danube defensive line southwest of the city. All roads leading west except for two to Esztergom and Szentendre were cut. The total encirclement of Budapest was only days away.

Gábor Vajna responded to the Soviet threat by ordering that all Jews in concealment outside the ghetto immediately go inside or face summary execution. After decreeing that any Budapest streets or squares named after Jews be renamed for Christian patriots he fled to join the Szálasi government in Sopron. He placed his cousin, Ernö Vajna, who shared his anti-Semitism, in charge of defending Budapest and handling the Jews.

Despite his boasts to Wallenberg about facing the Russian gallows, Eichmann also made preparations to flee. Just before leaving he organized a two-mile-long living chain of Jews to carry shells from an ammunition dump to German positions and ordered the removal of all children from the Red Cross shelters to the Central Ghetto. Although he would not be present to witness the destruction of the ghetto, he wanted to make certain that when it occurred, all of Budapest's Jews were included. He left instructions with the SS unit remaining behind in the capital that "No Jew must come out of the ghetto alive."

As an afterthought he ordered the Jewish Council to assemble on the evening of the twenty-second. Their execution would be his last act in Budapest. At nine o'clock, three of his SS officers raced into the Council building with revolvers drawn. No one was there and the doorkeeper explained that the Council had received a message to assemble at nine o'clock the next morning. One of the officers promised to shoot him and his daughter if the Council was not present at 9:00 A.M.

The Council survived. That night Eichmann withdrew his SS detachment through the last open road to the west, and two days later, on December 24, Russian troops reached the outskirts of Buda. They had broken through German defenses so quickly and unexpectedly that parents from the suburbs who had ventured into the capital to buy Christmas presents found themselves trapped and cut off. The day after Christmas the Russians severed the last open road to the west. Budapest was surrounded.

Caught inside the Russian circle were 750,000 Christians, 140,000 Jews, 80,000 German and Hungarian soldiers, several thousand Arrow Cross storm troopers, and a handful of neutral diplomats, among them Raoul Wallenberg.

Many of the civilians, particularly those in the working-class quarters of Pest, were apathetic or even neutral to the outcome of the siege. They hid in their cellars, venturing out as little as possible. The defending garrison had been ordered to hold out at all costs. "Defend Budapest to the last man," was their order. "Every street corner, every window must become a death-bringing fortress!" They were promised an airdrop of supplies and a counterattack to break the siege, and on December 29 they rejected a Russian plea to surrender.

Russian and Rumanian detachments nosed their way through the outskirts of Pest, driving back the defenders house by house with Tommy guns and grenades. Russian loudspeakers could be heard everywhere exhorting the Hungarians to desert the Germans and playing over and over again a Hungarian song with the lyrics "You are fleeing in vain."

The Arrow Cross government in Sopron conducted itself as if nothing were amiss. The parliament passed meaningless laws. Prime Minister Szálasi dictated his memoirs and ordered the government press to print thousands of pamphlets explaining the philosophical underpinnings of his "Hungarist" movement. He spent much of his time attending spiritualist séances during which he claimed to be in communication with John Campbell, a Scottish ghost who prophesied the imminent defeat of the Allies.

In Budapest, where there was virtually no government, the Arrow Cross was less preposterous and more dangerous. Gábor Vajna's cousin, Ernö, had the title of "Arrow Cross Official in Charge of the Defense of the Capital." In fact, power was held by gangs of young Arrow Cross toughs under the command of middle-aged psychopaths. Throughout the siege they perpetrated a reign of terror unmatched in Europe since the Dark Ages.

During the final weeks of December and the first weeks of January, Arrow Cross gangs, using the pretext of ferreting out Jews "in hiding," raided the ghettos and seized protected and unprotected Jews from homes, streets, hospitals, and air raid shelters. Execution squads marched many of those taken directly to the banks of the Danube and shot them. The rest were brought to the cellars of various Arrow Cross barracks, where they were stripped and tortured. Each cellar had its own specialty. In Tokoly Street they burned out eyes with hot nails. In the inquisition cellar in Andrássy Street known as the "Frozen Room," they beat Jews with leather straps and made them clean the toilet bowls with their tongues.

The Budapest Institute of Forensic Medicine, which collected some of the bodies, reported: "From the distorted faces of the corpses the conclusion could be drawn that their sufferings had been ghastly. Very few blown-out brains or heart-shots were to be found; on the other hand there was overwhelming evidence of the most brutal ill-treatment. Shooting out of eyes, scalping, deliberate breaking of bones, and abdominal knife wounds were Nyilas [Arrow Cross] specialties."

Among the most notorious leaders of the execution and torture squads was Kurt Rettman, a former telephone factory official who advocated the outright killing of Jews and who proclaimed in November, "It's a pity to go through all the bother of deportations and closing the Jews into ghettos. If we just shoot every Jew the problem is solved." Another infamous leader was Mrs. Vilmos Salzer, an upper-class matron who arrived every evening in the cellars wearing riding boots and carrying a whip and was fond of burning naked women with candles. Father András Kun, a Minorite monk, dressed in a black cape and, while carrying a crucifix in one hand and a revolver in the other, ordered the Danube executions with the words "In the name of Jesus Christ, fire!"

Jews who survived a night in the Arrow Cross cellars were

usually executed the following day. To save bullets, the death squads tied them into groups of three, shot the middle man or woman, and then pushed all three into the Danube, leaving the other two to drown. Some Jews were thrown into the river alive and then picked off by Arrow Cross boys who placed bets on who could hit the most floating targets.

The Arrow Cross squads were unpredictable. Jews never knew if they would merely check their identity cards, beat them on the spot, take them to the Danube, or, because they had been bribed by Wallenberg, protect them from a more vicious Arrow Cross unit. There was no law, no rational order to events. Lives depended on the whim of a fourteen-year-old boy with an armband and a gun.

On Christmas Eve the Arrow Cross stormed the Jewish children's homes run by the International Red Cross, shot children as young as a year and a half, and drove the survivors into the Danube. Four days later they attacked the Maros Street Hospital, tortured and killed patients, and massacred the doctors and nurses. They stormed the Swedish Legation and fired on Christian ambulancemen who came to the aid of wounded Jews. Different Arrow Cross units attacked and condemned each other to death during disputes over jurisdiction and the division of Jewish goods seized during the raids. One Arrow Cross squad of teenage boys even arrested and tortured a German officer during a frenzy of violence. No one was safe, least of all Wallenberg.

On December 26 an Arrow Squad commanded by Josef Reli arrested the baroness's former employer, Karl Müller. He was brought to the Frozen Room in Andrássy Street to be interrogated by Father Kun.

"Here is the right hand of that Jew-Messiah Wallenberg," Reli announced.

"So you're Wallenberg's right hand, are you?" bellowed Kun. "Well, then, let's see your right hand." Müller held it out. Kun whipped out a knife from his robes and slashed it open.

Müller survived his first interrogation and was later moved

across the river to the Arrow Cross headquarters on Nemetvolgyi Street in Buda. Here he saw to his horror that the local leader, Miklós Desi-Dregan, had reproduced dozens of pictures of Wallenberg and had plastered them on the walls and handed them to his squad leaders. At one point Müller overheard him tell his gangs that "if this low-class Jew-lover ever sets foot in Buda, shoot him on the spot."

Instead of hiding from the Arrow Cross death squads, Wallenberg counterattacked. He fought back as a diplomat, as a skilled administrator, and finally, when he had no other choice, as an underground guerilla.

As a diplomat he filed formal protests of the atrocities with the German military authorities and with Ernö Vajna and the other Arrow Cross officials theoretically in control of the capital. As the terror worsened in late December and early January his protest notes became more strident and threatening. In one of January 3 addressed to the German town commander, he characterized an Arrow Cross plan to move the protected Jews into the ghetto as "utterly crazy and inhuman," and added, "The Royal Swedish Legation is not aware of any similar plan ever having been carried out by any other civilized government."

Wallenberg was appalled at the prospect of having the thirty-five thousand protected Jews moved into the Central Ghetto. It was already seriously overcrowded, and its residents were close to starvation. He also worried that as the protected Jews moved, Arrow Cross bands would strip them of their clothing and remaining food supplies. Once in the ghetto they would also be more vulnerable to any last-minute pogrom. He knew from an informant that when Ernö Vajna had announced his plan to close the International Ghetto, he had told an aide that, in the Central Ghetto, all the Jews "would be exterminated with machine guns in due time."

Wallenberg's protests failed to influence either the Hungarians or the German military authorities, and on January 5, five thousand Swedish Jews, along with Jews living in other neutral houses, were marched into the Central Ghetto. The following morning the remaining thirty-seven hundred Swedish Jews were made to assemble in front of their houses in preparation for their transfer. At the last minute, however, they were permitted to return home. Wallenberg had persuaded Vajna to postpone their march for forty-eight hours.

On January 7 he and Vajna struck a deal: Vajna would allow the remaining Swedish Jews to stay in the International Ghetto, and in exchange Wallenberg would hand over to the government all of the food stored in the Swedish houses except that necessary to feed his Swedish Jews for the next three days. Wallenberg had purchased this precious food during the autumn and had hidden it in the basements of his houses. He was willing to sacrifice it now because he was certain the Russians would liberate Pest within a few days.

The letter that Wallenberg wrote to Vajna to confirm their bargain showed that, even at this late date and in the midst of the terror, he was adept at nurturing Arrow Cross fantasies that the government was a legitimate and civilized one, respected and taken seriously by other civilized states. Thus, even though two weeks earlier Arrow Cross toughs had sacked the Swedish Legation and sent the Swedish minister into hiding, Wallenberg began his letter by saying, "I would like to take the opportunity of informing you that I have acquainted His Excellency, the Swedish minister, with your very friendly remarks concerning Sweden. His Excellency has asked me to voice his deep gratitude and would like to assure you that the Swedish Legation will do everything in its power, during these difficult days as well as in the future, to help the needy and war-afflicted population of Hungary."

He closed with "May I take the opportunity of expressing my best wishes for the besieged capital and for yourself. I remain, with the highest esteem, Raoul Wallenberg."

At the same time as he was making these formal diplomatic

protests, Wallenberg was also overseeing and expanding his extensive humanitarian bureaucracy. By the end of December approximately fifteen thousand Jews held protective passes signed by him. A great many were quartered in the Swedish houses on Tátra Street and the Pozsonyi Roads in the International Ghetto. His Section C was responsible for feeding these Jews, providing them with medical care, and protecting them from the Arrow Cross. Whenever he could, he also smuggled food and medical supplies to the unprotected Jews in the Central Ghetto.

Wallenberg continued issuing Swedish passes throughout the terror. The Swiss had stopped after they reached the government-imposed limit of seventy-eight hundred, although by some estimates the Zionist underground operating out of the Glass House with the approval of Lutz and Krausz, had counterfeited as many as one hundred thousand Swiss passes. As a result, the Arrow Cross men were less likely to respect Swiss passes and staged their most frequent and ferocious attacks against Swiss-protected houses. On December 29, forty storm troopers invaded the Glass House and found twenty-seven hundred Jews living there under the pretext of Swiss protection. During the ensuing melee the Arrow Cross killed and wounded dozens and drove fifteen hundred into the streets.

The Swedish passes were more valuable. Wallenberg had exceeded his government quota by more than double, but each was an original document, signed by him personally. The Arrow Cross knew that he was the most energetic of the neutral diplomats in protecting "his" Jews.

Wallenberg's most important weapon in his one-man guerilla war against the death squads was information: information about which houses the Arrow Cross planned to attack and to which basement they had taken Jews seized in earlier raids. Members of the regular police force, the gendarmerie, and even the Arrow Cross itself provided this information because they were appalled by the anarchy and terror, because Wallenberg had cultivated their friendship, because of their fear of war crimes trials, or because he had bribed them.

He bribed them with Swedish protective passes, which they hoped to use to escape from the Soviets, or with money. He paid two hundred pengös a day to policemen who allowed Jews to escape from the Central Ghetto or who protected those living in the International Ghetto. He paid Oskar Görgenyi, the private secretary of the Arrow Cross official in charge of war mobilization, five thousand pengös for every advance copy of any order affecting the Jews.

His most important undercover informant was Pál Szalai, the Arrow Cross liaison officer with the regular Budapest police force. Even before the siege Szalai had become disillusioned with the Szálasi regime. During the reign of terror he organized small units of like-minded police, gendarmes, and Arrow Cross to protect the Jews living in the Central Ghetto. He intervened personally to save Jews, warned Wallenberg of impending Arrow Cross raids on the ghettos, and told him to which basement Swedish Jews had been taken after a successful raid. He often provided Wallenberg with a loyal police guard. Relations between them became so cordial that by the end of December they were meeting daily in the basement of the Üllöi Road office to discuss their plans over drinks or supper.

Acting on the information supplied by Szalai and others, Wallenberg spent most of his days and nights racing across Budapest, stopping executions on the banks of the Danube, rescuing Jews from Arrow Cross dungeons, and arranging for guards to protect Swedish houses targeted for an attack. His daring, his large and hardworking staff, his extensive financial resources, and his relationships with key members of the Arrow Cross and civilian police made him a man of considerable power in a city in which the traditional power centers were being destroyed. According to a prominent Hungarian jurist who later attended the Eichmann trial in Jerusalem, "At the time, he [Wallenberg] was probably the man with the greatest influence in Budapest."

He was not, however, the only force in Budapest concerned with saving Jews from the terror. The Zionist pioneers dressed some of its members in Arrow Cross uniforms and rescued Jews. Charles Lutz, Miklós Krausz, and Red Cross officials also labored heroically to protect their Jews. Christian religious orders such as the Benedictines, the Franciscans, and the Sisters of Mercy hid converted as well as unconverted Jews in their convents, monasteries, and churches. Nuns often slipped into the Jewish houses and shouted, "Tomorrow the priest is coming and will give you all baptism certificates with no formalities!" Of all these groups, however, Wallenberg was the most energetic and effective.

Throughout the terror he kept his knapsack in the back of his car and slept wherever he happened to be when he became too exhausted to continue. He seemed to be everywhere at once, but nowhere for very long. Every day he visited his offices at Üllöi Road and Jókai Street, coordinated his rescue activities with those of Miklós Krausz at the Swiss Glass House, and visited his Swedish houses. He was in perpetual motion and took incredible risks.

He carried a revolver despite the Arrow Cross practice of immediately executing any civilian found with a weapon.

He organized the theft of Arrow Cross identity papers by dressing his most Aryan-looking Jewish aides in Arrow Cross uniforms and instructing them to challenge the identity of real Arrow Cross men and confiscate their papers. He then distributed these papers to other Aryan-looking Jews.

He bribed regular policemen to fan out through the Central Ghetto, round up Jews holding Swedish passes, and then march them in military formation out of the ghetto, past the Arrow Cross guards, and back to the Swedish houses.

He set out on every expedition with numerous sets of license plates. He had a CD plate identifying him as a member of the consular corps and another which showed him to be a special courier. If he saw an Arrow Cross roadblock ahead he became a courier; when the Germans stopped him he was a diplomat.

To further confuse his enemy he put different numbered plates on the front and rear of his car. He once told his photographer, Tom Veres, "We ought to have license plate numbers that could be changed automatically by pushing a button inside the car."

He hid some of those he saved during his expeditions in a vault in the basement of a building which had once been a bank. On one occasion, while taking Pál Szalai on a tour of this building, he swung open the doors of this vault to reveal dozens of Jews sleeping on straw mats. "Did you ever see such treasure in a bank vault?" he asked. "Here we have something much more valuable than money: people!"

He felt a particular responsibility toward his immediate staff. When he heard that Johnny Moser, the young Jewish aide who had accompanied him to Hegyeshalom, had been seized by the SS for impersonating a German soldier, he ordered Langfelder to race to the SS checkpoint where Moser had been taken. They arrived as Moser was being led away. Langfelder slowed down and Wallenberg threw open the car door and shouted, "Johnny! Quick! Jump in!" Moser leaped into the car as Langfelder accelerated. They all escaped.

Although he concentrated his energies on saving the Swedish-protected Jews, he tried to rescue any Jew with whom he came into contact. On a number of occasions he saved Shalom Schwartz, a twenty-year-old who ran errands for the Swiss Legation's humanitarian section and had himself, while masquerading as a Nazi, saved dozens of Jews.

The Arrow Cross had caught Schwartz for the first time during one of the October labor roundups. The government had just learned that thousands of Swiss passes were counterfeit, and when Schwartz had presented papers showing he worked as a messenger for the Swiss Legation the storm troopers had beat him up and dragged him to Teleki Square to await deportation. He was saved at the last minute when Charles Lutz and Wallenberg made one of their visits to the square to rescue Jews holding Swiss and Swedish passes.

Wallenberg saved Schwartz a second time during the December terror. An Arrow Cross death squad seized him during a raid and took him to a notorious house located only a block from the Danube. Its proximity to the river encouraged even the laziest Arrow Cross men to join the frequent execution parties.

Throughout the night the Arrow Cross beat and tortured Schwartz and his companions. At daybreak, when he was "half-dead from the beatings they had given us," four Arrow Cross teenagers marched him and the others to the river. Because of his position in the Zionist underground he "knew what they did when they brought people to the banks of the Danube."

Seconds before he was to be executed, a car screeched to a halt a few yards away from the Arrow Cross boys. Wallenberg, Lutz, and a regular Hungarian police officer jumped out and began to talk to the Arrow Cross. Schwartz was close enough to hear the exchange. It was clear that Wallenberg was the spokesman.

He spoke in a low, soothing voice, like a long-suffering parent dealing with a child's temper tantrum, like a patient teacher trying to reason with a particularly dim-witted student. "I'm certain that all of these people," he said in German, "have protective passes. Do you know that it is therefore strictly forbidden, even illegal, for you to take them to the Danube?"

At first the four Arrow Cross boys scarcely listened to the Hungarian policeman's translation of Wallenberg's words. They shouted accusations at the Jews and screamed that they were to be executed.

Wallenberg was unflustered. "Even if these people do not have protective passes," he continued, "it is still forbidden for you to take them to the Danube. In fact, you have no right to kill anyone."

For an entire hour Schwartz listened as Wallenberg presented a series of simple, rational arguments designed to persuade the Arrow Cross boys to free the prisoners. Only at the very end did he become impatient and begin to raise his voice. Schwartz remembered later that "he wasn't exactly shouting at them but he had to speak loudly to be heard over their screaming. At the time I was amazed at how he had the courage to talk to them this way. They could have killed him at any time but he never seemed afraid. Finally, somehow, his arguments and his resourcefulness wore them down and they simply walked away. I thought it was a miracle!"

Lars Ernster, the medical student who belonged to the Swedish Labor Brigade, witnessed many of Wallenberg's "miracles" and explained them by saying, "These Arrow Cross were mostly very young boys and although they had been brainwashed to kill Jews some were still very unsure of themselves. When a Christian like Raoul dared to stand up to them he could intimidate, even frighten them. They knew it was perfectly all right to kill a Jew but they were afraid what might happen if they killed a non-Jew."

Despite Wallenberg's understanding of the Arrow Cross mentality, and despite his courage and energy, he was not always as successful as he had been in rescuing Shalom Schwartz. On January 3 he learned that on New Year's Day an Arrow Cross squad had seized Dr. Peter Sugar, one of his most trusted aides, from a Swedish-protected house on Magyar Street. He quickly collected one of his interpreters, Lázsló Hajmal, and raced to the Town Hall to force Arrow Cross officials to disclose Sugar's whereabouts.

When Wallenberg found Sedey, Budapest's chief of police, in the Town Hall air raid shelter, he momentarily forgot about his search for Dr. Sugar. The food situation in the Central Ghetto was desperate, and Sedey and General Hindy, the Hungarian general in command of Budapest, had recently announced that the ghetto Jews would receive food on a scale of nine hundred calories per person per day. This was at a time when members of the armed forces received three thousand calories and Christian inmates of the city's prisons were allocated fifteen hundred calories. Even the meager nine hundred calories accorded the Jews never reached the ghetto. It was either not sent or was plundered by the Arrow Cross. To prevent the Jews in the ghetto from starving, the International Red Cross, Wallenberg, and other neutral legations had supplied whatever food they could spare from their stores. Recently, however, government requisitions had depleted the Red Cross supplies. Wallenberg knew that unless more food was forthcoming from the government, thousands would soon die of starvation.

"Do you realize that you have personally sentenced to death the Jews of the Central Ghetto?" Wallenberg asked Sedey. "Many scarcely have enough food to last the day. If you don't supply them immediately they'll die." Wallenberg spoke in German, which he knew Sedey understood. Wallenberg's translator, Lázsló Hajmal, seeing that he was not needed, took notes on the conversation.

"We're unable to allocate more food to *any* of Budapest's inhabitants," Sedey replied.

"The other people in Budapest are not in the same position as the Jews!" Wallenberg shouted, seemingly oblivious to the heavily armed Arrow Cross boys who drifted in and out of the shelter while he spoke. "You have a special obligation to the Jews because you've imprisoned them in a ghetto. Jailors have a moral responsibility to feed their prisoners. I demand that you tell me now exactly how you propose to supply food to the ghetto."

Sedey was shocked by Wallenberg's outburst. He stammered so badly as he tried to formulate an answer that his words were incomprehensible. When Wallenberg realized he was thoroughly intimidated, he pushed a young clerk out of a chair and sat down and began typing a memorandum on Sedey's official stationery. When he finished he ripped the paper out of the typewriter and read its contents aloud. It was an official communiqué ordering the rationing board to supply food to the ghetto and holding it responsible if anyone died of starvation.

"Sign it!" Wallenberg ordered.

Sedey obeyed. Wallenberg snatched away the paper before Sedey could change his mind and told Hajmal to put it in his briefcase. Only now was he prepared to discuss Sugar's disappearance. "As soon as I leave here I plan to go to the Arrow Cross military headquarters at Városház Street to inquire about him," he said. "If I don't return here afterward you'll know that they've taken me prisoner as well."

"But how could you possibly think that they'd harm you, a neutral diplomat?" Sedey asked nervously.

"Yesterday Arrow Cross men struck the Swiss chargé d'affaires," Wallenberg shot back as he turned to leave. "Now you know where I'm going, and if I don't return, my government will hold you responsible."

Arrow Cross guards with machine guns stopped Wallenberg and Hajmal at the door of the Városház Street building, examined their papers, and wrote down their names and addresses. "You'll have to show us a written authorization from Nidosi [the Arrow Cross commandant] if you want to leave the building alive," one warned.

The upstairs rooms were deserted. Wallenberg and Hajmal descended into the dimly lit basement. Everywhere Jewish prisoners—men, women, and children—had been packed into closets and storage rooms. Through the open doors Wallenberg and Hajmal could see Arrow Cross youths torturing naked prisoners. Screams echoed through the corridors. None of the senior Arrow Cross leaders were visible.

Wallenberg cupped his hands around his mouth and shouted at the top of his voice, "Nidosi! Nidosi!" He paused and looked up and down the dim hallway. No one answered.

He cupped his hands again and shouted, "Kurt Rettman! Kurt Rettman!" Again there was no reply. Either they had left or, more likely, not wanting Wallenberg to be able to link them with the barbarities, they had gone into hiding.

Wallenberg turned to Hajmal and said, "We won't be able to accomplish anything here. I guess I can escape one way or the other, but how about you? We'd better go upstairs together."

By the time they reached the door Wallenberg had an idea. He suddenly shouted to Hajmal in German, "Go back to Hindy's office and wait there until I return." The Arrow Cross guards did not understand German but, as Wallenberg had anticipated, they were so impressed by Hindy's name that they allowed Hajmal to leave.

Wallenberg returned to the cellar to make one last search for Sugar. Two hours later he escaped from the building after shouting German commands at the bewildered guards. He was disconsolate that he had failed to save Sugar. "Everything was in vain," he told Hajmal. "I've failed and I'm afraid we'll never see him again."

Despite the Arrow Cross raids on Swedish houses and the abduction of Jews such as Sugar who held Swedish passes, Wallenberg continued to believe that Jews with passes who remained in the International Ghetto were more likely to survive the terror. Pál Szalai constantly urged him to move his Swedish Jews into the Central Ghetto and argued that the regular police guards on the ghetto's four gates had reduced raids by the Arrow Cross death squads and had made it safer than the International Ghetto.

Wallenberg disagreed. He still feared that the SS and Arrow Cross planned to destroy the Central Ghetto during their retreat through Pest. For the time being, the Jews in Swedish houses might be more vulnerable and some would undoubtedly perish in the Arrow Cross cellars. If, however, he moved them into the ghetto they might stand no chance at all of surviving. He resisted Szalai's advice and continued to place Jews in Swedish houses and to issue new protective passes.

Arrow Cross squads searched in vain for the underground Section C offices which manufactured the Swedish passes. Wallenberg foiled them by shifting his clerks and messengers to different locations every evening. One of these clerks, a young woman named Agnes Adachi, finally met Wallenberg when he came to supervise their operations and to warn them that the moonlit villa in which they were working was next door to an SS headquarters. "No talking—and, please," Wallenberg said as he looked over Adachi's shoulder, "write lightly."

When the clerks had written their quota for the evening, Wallenberg divided the passes between them. He insisted that the passes be delivered that same night. They might protect someone from arrest during a predawn raid.

These nighttime delivery runs were particularly dangerous. The clerks, all of them Jews, were violating the curfew and if caught they risked immediate execution. Adachi could remember going out alone, night after night, her pockets stuffed with passes, her heels click-clacking loudly as she raced across the Danube bridges, an easy target in the bright moonlight, and yet she felt no fear. "It was impossible for us to be afraid with Wallenberg as our leader," she said, "because we thought that if he could take such risks, then so could we. His calm relaxed us and I can remember thinking, 'Boy! It would be easy to fall in love with a man like this.' "

Others who worked with Wallenberg or were saved by him were also mesmerized by his courage and his serenity.

One of his drivers, Sándor Ardai, said, "I never heard Wallenberg speak an unnecessary word during the month and a half that I and Langfelder took turns as driver. Not a single comment, never a complaint, even if he could not sleep more than a few hours for several days. Only once did I see him more distressed than usual."

According to Shalom Schwartz: "He was filled with such patience it was just unbelievable."

Another aide said, "He was a modest, unassuming boy with an iron will."

Tom Veres considered him "my idol," and said, "To me he didn't even seem human."

One person he saved remembered that "Wallenberg was very elegant yet also very natural. I thought that it was fantastic that such a man would suddenly appear in the middle of the night to save Jews, as if he had done it all his life."

"He kept telling me he was afraid," said Per Anger. "And I thought that only a man who can admit that is probably genuinely courageous."

"He must have been the loneliest man in the world because there was nothing behind him," remembered another acquaintance. "They could have shot him down in the street and no one would have known about it."

Wallenberg told one aide: "I like this dangerous game. I love this dangerous game."

He told another: "Ah! I see that you and I are both still alive. That is a mere coincidence."

11

January 7–16, 1945

"You should disappear as soon as possible," Pál Szalai warned Wallenberg on January 7. "The Arrow Cross leaders who might have kept order have fled or gone underground. The worst elements have taken over and Vajna is under their influence. They've also taken over the Foreign Ministry. If you go there to make diplomatic protests, you may never come out alive. You can also anticipate that the Arrow Cross will now attack individual members of the Swedish Legation; they'll send even more violent search parties to the Swedish houses."

The next morning Szalai's prophecies began coming true. An Arrow Cross squad commanded by Vörösváry, the headwaiter at the Kaduna restaurant, attacked the Swedish house at 1 Jókai Street where Wallenberg had gathered many of his closest aides. Among them were some of the wealthiest bankers and industrialists in Budapest, men who had provided the experience and skills to make Section C so effective. They felt relatively secure in Jókai Street. They had been permitted to remove the Yellow Star and fly the blue and yellow Swedish flag. Most were protected both by Swedish protective passes and by identity cards stating that they were employees of the Swedish Legation. There had

144

been a small Arrow Cross raid on the house in December, but since then Wallenberg had mounted a special guard consisting of a regular policeman, two Jewish aides, and six gendarmes.

During the night of January 7 the gendarmes protecting the Jókai Street house mysteriously disappeared. At the same time the building's janitor, a secret Arrow Cross sympathizer, approached the regular policeman and asked if he would resist an Arrow Cross raid. He said he would not. In the middle of the night, while the Jews slept, the janitor opened the door and admitted an Arrow Cross terror squad. They swept through the building, firing pistols into the air and screaming obscenities.

They had come for Wallenberg. They burst into the cellar where most of the three hundred residents of Jókai Street lay sleeping on straw mats. They tore apart every room, beating everybody in sight and ordering them to line up against the wall of the courtyard. A cripple who did not move quickly enough was shot and killed. Their information about Wallenberg had been wrong: He never slept at Jókai Street. The raiders took out their frustration on the building's inhabitants.

Twelve-year-old Kate Wacz had lived at Jókai Street for only a couple of days with her mother, brother, grandparents, aunt, and uncle. They had formerly been quartered at the Üllői Road Swedish house and her mother was bitter about the move. "First we were at Üllői Road," she said after the war. "But then even richer Jews than we came along and we were therefore moved from there to Jókai Street." Kate passed her days at both Üllői Road and Jókai Street playing "spirit games" with the other children. They sat around a table in a darkened room, their eyes shut and holding hands, in a séance; they jiggled the table with their legs and pretended to have made contact with the spirits of their dead parents, brothers, sisters, cousins, and grandparents.

The Arrow Cross found Kate and her mother cowering behind a partition in their bedroom. As Kate scrambled out, a tall blond woman wearing a leather coat and riding boots, the infamous

Mrs. Vilmos Salzer, screamed, "Outside! Outside or we'll kill you in here!"

In the courtyard Kate and her mother, brother, and 280 residents of Jókai Street—only 20 had managed to hide or escape—were made to stand with their faces pressed against the wall while the Arrow Cross separated them into three groups: men, women and children, women without children. Kate's mother was frantic: Should her fifteen-year-old son join the men or the women with children? Which group was most likely to be taken to the Central Ghetto and released? Driven into the Danube? Made to work? She told her son to join the men. He ignored her and hunched over so that the Arrow Cross would think he was younger. She begged him to leave and finally he obeyed—but he sneaked back to his mother and sister.

The Arrow Cross marched most of the Jókai Street Jews to the cellars of their Városház Street building and turned them over to Father Kun. They arrived in the dark and during an artillery barrage. The Arrow Cross men at Városház Street were drunk; some had passed out. As the Jews were marched into the building, the men beat them and warned them to turn over their hidden valuables so that "the fish in the Danube don't eat them."

The cellar was too crowded to accommodate the Jews, so the Arrow Cross took Kate and the others upstairs and shoved them into a small, dark room. One guard warned, "We'll shoot anyone who doesn't fit into this room, anyone who complains." Everyone fought and pushed to cram themselves inside. For the rest of the evening they remained standing in this room, without space to turn around and, except for a few children who cried, silent.

The following morning the Arrow Cross pulled them out one by one, questioned, stripped, and searched them—and, if they were found to have concealed valuables, beat them with rifle butts. An Arrow Cross woman shouted at Kate to empty her pockets. She dug into the pocket of her brown pullover and brought out her only possession, a handful of peanuts. The woman confiscated them and then ordered her to remove her shoes.

"No! You can't take away my only shoes!" she protested. "How will I be able to walk anywhere?"

"Take them off or we'll kill you," the woman threatened.

Kate obeyed. Later that evening she, her mother, and several dozen other women and children from Jókai Street were marched into the Central Ghetto. The men and other women remained at Városház Street. During the coming week, as the Russians advanced through Pest, the Arrow Cross led groups of Jókai Street Jews outside to dig trenches, cut wood, clear rubble, and roll drums of gasoline to defensive positions during artillery bombardments. At the end of each day the group was taken to the Danube and executed. A few individuals escaped by convincing their executioners that they were Christians or by promising to lead them to caches of hidden valuables. Several committed suicide by jumping from windows. Within a week 180 of the 280 taken from Jókai Street had perished.

The Jókai Street massacre was Wallenberg's greatest defeat. On January 8 the Arrow Cross had also raided Üllöi Road and carried off 156 of his Jews to the Maria Theresa barracks. All of these, however, were saved by Pál Szalai and a detachment of regular policemen. The scope of these two attacks, the constant Russian shelling, and the seizure of power by the most fanatical Arrow Cross terrorists all reduced Wallenberg's mobility and effectiveness. Nevertheless he refused to go into hiding until the very end.

He saw Per Anger for the last time on January 10 when they drove together to SS headquarters. Wallenberg wanted guarantees that his Swedish houses would not be liquidated at the last minute; Anger wanted to persuade the Germans to protect members of the Legation staff during the siege. Since the Arrow Cross attack on Christmas Eve the Swedish Legation had ceased to function and its diplomats had separated for their own protection. Danielsson and the female typists moved into the Swiss Legation; Carlsson and Berg returned to the Swedish Legation building as care-takers after a force of gendarmes had retaken it from the Arrow Cross; and Anger took refuge in his Uri Street apartment. Only Wallenberg insisted on staying in the open and remaining in Pest, with his Jews.

As he drove to SS headquarters, Anger tried to persuade Wallenberg to join the other Swedes in Buda. "It's safer for all of us if we stick together," he said. "Why not come to the other side of the river?"

Wallenberg shook his head. The Russian shells had toppled trees and carved huge craters in the asphalt. Shattered and smoldering buildings, dead horses, and human corpses lined the side of the road; bombs exploded near the car.

"Aren't you ever scared?" Anger asked.

"Sure, I get scared sometimes," Wallenberg answered. "But I don't have any choice. I took on this mission, and now I could never go back to Stockholm unless I knew inside myself that I'd done everything to save as many Jews as possible."

The next day, January 11, he and Vilmos Langfelder were finally forced to seek refuge from the Arrow Cross and the Russian shelling. They chose as their hideout a house on Benczur Street that was under the protection of the International Red Cross and near the advancing Russian columns. The house belonged to László Ocskay, an aristocrat who had been the Hungarian manager of the Socony Vacuum Oil Company. Many of his business colleagues and about two dozen other Jews, mostly wealthy industrialists, had also found refuge in his two-story stone house. They were protected by the Red Cross and by a German colonel and his adjutant who were frequent dinner guests and appeared to enjoy eating with so many cultured Jews. The colonel had posted an SS guard outside the house to fend off attacks by the Arrow Cross.

Dr. György Wilhelm, the son of the vice-chairman of the Jewish Council, Károly Wilhelm, was the senior Jewish leader in the house. Both Wilhelms knew Wallenberg well and had often coordinated their own rescue activities with his. Upon arriving at Benczur Street, Wallenberg told Wilhelm, "I'd like to stay here a few days. I don't feel very secure in my other houses and apartments, and I also think that this district will be among the first in central Pest to be liberated by the Russians. I want to make contact with them as soon as possible so I can begin relief activities on behalf of the Jews."

Wallenberg had already formulated a detailed and ambitious plan for setting up a postwar relief organization to assist Hungarian Jews. He assumed that thousands of Jews who had fled the country would try to return to their former homes; most would be penniless and many would find that their families had vanished. His organization would find them jobs, reunite them with surviving family members, and assist those who were destitute. It would also compensate those who had survived the siege of Budapest but had lost their livelihood and property.

Wallenberg interested himself in the most minute details of his projected humanitarian foundation and had even drafted an organizational plan that divided it into three sections: one for employment, foreign representation, and repatriation of Jews from abroad; a second for financing the reacquisition of Jewish assets and property; and a third for searching out missing relatives, finding housing, and providing counseling.

He hoped that the postwar Hungarian government would approve and subsidize his foundation. To this end he wanted to make contact with the Soviet Army as soon as possible and visit its headquarters at Debrecen in order to win over the Soviet commander, Marshall Malinovsky, and General Miklós, an anti-Nazi Hungarian who was likely to assume power after the Russian victory.

If the Soviets and Miklós refused to assist him, Wallenberg had devised a contingency plan for financing what he called the "Wallenberg Institute for Support and Reconstruction." He would operate it with funds from the War Refugee Board, donations from wealthy Hungarians, and money raised through a national appeal. He had already prepared the text of a fund-raising appeal to the Hungarian people.

He planned to introduce his appeal by saying:

I ask your indulgence if I use the first person to address you. I promise that this will be the first and last time and I am only doing it because I am well known as the head of the Humanitarian Section of the Royal Swedish Legation. Thousands of you have helped organize my rescue operations and now I am appealing for your continued assistance for relief work. As you know, I am a citizen of a neutral country, but I think it is fair to say that neither I nor my country have ever looked on neutrality as a comfortable, easy way to avoid suffering. On the contrary, my countrymen have often proven themselves even more sensitive to human suffering than those who suffer. For many months now I have witnessed the suffering of the Hungarian people and, if it is not too presumptuous to say so, I think I have participated in it spiritually to such an extent that it has now become my suffering. Because of my involvement, I have been able to recognize the great need for speedy humanitarian relief and reconstruction activities.

After this preamble, Wallenberg planned to describe in detail the relief work his institute would undertake:

We have decided to create an organization whose name and purpose I will now present to the public. It is not a purely humanitarian organization, but also an economic one since, as we view the situation, a humanitarian action without the corresponding economic assistance organization would be limited, and in many ways ineffective.

Following the wishes of my collaborators, we intend to call this organization the "Wallenberg Institute for Support and Reconstruction." It should be an organization which will ena-

*ble all participants to help themselves in a cooperative manner.
I have an administration and a staff for this organization.
I have come to know my collaborators in a time of very great
need. In choosing them I have looked for three things: compassion, honesty and initiative.*

*In our action we want to use the effective means which
are provided by private action and private control. We will
accept government and national assistance and incorporate
it into our activities, provided that this will cause no delay
in providing help. I will mention only the more important
areas of our activity:*

*Search for lost members of families, in particular returning
children to their parents; the reestablishment of identity; legal
help to war victims; reestablishment and renewal of business
relations; creation of employment; food distribution; help with
housing; collection and distribution of furniture; repatriation
and emigration (a special department for assisting Jews and
reestablishing their means of support); care of orphans; saving
of cultural values; medical care for individuals and villages;
fighting epidemics; establishing medical institutions and providing medicines; planning and construction of villages and
industries, temporary housing and temporary hospitals; unem-
ployment assistance . . . and a humanitarian and economic
information service.*

Despite the dangers from Arrow Cross terror squads and Russian artillery bombardment, Wallenberg made a final sortie from
the Benczur Street house on January 12. He went first to his
Üllöi Road office and signed a last batch of protective passes.
Some workers in this office carried Swedish provisional passports
due to expire on January 15 and they asked him to extend them.
He agreed, but added that he "did not think it was really necessary
since the Russians are sure to be here by then."

He next visited the Town Hall, where he met with Pál Szalai
and asked him to do his best to protect the Jews in Buda if he

decided to cross the Danube to escape from the Soviets. He also told Szalai: "I don't think I'm safe in any of the Swedish houses, so I've moved to the home of a friend to await the liberation. After the Russians take Buda, I hope you'll be able to make your way to my Üllöi Road office. From there we'll go together to visit Malinovsky. Afterward I'll take you with me to Sweden and introduce you to the king."

Late that afternoon he stopped at the Swiss Legation to say goodbye to his collaborator Miklós Krausz, and to collect a file of documents and 200,000 pengös that he had entrusted to Krausz for safekeeping.

The same evening Russian columns came within several hundred yards of the Benczur Street house, forcing everyone inside—including Wallenberg and Langfelder—to take refuge in the basement kitchen. There they spent the night huddled against the stoves and cold chests, awaiting their liberators. Early the next morning they heard pounding and foreign voices coming from the cellar of a neighboring house. Underground passages, cisterns, and corridors, some built by the Turks, connected many Budapest buildings. Whenever possible, the Russians tried to advance through them, thereby minimizing casualties and surprising the enemy from the rear.

Early on the morning of the thirteenth, the basement walls of the Benczur Street house shook and cracked; chunks of cement crashed to the floor and clouds of dust enveloped the kitchen. When the dust cleared, a Russian soldier poked his head through a hole in the wall and inspected the kitchen. Wallenberg had his first glimpse of his "liberators."

More pounding followed. When the hole became large enough, fifteen Russian soldiers climbed through into the kitchen. Two of them quickly whispered to the assembled Jews: "We are also Jews, but don't tell anyone because there are a lot of anti-Semites amongst us."

"Does anyone speak German?" Wallenberg asked the Russians.

When one of the soldiers admitted that he did, Wallenberg

said, "I am a Swedish diplomat," and then pulled papers in Russian and German from his pocket certifying that he, like all Swedish diplomats in Budapest, had been responsible for representing the Soviet Union and protecting its property during the war.

After examining the documents the soldier said, "You'll have to speak with my commanding officer." He returned several hours later with two high-ranking Soviet officers who took Wallenberg into a room and questioned him. When they emerged Wallenberg told the Jews: "I'm going to accompany them, but I don't think I shall be away for the night."

During the next three days he was interrogated several times by Soviet NKVD (secret police) and Army officers, who may have belonged to the special political branch of the Russian 18th Army, under the command of Major General Leonid I. Brezhnev. One of his secretaries, Gabriella Zekany, witnessed an interrogation held in Russian headquarters. On this occasion, Wallenberg told the Soviets that many of the Swedish houses were protected by armed guards and that the Russian forces should take particular care not to mistake them for Hungarian soldiers. "At the beginning the Soviet officer was rather cordial," Zekany remembered later, "but at some point in the interview he began to suspect that Wallenberg, who after all did speak excellent German, was really a German, perhaps a spy. At this point the officer dismissed me and said that he had to check Wallenberg's identity. This officer spoke German with a Yiddish accent and he told me he came from Georgia. I think he could have been Jewish."

According to another account of these interrogations, Wallenberg tried to persuade the Russians to mount an immediate and massive relief effort to aid Jews in liberated Pest; according to still another account, he tried to persuade the Russians to stop shelling the Swedish Legation in Buda and pointed out that the building lacked bombproof shelters. It is also probable that he mentioned his grandiose schemes for postwar relief and reconstruction and that the Russians believed that these threatened plans of their own. The Russians must also have been surprised that thousands of Hungarian Jews held Swedish passports and claimed Swedish citizenship, and that Wallenberg had come to Budapest for the sole purpose of saving Jews. They searched for other motives.

Between interrogations Wallenberg was permitted to move about the liberated districts of Pest. Accompanied by Langfelder and Soviet officers, he visited his offices and his friends. During these three days he met with Karl Müller, who had escaped from the Arrow Cross headquarters in Buda by bribing a guard. Wallenberg hugged him and explained that he had been unable to come to his rescue because no one had been able to discover where he had been imprisoned. Müller reported on the terrible condition of the Jews in Buda, and Wallenberg promised to go there as soon as possible. When Müller warned that Wallenberg's picture had been distributed to Arrow Cross units in Buda, Wallenberg said, "My life is one life, but this is a matter of saving thousands of lives."

While Wallenberg was being interrogated, the Germans and their Arrow Cross allies made plans to exterminate the seventy thousand Jews still under their control in the Central Ghetto. In the late afternoon of January 15, two days after Wallenberg had been "liberated" by the Russians, a policeman dashed into Pál Szalai's office in the Town Hall air raid shelter and informed him that the liquidation of the ghetto was imminent. A force of five hundred German soldiers and twenty-two Arrow Cross men had already gathered at the Royal Hotel, and two hundred policemen had been mobilized to join them. Within the hour they would attack the Central Ghetto and machine-gun its inhabitants. The last-minute pogrom which Wallenberg had feared was about to occur.

Many senior German generals and Arrow Cross leaders had also taken refuge in the Town Hall shelter. Szalai raced over to Ernö Vajna and implored him to call off this mass murder.

P

Vajna said that he knew about the operation and was unwilling to stop it.

In another part of the same cellar Szalai found General Schmidthuber, commandant of one of the German SS divisions defending Budapest. "I asked him whether he was aware of the operation planned for the ghetto," Szalai said later, "and I also informed him that members of his unit were among those mobilized at the Royal Hotel. I warned him that, according to Wallenberg's communication, if he did not prevent this crime he would be held responsible and would be called to account not as a soldier but as a murderer."

Schmidthuber immediately summoned Vajna, Police Commissioner Kubissy, and a German captain and ordered them to cancel the operation. Wallenberg had not actually been in communication with Szalai on this particular matter, but his threats of postwar criminal trials were well known to Germans such as Schmidthuber. Simply by invoking his name, Szalai had managed to save the Jews of the Central Ghetto. One day later, on January 16, the Soviet Army liberated the International Ghetto. On the evening of the seventeenth they reached the seventy thousand Jews living in the Central Ghetto. By then, however, Wallenberg was gone.

January 16–17, 1945

On the evening of January 16, shortly after the Russians had liberated the International Ghetto, Wallenberg visited Miklós Krausz at the Swiss house (the building had formerly housed the American Embassy) on Szabodsag Square and told him of his plans to drive to Debrecen. He explained that he wanted to persuade Marshall Malinovsky and General Miklós to liberate the Central Ghetto before its inhabitants were executed. He also hoped to secure their endorsement for the Wallenberg Institute for Support and Reconstruction.

Krausz begged him to stay in Budapest. "We now have a hundred and fifty armed policemen guarding the ghetto," he said. "And anyway, why do you want to leave just now, at the very moment the Russians are liberating the city?"

"Debrecen is where the Russians and Hungarians have their headquarters," Wallenberg replied. "I think I'm the best person to explain the Swedish houses and passes to them as well as to persuade them not to mistreat the liberated Jews."

Krausz had always considered Wallenberg naive, but this plan was incredible. "And how do you expect to be able to accomplish all this?" he asked.

"Don't forget that my government has been responsible for protecting Russian property in Hungary throughout the war," Wallenberg said. "The Russians are certain to respect the suggestions of a Swedish diplomat."

"I think it's a waste of time," Krausz replied, "and dangerous, too. You'll be traveling on open roads and there's still a great deal of fighting everywhere."

None of these arguments made the slightest impression. Wallenberg was determined. Before leaving he told Krausz, "If Buda is liberated before I return from Debrecen, please tell Danielsson where I've gone."

Late that same evening, Wallenberg, Langfelder, and one of Wallenberg's Jewish aides, György Szöllős, gathered at a garage on Muzeum Street to prepare his car for the trip to Debrecen. Just after the war Szöllős told the Hungarian historian Jenö Lévai that they had packed the car with food parcels and that "in the fuel tank we hid a great quantity of gold and jewels that Wallenberg was taking with him." Presumably these valuables belonged to Jews who had entrusted them to Wallenberg for safekeeping or had donated them to help finance his rescue operations. Some may have belonged to the 180 Jews who had perished in the recent Jókai Street raid.

On January 17, before leaving for Debrecen, Wallenberg revisited Miklós Krausz. "Well, what happened?" Krausz asked. "I thought you were going to Russian headquarters. Were you unsuccessful?"

"On the contrary," Wallenberg replied. "I wanted to stop by to tell you that I'm leaving today. I appear to have established a good relationship with the Russian military."

On January 17, Wallenberg and Langfelder also visited the Benczur Street house where they had previously taken refuge. "I need to pick up all my possessions because I'm leaving today for Debrecen," Wallenberg told György Wilhelm. "Please thank everyone for their hospitality and tell them I'll call on you as soon as I return." He then collected his rucksacks and sleeping bag and the 200,000 pengös he had given to Wilhelm for safekeeping after reclaiming them from Miklós Krausz the week before.

László Petö, the son of a member of the Jewish Council and a personal friend of Wallenberg's before the war, happened to be visiting Benczur Street at the same time. He found Wallenberg "in a great mood, a brilliant mood."

Wallenberg took Petö outside and pointed out the Russian motorcycle and sidecar that had been detailed to escort him to Debrecen. The driver was in full battle dress, and another fully armed soldier sat behind him; an officer rode in the sidecar. "They've been ordered up just for me," Wallenberg joked. "But I still don't know if they're coming along to protect me or guard me. Am I a guest, or a prisoner?"

Petö accompanied Wallenberg and his escort to their next stop, the Swedish house on Tátra Street. The house had been liberated the night before and Petö was anxious to contact his friends there. Wallenberg wanted to find out how its residents weathered the fighting. While the Russian officer paced up and down the sidewalk, Petö and Wallenberg climbed to an office on the second floor and met with the building's leader, Rezsö Müller.

Wallenberg gave Müller 100,000 pengös, half of what he had collected from Wilhelm, and instructed him to use them to buy food and protection for the Swedish Jews. He said that he expected to return from Debrecen in about eight days.

As they left Tátra Street, Petö decided to accompany Wallenberg to Debrecen. Their last stop before leaving Budapest was the Swedish hospital on Negrady Street. The hospital's manager, Pál Nevi, greeted Wallenberg at the door and walked with him along Negrady Street, discussing the condition of the building and the patients. It is possible that Wallenberg used this opportunity to give Nevi some or all of the 100,000 pengös remaining in his possession so that the hospital could function while he was away.

Outside the Duna Park café, Wallenberg slipped and fell on the icy sidewalk, injuring himself. As he struggled to his feet he saw three Jews still wearing Yellow Stars emerge from a nearby building. He immediately forgot his injuries and, while staring at the Jews with tears in his eyes, told Nevi, "So you see, I *have* succeeded; my work has not been in vain."

These three Jews were among the 120,000 in Budapest who had survived Eichmann's attempts to deport them, the Arrow Cross terror, and the hardships of the final siege. In the Central Ghetto 70,000 survived, in the International Ghetto, 25,000 survived, and so did another 25,000 who had been hiding in private homes and churches throughout the city. Wallenberg could claim to have rescued personally the 15,000 to 20,000 Jews who held Swedish papers. In addition, his soup kitchens and hospitals; his constant lobbying, bribing, and intriguing; and his confrontations at the execution and deportation points had all played a vital role in saving the non-Swedish Jews. When he left Budapest on January 17, he left behind the largest Jewish community in Europe to have survived the Nazi domination.

Near the Swedish hospital Langfelder collided with a truck carrying Russian soldiers to the front. Although the damage was minor, the soldiers jumped out, seized Langfelder, and began shouting and threatening him. The Russian officer leaped from the sidecar and ordered him released. He explained to the soldiers that Langfelder was driving a foreign diplomat whose privileges had to be respected.

When they resumed the journey, Petö changed his mind about going to Debrecen. He had overheard the Russians saying that they would soon be liberating Buda. His parents were hiding there and he wanted to see them as soon as possible.

He climbed out of the car at the corner of Arena Road and Benczur Street, said farewell to Langfelder and Wallenberg, and watched them speed off toward Debrecen. His decision to stay in Budapest saved his life.

Raoul Wallenberg at age three, held by his mother. (Collection of Frederick E. Werbell)

Raoul Wallenberg in the uniform of the Swedish Home Guard. (Pressens Bild/
Photoreporters)

Adolf Eichmann. (Courtesty of Yivo Institute of Jewish Studies)

Admiral Miklós Horthy, the Hungarian regent, with Adolf Hitler in Berlin
in 1938. Horthy was Hungary's ruler when Wallenberg arrived in Budapest
in 1944.

Raoul Wallenberg holding a meeting with his senior Jewish aides in Budapest sometime during the last five months of 1944. (Jenö Lévai, *Raoul Wallenberg*)

Raoul Wallenberg's colleague Per Anger, at the Danube River. Anger was the last Swedish diplomat to see Wallenberg alive. (Per Anger, *With Raoul Wallenberg in Budapest*)

A Jewish labor brigade on its way to remove rubble caused by an Allied air raid on Budapest. (Per Anger, *With Raoul Wallenberg in Budapest*)

November 1944. On the platform of Jósefváros Station in Budapest, Raoul Wallenberg (marked with an *X*) saves Jewish laborers with Swedish papers from deportation and almost certain death. To the left of Wallenberg is a German soldier; to his right, a Jew holding a Swedish pass. (White Papers, Swedish Foreign Office)

November 1944. Elderly Jews driven from the Yellow Star houses in Budapest begin their death march to Hegyeshalom. (White Papers, Swedish Foreign Office)

Hungarian Jews, all women and children, about to be loaded into boxcars at a Hungarian railway station. (White Papers, Swedish Foreign Office)

Ivan Danielsson, the senior Swedish diplomat
in Budapest during Wallenberg's time. (Per
Anger, *With Raoul Wallenberg in Budapest*)

The Swedish Legation in Budapest. (Jenö
Lévai, *Raoul Wallenberg*)

Last photograph known to have been taken of Raoul Wallenberg. He is sitting at his desk in Budapest on November 26, 1944. (Collection of Frederick E. Werbell)

One of the Swedish protective passes designed by Raoul Wallenberg and signed by the Swedish minister, Ivan Danielsson. (Eric Sjöquist, *Affären Raoul Wallenberg*)

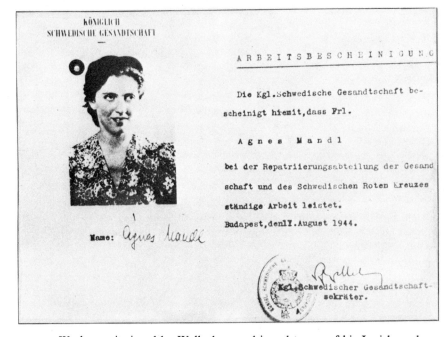

Work permit signed by Wallenberg and issued to one of his Jewish workers, Agnes Mandl (later Agnes Adachi). (Collection of Frederick E. Werbell)

Budapest Jews lined up in front of the Swedish Legation in hopes of obtaining Swedish passes. (Per Anger, *With Raoul Wallenberg in Budapest*)

Dr. Nanna Svartz, internationally renowned doctor whose testimonies have shed light on Wallenberg's fate, at the January 1981 Wallenberg hearings in Stockholm. (Pressens Bild/Photoreporters)

Former Swedish Prime Minister (1944–1969) Tage Erlander and his wife, Aina. Erlander was prime minister during the years of Wallenberg's incarceration in the Soviet Union. (Pressens Bild/Photoreporters)

Steffan Söderblom, Swedish ambassador to
Moscow in 1945, the year Wallenberg was
arrested by the Russians. His interview with
Stalin in 1945 was crucial in determining
Wallenberg's fate. (Pressens Bild/
Photoreporters)

Former KGB agent Efim Moshinsky,
who claimed to have met Wallenberg on
Wrangell's Island in 1961. (Eric Sjöquist,
Affären Raoul Wallenberg)

Raoul Wallenberg's mother, Maj von Dardel, holding a picture of her son in 1972. Seven years later she died at the age of eighty-seven; her husband, Fredrik von Dardel, died in the same month at age ninety-three. (Collection of Frederick E. Werbell)

Lubyanka, whose buildings housed the headquarters of the NKVD (Stalin's secret police) and also the prison where Raoul Wallenberg was incarcerated upon his arrival in Moscow in 1945. (Pressens Bild/Photoreporters)

Commemorative marker on the Budapest street named after Raoul Wallenberg. (Pressens Bild/Photoreporters)

Monument to Raoul Wallenberg erected in Budapest's St. Istvan Park which portrays him struggling against a serpent carrying a swastika on its head. The night before the monument's official dedication it was dismantled and removed by the Soviets. (Eric Sjöquist, *Affären Raoul Wallenberg*)

PART THREE

PRISONER

13

January 1945–Spring 1947

LUBYANKA AND LEFORTOVSKAYA,

MOSCOW

Green-uniformed NKVD agents stopped Wallenberg, Langfelder, and their Soviet military escort outside Budapest. They slashed the tires of their car, ordered them out, and dismissed the escort. The NKVD would take Wallenberg and Langfelder to Debrecen.

At Debrecen, Marshall Malinovsky did not receive them; an NKVD officer explained that they must meet with higher authorities in the Soviet Union. They were sent by train, still accompanied by NKVD guards, to Bessarabia, a Rumanian region that borders the Soviet Union. They stopped briefly at an internment camp for foreigners near Focsani and changed trains. In the border town of Iasi they left the train to dine at a local restaurant. That evening the train turned north into the Ukraine, toward Moscow. Throughout the trip their guards were polite. Wartime train travel was slow and unreliable, and the journey of fifteen hundred miles took two weeks. On January 31 they arrived in Moscow.

The guards transferred them to the subway and, as they neared their final destination, proudly pointed out the revolutionary murals in the underground stations. They alighted at Dzerzhinskaya Station and emerged into Dzerzhinskii Square. On one side was the former office of the Rossiya Insurance Company, a four-story building adorned with stone water nymphs; next door was a taller modern building with a windowless top floor. Together the buildings were known as Lubyanka, headquarters for the NKVD.

If Wallenberg and Langfelder had entertained doubts as to whether they were guests or prisoners, they knew the truth as soon as they arrived in Lubyanka. A guard marched them to separate cells and they parted, never again to see one another. Next, like all new prisoners at Lubyanka, they bathed and then waited alone in an airless "box" until called for their first interrogation.

The interrogators worked in the spacious, high-ceilinged offices designed for insurance executives before the Revolution. They accused Wallenberg of spying for the Germans and of helping Gestapo members escape the punishment they deserved for their anti-Soviet activities.

"I am a diplomat and a Swedish citizen," Wallenberg protested. "I was working in Budapest to save Jews from Nazi persecution. I even represented Soviet interests in Hungary."

"What would you be doing working for Soviet interests?" they said. "We know who you are. You're a member of an important capitalist family in Sweden."

When the interrogation ended, a guard marched Wallenberg up to the fifth floor and led him to cell 123. In 1945 many of the inmates of Lubyanka were Germans and other Axis citizens who had been captured by the Red Army in Eastern Europe. Wallenberg joined two such prisoners: Gustav Richter, a former policeman at the German Embassy in Bucharest, and Otto Scheuer, an Austrian lieutenant.

While in his cell, Wallenberg was watched as closely as he had been during the journey to Moscow. Every minute a guard looked through his peephole to see if he or his cellmates were dozing, knocking on the wall, or moving too close to the only window, a tiny opening high in the wall. Every day guards took him and his cellmates to a yard on top of the building. The eighteen-foot walls prevented them from looking out, but they could hear the traffic on Dzerzhinskii Square, feel the sun, and see the sky. Hands behind their backs, they marched in pairs, forbidden to stop or talk and always covered by an armed guard.

Talking was also forbidden at night as they strained to sleep under the glare of the cell's two-hundred-watt bulb. Only during the day and inside the cell was talk permitted. Wallenberg told his cellmates about his adventures in Budapest and his subsequent arrest. He worried continually that his imprisonment would harm his reputation. "What on earth will my relatives say when they hear that I've been in prison?" he asked.

Richter, the former German policeman, reassured him. "In the circumstances, it is certainly no cause for embarrassment. I don't think it will damage your good name."

Twice every month Lubyanka prisoners were permitted to write petitions to any Soviet officials, even to Stalin. Wallenberg took advantage of this privilege at the first opportunity. He addressed his petition to the prison director; in it he protested his arrest and treatment and demanded that he be allowed to contact the Swedish Embassy. Most prisoners never received a response to their petitions; Wallenberg was no exception.

His anger at his predicament did not diminish his spirits, and throughout February 1945 he remained healthy on the prison diet of bread, tea, and thin porridge. The guards treated him well, and only once during the month was he subjected to an interrogation. During it he was accused of spying and of being a "big capitalist."

In the middle of March a guard ordered him to gather his belongings and transferred him to another cell. His new cellmates were Hans Loyda, a Czech-born interpreter who had been attached to the German Army, and Wilhelm Roedel, the former counselor at the German Embassy in Bucharest. Both immediately recognized him from the description given by their previous cellmate, Vilmos Langfelder. He was relieved to hear news of Langfelder and asked the prison duty officer to deliver his own cigarette ration to his driver. Langfelder, however, never received the cigarettes. He had left Lubyanka. He was never heard from again.

Wallenberg himself did not remain in Lubyanka for long. In early April, soon after he had changed cells, he and Roedel were driven across Moscow in a prison van to the Baumanskii district. The van halted outside a polished brick building and they were taken inside a four-story structure built in the shape of the letter K, the Lefortovskaya prison.

A guard led them up two flights of stairs and past heavy wire netting stretched across the stairwell at each landing to prevent prisoners from committing suicide by jumping from the upper stories. They turned left on the third floor into a narrow gallery with metal doors on one side and a dark shaft on the other. The guard unlocked the third door, cell 151, and Wallenberg and Roedel went inside.

By the standards of Soviet prisons their cell was spacious. They shared a space ten feet long by eight feet wide containing three beds, one against each side wall and one under the window, a small table, and a basin with running water. The window had a grating and a metal cover on three sides so that light could only enter the cell from above. As at Lubyanka, a guard could observe them through an eye-level peephole. Surveillance at Lefortovskaya, however, was less strict; a guard checked them only once every two or three minutes.

Wallenberg was lucky to have been placed on the third floor. The lower cells were perpetually cold and damp. Ice formed on their walls in midsummer and the guards wore padded jackets and felt boots throughout the year. The solitary cells in the basement were flooded with ankle-deep cold water; the "psychological cells" on a higher floor were painted black so their walls could absorb the light from their twenty-five-watt bulbs.

In the days following his arrival Wallenberg was summoned frequently for questioning. The interrogation rooms were in a building located at the center of the courtyard and linked to the surrounding cell blocks by a covered bridge. When he moved between his cell and the interrogation rooms he saw no other prisoners. Lefortovskaya had a system to prevent chance meetings. A flagman stood at a point from which he could observe all the cell doors and the galleries between them. No guard could move a prisoner without a signal from him that the gallery was clear.

The Lefortovskaya interrogators asked Wallenberg the same questions: What was he doing in Budapest? Would he give them details of his work on behalf of the fascists?

He protested that he was a citizen of Sweden, a neutral country which had even represented Soviet interests in Hungary. He was a diplomat; his activities in Budapest were purely humanitarian; he had done nothing to deserve arrest and detention.

Many of Wallenberg's fellow prisoners were high-ranking prisoners of war and Axis diplomats who had been arrested in Eastern Europe. Since there were fewer guards at Lefortovskaya than at Lubyanka, it was easier for the prisoners to converse with neighboring cells by knocking on the walls. The inmates of cells 153, 152, and 151 "talked" regularly.

Claudio de Mohr, an Italian diplomat formerly posted to Bulgaria, occupied cell 152. Early one morning he heard knocking coming from cell 151. Slowly he began to understand the message. It was in German. One of the prisoners in 151 had been captured by the Russians in Budapest in January 1945. He was a Swedish diplomat.

It seemed impossible. De Mohr knocked back: "Are you really a Swedish diplomat?"

"Yes, a Swedish diplomat."

The news passed from cell to cell. All who heard it were astonished and wanted confirmation. It must be a mistake. Why would a diplomat from a neutral country be in a Moscow jail?

Wallenberg remained in Lefortovskaya from April 1945 until the spring of 1947. Shortly after his arrival he and Roedel were moved to cell 203 on the prison's fourth floor, directly above their original home, cell 151. Throughout Wallenberg's two-year stay in Lefortovskaya he left his cell for only twenty minutes a day, when he and Roedel were taken to exercise in one of the small yards in the prison courtyard. The yards measured fifteen feet by ten feet and were surrounded by a ten-foot wooden fence to prevent prisoners from seeing anyone in an adjoining yard.

Wallenberg's only contact with other inmates came through the "prison telegraph." The water pressure was so low on the upper floors of Lefortovskaya that the water pipes were often empty. Wallenberg could converse with cells on the same pipeline simply by opening his tap and talking into it. Even when the pipes were full they were effective conductors. The vaulted ceilings and brick walls of the cells also magnified sound, and most prisoners beat out messages with the handles of their toothbrushes.

They developed several codes. One was the "square system" in which the letters of the alphabet were written out in a square, five letters by five letters. For each letter two sets of knocks were given: the first to specify the row, the second for the column. Thus three knocks followed shortly by two knocks represented the letter L. Even more popular was the "idiot code." Under this system a single knock meant A, two knocks B, and so on.

Wallenberg was a keen knocker and he communicated in both French and German. He always introduced himself by five knocks and held involved conversations with the occupants of surrounding cells. An experienced prisoner learned to beat out his messages while sitting on his bed with his back to the wall and a book on his knee. He would arrange the sleeve of his coat in such a way that it seemed that his arm was resting on the book. In fact he would be tapping on the wall and the sleeve would be empty.

Wallenberg renewed contact with Rensinghoff, Wallenstein, and von Rantzau, three German diplomats whose cell had adjoined his on the third floor and who were now diagonally below him. He had resolved to write a protest to Stalin and every day he "discussed" its contents with them.

They agreed the letter should be in French. Wallenberg should emphasize his diplomatic status and request a hearing at which he would demand to know the accusations against him, and would then rebut them. He would also ask permission to contact the Swedish Embassy or the Red Cross, preferably in person, but otherwise in writing. Wallenstein recommended an appropriately respectful opening: "Agréez, Monsieur le Président, l'expression de ma trés haute considération." In the idiot code "consideration" alone required 146 knocks.

When Wallenberg completed the letter he gave it to a guard with instructions to forward it to Stalin. His arrest, he thought, must be a mistake. Stalin would correct it.

There was no reply to his letter.

During the spring of 1946 the Lefortovskaya guards again fetched Wallenberg for interrogation. Again NKVD officers accused him of collaborating with the Nazis, and again he protested and reminded them that he was a Swedish diplomat.

One interrogator said: "Your case is quite clear. You are a political case. If you think you are innocent, you must prove it. The best proof of your guilt is that the Swedish government and the Swedish Embassy have done nothing for you."

"I have asked many times to be allowed to contact the Embassy. I am asking again," Wallenberg said. "Or let me get in touch with the Red Cross."

"No one is at all interested in you. If the Swedish government or the Embassy cared about you, *they* would have contacted *you* ages ago."

Wallenberg demanded to know what they planned to do with him. The interrogator replied: "For political reasons, you will never be sentenced."

Wallenberg recounted this exchange to his neighbors. He was bitter; everyone appeared to have forsaken him: the Americans who had sent him to Budapest, the Jews he had saved, and his own government.

Sometime during the spring of 1947 he knocked out his last

message to the occupants of a neighboring cell: "They are taking us away."

A guard unlocked the cell door and summoned Roedel and Wallenberg outside. As Wallenberg left, he banged the wall two last times with his fist.

He was taken from his cell to the transit room at Lefortovskaya and crowded together with fifty other prisoners, almost all Russians. His presence in this room was unusual; few foreigners were transferred from the relative comfort of the Moscow area prisons.

A deportation for Siberia was assembled from among the prisoners in the transit room. Those forced to join it were of all ages: youths who had written cynical letters to their friends, old men who had reminisced too fondly about the days before 1917. Most had violated Article 58 of the Soviet Criminal Code, prohibiting espionage and "counterrevolutionary activities." In the eyes of the law they were all subversives, traitors, saboteurs, and bourgeois separatists, and many had been sentenced to years of hard labor. Wallenberg had previously only been imprisoned with other foreigners. As long as they stayed together, the hope of help from Germany or Italy or Sweden lived on. Now he was with Russians.

An official entered the transit room waving a list and shouting, "Deportation to Vorkuta! Deportation to Vorkuta!" He yelled out names and signaled those called to gather in one corner of the room. As Wallenberg joined the group being deported, he said, "They just want to make me disappear into darkness and fog."

14

Spring 1947–January 1953

VORKUTA, KHAL'MER YU, AND VERKHNEURAL'SK,

SIBERIA

When Wallenberg arrived at the Pechora transit camp en route to Vorkuta, officials reduced his rations and placed him in a punishment cell for three and a half days. He became weak at first but soon recovered, and a fellow prisoner reported later that he appeared "sprightly" and "energetic." He was thirty-four years old.

From the transit camp he was sent to the town of Vorkuta in the northern Urals, seventy miles north of the Arctic Circle. The surrounding area is rich in coal, oil, gold, and other metals, but few Russians can be persuaded to volunteer to work in its harsh climate. To exploit the region's natural resources the government has to use slave labor. The earliest deportations of laborers to Vorkuta traveled on barges infested with lice. When the river froze, trapping the barges, their guards ordered them ashore—to live in tepees made of animal hide. These first prisoners built railroads, prison camps, settlements for guards and other camp workers, mines, and industrial complexes. Once this work was completed, they labored twelve hours a day in the coal mines.

Each prisoner in the Vorkuta camp was identified by a letter of the alphabet and three digits. There were a thousand people to each letter and twenty-eight letters in the Russian alphabet; thus, each prison "alphabet" contained twenty-eight thousand men. The members of the first "alphabet" all died within their first year at Vorkuta.

While Wallenberg was at Vorkuta the NKVD interrogated everyone who had shared a cell with him in Moscow. On the morning of July 27, 1947, a guard led Gustav Richter out of his cell in Lefortovskaya Prison, over the covered bridge, and into an interrogation room that was already occupied by two NKVD officers. The senior officer, a colonel, questioned Richter in Russian while a lieutenant colonel translated into German.

"Name your cellmates since you have been in prison," the colonel commanded.

Richter began reciting a long list of names. He had been a prisoner for three years and had been moved often. When he came to Wallenberg, his cellmate in Lubyanka in February 1945, the colonel interrupted him and demanded a detailed account of everything Wallenberg had said and a list of those prisoners with whom Richter had discussed Wallenberg. The entire interrogation now centered around Wallenberg.

When Richter had finished, he was taken to one of the freezing isolation cells in Lefortovskaya's basement. He served seven months of solitary confinement, first in the basement cell without ever being allowed out for exercise, and then in a dark cell in the women's division on the second floor. He saw no other prisoners until February 1948.

Another German prisoner, Horst Kitschmann, was brought to Lefortovskaya from Lubyanka on July 27, the same day Richter was interrogated. An NKVD colonel also asked Kitschmann to list his former cellmates. When he reached the name of Vilmos Langfelder, Wallenberg's driver, the colonel interrupted and asked, "What did Langfelder tell you?" When Kitschmann mentioned Langfelder's stories of Wallenberg, the colonel asked if he had repeated them to other prisoners.

As "punishment for discussing Wallenberg and Langfelder with other prisoners" Kitschmann also was placed in an isolation cell for seven months.

The NKVD interrogated every prisoner who had met Wallenberg or Langfelder. Ernst Huber, who had been with Langfelder in 1945, was shipped from a prison in the Ural Mountains to Moscow for questioning, a distance of over a thousand miles. A Captain Wolfgang Richter was also sent from the Urals under the mistaken impression that he was the same Richter who had shared a cell with Wallenberg at Lubyanka.

All of these prisoners were interrogated in Lefortovskaya on the twenty-seventh of July. All were asked the same questions: "With whom did you share a cell?" "What did Wallenberg and Langfelder tell you?" "Did you discuss Wallenberg and Langfelder with other prisoners?" All were isolated in punishment cells for several months afterward.

By the summer of 1948, a year after the Russians had informed the Swedish ambassador to Moscow that "Wallenberg is not in the Soviet Union and is unknown to us," Wallenberg had been transferred from Vorkuta to a labor camp farther north at Khal'mer Yu. Here he met Dr. Menachem Meltzer, a camp physician who examined prisoners to see if they were suitable for construction work.

Camp guards brought Wallenberg into Meltzer's office. Meltzer placed a stethoscope against his chest and noted that he had a strong heart. He then looked at his patient's file and said, "Your name is Paul, correct?"

"No," Wallenberg replied. "My name is Raoul. I'm Swedish."

In January 1951 Wallenberg was transferred from Khal'mer Yu to a more comfortable camp for political prisoners at Verkhneural'sk near the city of Chelyabinsk in the southern Urals.

Verkhneural'sk is less than a thousand miles from Khal'mer

Yu, but the railway journey between the two is more than twenty-five hundred miles. Wallenberg first had to travel fifteen hundred miles southwest to Moscow and then a thousand miles east to Verkhneural'sk. He broke the journey at Moscow's Butyrka Prison.

During his week at Butyrka he became more healthy and cheerful. The guards treated him well, bringing him extra rations and also cigarettes. One day he was taken from his cell to another room in the prison, where a barber shaved his head with a razor. This astonished his cellmate, a Hungarian professor named Zoltan Rivo. He and the other prisoners never received such treatment; the guards shaved them bald with electric clippers. After a week at Butyrka, Wallenberg was issued civilian clothes and escorted under guard to Verkhneural'sk.

He remained at Verkhneural'sk for two years. Unlike Vorkuta, which was a labor camp where prisoners had many opportunities to see one another, Verkhneural'sk was a strongly guarded prison where inmates only met if they shared a cell or passed on the way to the bath or their exercise cubicles. For part of the time Wallenberg shared a cell with David Vendrovsky, a Russian who had once been a correspondent for the European Press Agency in Moscow.

Vendrovsky later shared a cell with Abraham Kalinski, a former Polish military attaché in Moscow who was serving twenty-five years in Soviet prisons for allegedly spying for the United States. His crime had been to write a letter to President Roosevelt in which he protested the 1940 massacre of twelve thousand Polish soldiers at Katyn. The Soviet authorities had intercepted his letter, arrested him, and later sent him to Verkhneural'sk Prison.

Kalinski was considered a dangerous prisoner and was kept in solitary confinement during most of his incarceration. From time to time, however, prison authorities gave him a companion to prevent him from becoming insane. On one occasion they brought in Vendrovsky. Pleased to have someone to talk with,

Kalinski asked Vendrovsky what other prisoners he had met at Verkhneural'sk.

"I have been sitting with a very interesting and unusually sympathetic Swede," Vendrovsky answered. "He is noble and innocent and cannot understand why he is accused of being a spy. He is the former diplomat, Raoul Wallenberg."

Kalinski said that he had heard about Wallenberg but had not yet seen him.

One day in 1953 the guards ordered all the political prisoners in Verkhneural'sk to prepare to leave. A rumor circulated: Stalin was dead and Beria, his security chief, was to be executed; they were to be moved to make room for Beria's aides.

All of the prisoners, including Wallenberg and Kalinski, were marched to the railroad siding, where a train with open boxcars stood ready to receive them. In the crowd waiting to board, Kalinski spotted a distinguished-looking figure in a brown padded jacket. The man seemed somehow familiar, yet Kalinski was sure he had never seen him before. Suddenly he realized that he had recognized him from the descriptions of his fellow prisoners. It was the Swedish diplomat, Raoul Wallenberg.

15

1953–1960

When Wallenberg, Kalinski, and many of the other prisoners from Verkhneural'sk arrived in Moscow, they were placed in vans—one bore the words "Khlebkombinat" ("Bread Company")—and driven 150 miles east to the ancient cathedral city of Vladimir. During the reign of Catherine the Great it had been a staging point for prisoners being marched to Siberia. The original Vladimir jail, a two-hundred-year-old brick structure, was now only one of four buildings comprising the modern Vladimir prison complex.

In the early 1950s this entire complex held about six hundred foreigners. There were Germans and Austrians (including some of Wallenberg's old neighbors from Lefortovskaya), Rumanians, Hungarians, Poles, a Frenchman, an Englishman, and an American. Many of these foreigners shared cells; sometimes there were as many as sixteen in a single large cell at the same time. Together they managed to ease the boredom of prison life. Vladimir had an excellent library, which included the works of Balzac and Victor Hugo as well as those of Marx, Engels, and Lenin, and in one cell a different prisoner lectured each evening on a chosen theme. They also celebrated Christmas and the arrival of food parcels.

Wallenberg and Kalinski were both assigned to different cells in building 2, the Vladimir TON (Tyurma Osobogo Naznadeniya—"Special Purpose Prison"), the strictest isolation prison in the Soviet system. The TON was a prison within a prison, a red brick building surrounded by high walls that were surrounded by the even higher walls of the Vladimir complex. Here the routine was vastly different from that enjoyed by foreign prisoners in the other Vladimir buildings. Wallenberg, for example, could not receive parcels or letters. When he was not in solitary confinement his cellmates were always Russians sentenced to long terms. If and when they were released the authorities could persuade them never to mention their Swedish companion.

Like all prisoners in the TON, Wallenberg was permitted to see only his cellmate. Twice a day a guard took him and this cellmate away from their cell, away from the hundred-watt bulb burning night and day, and away from the speaker broadcasting music and propaganda from Radio Moscow sixteen hours a day. He led them down to the second-floor corridor to the toilet, waited until they were finished, and then returned them to their cell. He then went back to the toilet and shined a flashlight onto its walls and into its plumbing. Only when he was certain they had not scrawled graffiti or hidden messages did he bring in the next pair of prisoners.

Once a day a guard brought them downstairs, around the front of the TON, and into an exercise pen.

Every ten days a guard escorted them through the arched gateway in the red brick walls that separated the TON from the rest of Vladimir Prison. He led them across an open yard and into a one-story bathhouse and then locked each one into a shower stall. The guards patroling the fifteen-foot walls encircling the entire prison had orders to shoot on sight prisoners who crossed the open yard without an escort.

Once a month a guard led them into the projection booth of a small prison auditorium. Through one-way glass they could see thirty or forty prisoners from the Vladimir work camp sitting on wooden benches, also watching the monthly movie.

These strict precautions made it theoretically impossible for a TON prisoner to see anyone but his cellmate. Sometimes, however, guards made mistakes, deviated from routes and schedules, and chance encounters occurred before they could shout "Look at your feet!" Sometimes resourceful and daring prisoners circumvented the rules, and then what the guards feared most occurred: The prisoners of the Vladimir TON, some of whom the state had declared dead or missing, saw or communicated with one another.

As in Lefortovskaya, Wallenberg tried to communicate by tapping on his wall. Sometime in 1954 he succeeded in making contact with Emile Brugger, a Swiss citizen who had been kidnapped by the Soviets in Vienna, where he had been working for the American occupation forces. He had been taken shortly after the war and had been in Soviet prisons ever since. Like Wallenberg, he had been transferred from Verkhneural'sk in 1953 in order to make room for Beria's disgraced collaborators. At first he had been assigned to block 3 and placed in a cell opposite the kitchens. In summer the food attracted plagues of flies to his cell. They buzzed against the tiny window and settled on prisoners' faces. By July 1954 an eye disease carried by the flies had made Brugger temporarily blind. As a result he was moved to the TON. It contained the prison hospital as well as the special isolation prison for political "criminals."

Brugger was suspicious when he first heard Wallenberg tapping on his wall. The guards often planted spies who tried to persuade other prisoners to knock. Finally his curiosity overcame his fears. "Who is there?" he knocked back in German.

Wallenberg was equally suspicious. "Who are you?" he knocked.

"Swiss."

"Swedish."

The next day they resumed their conversation:

"Wallenberg, first secretary at the Swedish Embassy in Budapest, deported 1945."

"Brugger, deported 1948, Vienna."

The next day Wallenberg tapped: "When you are freed, report to a Swedish consulate or legation; I am not allowed to write and don't receive letters."

Soon afterward Brugger recovered his sight and was returned to his cell in block 3.

The following year, 1955, an Austrian prisoner named Schöggl who had undergone an operation in the Vladimir prison hospital was placed in Wallenberg's cell by mistake. Wallenberg told Schöggl that he had been kept in solitary confinement for several years and begged him, if he was ever released, to tell any Swedish legation that he had met Raoul Wallenberg. If he could not remember the name, it would be enough to say "a Swede from Budapest."

The next morning a political officer inspected the cell. When he saw Schöggl, he was furious and ordered a guard to transfer him to another cell. Later he came to Schöggl's cell and warned him never to tell anybody about his meeting with Wallenberg. Years later, when Schöggl returned to the West, he so feared Russian reprisals that he would only recount his story anonymously.

The authorities at Vladimir may have been able to isolate Wallenberg, but they could not prevent information about him from circulating among the other prisoners. A Georgian social democrat, Simon Gogobaritze, had shared a cell with Wallenberg at various times between 1948 and 1953. One day during the winter of 1956 Gogobaritze was moved into cell 21 of the Vladimir TON. His new cellmate was Abraham Kalinski.

Minutes after arriving in Kalinski's cell, Gogobaritze pressed his cheek against the window and stared out through a crack in one of the frosted panes. Only the bottom half of the window was frosted; the upper half was clear. In order to gaze through the clear half Gogobaritze would have had to climb onto the bureau while Kalinski stood in front of the door, blocking the peephole. This was dangerous. Guards had orders to unlock and enter a cell the moment they encountered a blocked peephole. Looking through the clear panes was a serious offense, punishable by five days' isolation in a freezing cell. It was less hazardous to stare through the crack, but the field of vision was narrowed.

Six inches beyond the crack in the frosted pane Gogobaritze could see a clear glass window; twelve inches beyond that were thick bars. Beyond the bars he could see his former cellmate, Raoul Wallenberg, exercising in one of the pens located in the yard below. "It's Wallenberg!" he told Kalinski.

Kalinski looked through the crack in the window. Wallenberg had pulled off his khaki jacket and, dressed only in overalls and an undershirt, was scooping up handfuls of snow and rubbing them onto his face, chest, and arms. Once the snow had warmed him he jumped in the air and clapped his hands over his head. He ran in place, bent over and touched his toes, rotated his arms in circles like airplane propellers, fell to the ground, did push-ups, and then strode around the walls of the exercise pen. The walls were eight feet high and enclosed a twenty-by-twenty-five-foot space. It took ten seconds to make a complete circuit, twenty minutes to walk a mile. His cellmate, Mamulov, a former aide to Beria, Stalin's chief of police, stood and watched.

Above them a guard with a submachine gun paced along a catwalk overlooking all eight exercise pens. He was not there to prevent escape—that was impossible—but to keep prisoners in neighboring pens from shouting, throwing messages, or hoisting themselves up to peer over the walls. He frequently shouted at the men below to "Look at your feet!"

In the years that followed, Kalinski watched the Swede exercise in the yard in every type of weather and with a number of different companions. Once he was with Munters, the former foreign minister of Free Latvia; another time, Shariya, former secretary of the central committee of the Georgian Communist party. Always he was accompanied by a Soviet political prisoner, never a foreigner.

As part of the liberalization after Stalin's death many foreign prisoners had gained the right to correspond with their families at home. They used "answer postcards" provided by the Red Cross, on which they were allowed to write twenty lines. A German prisoner in the cell above Kalinski had correspondence privileges. Once a month he tied a card to a thread and lowered it through a vent into Kalinski's cell. Kalinski wrote the card and the German retrieved it with the thread and dispatched it as his own.

The cards were bound to be censored, Kalinski thought, so he used a code. He used Hebrew letters, but the words they spelled out had meaning only in Yiddish. First he wrote to the Jewish community in Vienna that he was alive and needed food parcels. They contacted his sister, who had moved to Israel but had not changed her last name in the hope that her brother, whom the Soviets had declared dead in 1945, might reappear and search for her. Later Kalinski wrote to her directly: "I am living in this hotel and I don't know when I'll move. With me there is an Italian, a Swede who saved a thousand Jews in Rumania [sic]. . . . Those who are here have never committed any crime and have never been before a court!"

His sister tore off the answer portion of the folded card and returned it. "Is there no justice?" she asked.

"Justice?" Kalinski replied. "How can I answer your question when there is a Swede sitting in prison who has saved tens of thousands of Jews, while Gestapo murderers and Russian collaborators with the Gestapo go free?"

Kalinski was not entirely correct. Most of Wallenberg's enemies among the Hungarian fascists had been tried and executed shortly after the war. Among them were former Prime Minister Döme Sztójay and the "three Lászlós"—Baky, Endre, and Ferenczy—who had coordinated the deportation of the provincial Jews to Auschwitz during the spring of 1944; Father Kun, Kurt Rettman, and the other local Arrow Cross responsible for the terror; and Arrow Cross leaders Ferenc Szálasi, Gábor Kemény, and Gábor Vajna.

The Germans who had directed and encouraged their crimes fared much better. At the time that Kalinski wrote his indignant postcard, 1956, most of Wallenberg's German enemies had enjoyed a decade of freedom. Theodore Grell, the German diplomat who had threatened him with death, and Otto Winkelmann, the senior SS and police leader in Hungary, both escaped prosecution. The Reich plenipotentiary, Dr. Edmund Veesenmayer, was convicted to twenty years imprisonment by an Allied war crimes tribunal in 1949. Two years later his sentence was reduced to ten years, and he was freed in 1952 on the recommendation of an American board of clemency. Two of Eichmann's senior aides, Hermann Krumey and Otto Hunsche, and his transportation officer, Franz Novak, were not apprehended until the early 1960s. Afterward they went through a decade of trials and appeals in the West German courts which resulted in prison sentences of varying lengths.

Eichmann himself hid in Europe for five years after the war and then escaped to Argentina in 1950. There he managed a rabbit farm, worked as a mechanic, and reunited with his wife and children, fathered a son, and enjoyed ten years of freedom. In 1960 he was kidnapped by Israeli agents and flown to Jerusalem. He was sentenced to death after a fourteen-week trial and hanged in 1962. Wallenberg would outlive him, but not by much.

Wallenberg remained in Vladimir through the end of the decade. When Kalinski saw him for the last time before his own release from prison, on October 22, 1959, he thought Wallenberg looked "young and fit."

Wallenberg did not stay young and fit for long. Sometime soon after Kalinski's release in 1959, he became so desperate that he went on a hunger strike. When he became ill due to this hunger strike, he was transferred to Moscow, to the hospital wing of the enormous Butyrka Prison where he had received such privileged treatment in 1948.

While in Moscow he was examined by Dr. A. L. Myasnikov, chairman of the Soviet Academy of Medical Science and chief of the Department of Internal Medicine at Moscow's University Hospital. Wallenberg would never know that in one very important respect his hunger strike had succeeded. By forcing Soviet authorities to shift him to Moscow it had placed him in contact with Myasnikov. Soon Myasnikov would become instrumental in conveying important news of his incarceration and condition to the West. Some of this news would become known almost immediately; the rest would remain secret until 1981.

At one point during his stay in Butyrka, Wallenberg was given an American cellmate, Cecil Stowner, who was as pleased as Wallenberg to have the opportunity to converse in English. This encounter may, however, have been a mistake on the part of the guards, since the two men were separated soon afterward. Except for this brief period with Stowner and except for the day when the Soviets had mistakenly placed the Austrian, Schöggl, in his cell, Wallenberg had spent the last decade only in the company of Russian citizens serving long sentences. He had had no opportunity to speak Swedish, English, or German. He had not written or received a letter. He had no idea what, if any, attempts had been or were being made by the Swedish government to free him. His ignorance on this subject, however, may have been a blessing. If he had known the truth he might have sunk into even greater despair.

PART IV

THE SEARCH

16

1945

The truth was that during the first decade of Wallenberg's incarceration, those who should have done the most to press for his release, did the least. The Swedish government had sent him to Budapest as an accredited member of its diplomatic corps; the United States had promoted his rescue mission and backed it with funds; Israel had become the home for many of those he saved. All failed him during this first decade. Only his family and friends mounted the kind of sustained and diligent effort which, if emulated by others during the crucial early period of his captivity, might have produced results.

This early period was crucial because the longer Sweden and the United States waited to press for his release, the more the Soviets were encouraged to believe that, for the West, his fate was a matter of little consequence. Meanwhile, the longer the Soviets held him, the more difficult it became for them to set him free without suffering a propaganda defeat at a time of increasing Cold War tensions. Even if the Soviets did not consider Wallenberg a hero, it was not long before they learned that the West did. It was, ironically, the energetic private campaign mounted by his family, friends, and colleagues, after they had despaired of government actions, that increased Wallenberg's heroic stature and made it more difficult for the Soviets even to admit that they had arrested him.

The factors which must have prompted the Soviets to arrest Wallenberg are more understandable than the failure of his own government to obtain his release.

First of all, there was no lack of evidence to prove the Soviet accusation that he had spied for the Nazis. His activities in Budapest had required extensive contact with Nazis and Arrow Cross at the highest levels, and during the terror he had given them Swedish passes in exchange for favors and information. When the NKVD encountered fascists carrying his protective passes, they concluded that his "humanitarian activities" were simply a cover for anti-Soviet collaboration. Repeated interrogation of his aides produced no evidence for this charge, but did not allay Soviet suspicions.

After the liberation Per Anger observed that "the Russian military authorities were very irritated by continually encountering people furnished with foreign documents. The situation was not made any better by the fact that a substantial number of falsified protective passports, both Swiss and Swedish, were in circulation. Quite a few of these had ended up in the hands of Arrow Cross men and others of the Nazi persuasion. They brought high prices on the black market and had contributed heavily to the inflation of foreign identification papers."

Another likely reason for Wallenberg's arrest was his connection with the United States. He had studied in America for four years and had traveled to Budapest on a mission backed by President Roosevelt. While in Hungary, he had unwisely told his closest aides of his American backing. Some must have repeated these conversations when they were interrogated by the NKVD. Wallenberg, too, in order to defend himself against the accusations of German espionage, had undoubtedly argued that his activities in Budapest were fully supported by an ally of the Soviet Union, the United States. He could hardly have known that he was about to be one of the first victims of the Cold War.

The Soviets regarded Hungary as part of their sphere of influence and were determined to control its postwar development. Their plans to install a communist regime had already been threatened by Horthy's attempt to arrange a separate armistice with the Western allies. They continued to be suspicious of efforts by Britain and America to gain influence in Hungary. Wallenberg, even though he identified himself as a neutral diplomat, appeared to threaten Soviet plans. He proposed his own scheme for Jewish relief and the return of Jewish property—a scheme that he proposed to manage himself. The Soviets did not want a member of an important capitalist banking family with mysterious American connections and a substantial personal following in Budapest to play an important role in postwar Hungary.

According to one anecdote, when Marshall Malinovsky entered Pest and saw all the foreign flags waving over hundreds of buildings, many of which had no right to be under foreign protection, he said, "Apparently I have come to a Swiss or Swedish city, not a Hungarian one."

Wallenberg's explanation for his presence in Budapest, the Swedish flags, the thousands of Swedish passes, and his American connections was that he was carrying out a purely humanitarian mission to save Jews. This was beyond the comprehension of his interrogators. After a war which had cost millions of Russian lives and terrible suffering, it was incomprehensible that a citizen of a neutral country would voluntarily risk suffering and danger for a humanitarian mission. That the purpose of this humanitarian mission was to save Jews made it even more impossible to believe.

The Soviet authorities at Debrecen must have become even more suspicious of Wallenberg when they discovered the gold and valuables hidden in his car. They must have wondered why a Swedish diplomat was leaving Budapest with valuables hidden in his fuel tank. Was this payment for spying for the Nazis? For the Americans? Was it fascist loot? Was he stealing it?

After the war the Soviets never accounted for these valuables, and it can be assumed that they were either confiscated by the government or stolen by officials at Debrecen.

Wallenberg's initial failure to return to Budapest from Debrecen in January of 1945 did not immediately surprise the Swedish government or his Swedish and Hungarian colleagues. For weeks the Soviet Army had been rounding up and detaining Arrow Cross men, Germans, and neutral foreigners. Many people had disappeared; Wallenberg might be anywhere.

Within several weeks, however, this early complacency about his fate began to vanish. One day in February 1945 a Soviet officer stormed into Budapest's Vaterlandische Bank and interrogated Paul Hegedus, one of Wallenberg's former aides. The officer explained that he was searching for Waldemar Langlet, the Swedish Red Cross representative in Budapest. Apparently Langlet had written a letter to the Soviet military police in which he mentioned that Wallenberg had left Budapest to visit Marshall Malinovsky. "How did Langlet know about that journey?" the officer demanded.

Hegedus recognized from the officer's accent that he was a Ukrainian and answered back in their common language. The officer switched to Ukrainian and told him that his name was Pless. Hegedus guided him to Langlet's office at 22 Üllöi Road. Pless questioned Langlet, searched his house, stole his Cyrillic typewriter, and then ordered Hegedus and Mr. and Mrs. Langlet to accompany him to NKVD headquarters.

As they drove through Budapest, they witnessed Russian soldiers robbing pedestrians at gunpoint. Pless told his driver to halt and shouted, "Stop that at once!" to a captain who had joined in the pillage.

The captain hesitated. "I am with counterintelligence," Pless bellowed. The captain turned pale and obeyed.

At NKVD headquarters Pless ordered Hegedus and the Langlets into a bedroom already occupied by eight other prisoners. One of them, a Jew who introduced himself as Stern, was an official of the Hungarian Communist party who had once attended a party school in Moscow. He was distressed. Why were his comrades, the Soviets, treating him like an enemy?

They waited for hours. Langlet, seventy years old and in poor health, dozed with his head on a table. Finally an officer strode into the room and took the Langlets away. Soon afterward he returned and led Hegedus across the road to the upper story of a building occupied by dozens of armed Russian soldiers. Here the interrogation began.

"Who is this Wallenberg," the NKVD officer asked, "and what was he doing in Budapest?"

"He came here to save Jews," Hegedus answered simply.

"Lies! Raoul Wallenberg was a German spy. Why else would he have come here if he wasn't in the pay of German espionage? All this so-called work to save Jews—that was just a cover for the spying the Swedes were doing for the fascists."

The officer was polite, but frequently tried to catch Hegedus with trick questions. Again and again he asserted that Wallenberg was a fascist spy.

The next morning the interrogation became more rigorous. An officer emptied Hegedus's pockets and confiscated every scrap of paper. A medical prescription aroused his suspicion. "What does this mean?" he demanded before resuming the formal interrogation.

"Wallenberg helped the fascists and the Arrow Cross by giving them protective passes," he charged.

Hegedus protested. "Raoul may have given a few passes to his enemies if by doing so he could stop thousands of Jews being deported. In any case, the fascists could easily make their own passes, by stealing them from Jews and changing the names." The officer dismissed these explanations as rubbish.

During the afternoon session one interrogator said, "It was not just Wallenberg; Berg was a spy, too, and the whole Swedish Legation. They were all German spies. Why else would they stay in Budapest after the Nazis and Arrow Cross came to power?"

Again Hegedus tried to explain. When the Nazis came to power, people needed help all the more and the neutral diplomats were best able to give it.

The officer roared with laughter. "Do you really think any sensible person would believe that people would stay in this town, under siege, just for 'humanitarian purposes' when they could have returned to their nice peaceful neutral country!"

The officer demanded details of Wallenberg's activities. "Where did he go? Who came to his office? Which officials at the Legation did he work with? Which Hungarians were in contact with him?"

Again Hegedus was marched to the waiting room. Again he was hauled out for questioning. In the middle of the night Pless reappeared. "Come on, now," he coaxed, "I am Jewish like you; we both speak Ukrainian. Now, are you going to help us or not? Wallenberg was a spy, Berg was a spy, the whole Swedish Legation was a spying operation. It has cost us many lives. If you help us, we'll look after you well."

Pless pleaded with Hegedus for several hours. He needed evidence against the fascist Wallenberg. A terrible enemy of humanity must be prevented from doing any more damage. Finally he lost his temper, slapped Hegedus, and left.

The following day Hegedus was freed. He was not the only one of Wallenberg's co-workers to be arrested and questioned. The Russians bullied some into agreeing with their accusations and charging that Wallenberg had sold protective passes for one thousand to fifteen hundred pengös without the Legation stamp and for five thousand pengös with an official stamp on the photograph.

The NKVD also interrogated Wallenberg's Swedish colleagues. They told Lars Berg that they knew that he and Wallenberg had used their departments as a cover for fascist spying and accused him of giving out protective passes to non-Jews and of not being active enough in protecting Soviet interests. They pressed him for evidence against Wallenberg.

Göte Carlsson received the same treatment. When he tried to explain Wallenberg's real mission, the officer interrogating him raged: "It is totally illogical for someone like Wallenberg to leave peaceful Sweden to come and risk his life in Budapest to save strangers!"

In mid-March the Russians moved Minister Danielsson and other Legation personnel to the Red Cross headquarters at Üllöi Road. Berg joined them later. Still there was no news of Wallenberg.

At the end of the month the Swedes were taken to the station and put on a train which followed the same route that Wallenberg had taken two months earlier. When they arrived in Moscow, their hosts arranged a tour of the city which included the NKVD headquarters, Lubyanka. (Lubyanka also housed the NKVD prison in which Wallenberg was incarcerated at the time of the Swedish diplomat's "tour.") Finally the Russians permitted them to leave Moscow and return to Sweden on board a Finnish ship. On April 18, 1945, two months after the liberation of Budapest and three months after Wallenberg's departure for Debrecen, they arrived home safely. During most of this time the Soviets had told their friends and relatives almost nothing about their condition. There had been more news of Wallenberg.

On January 16, Soviet Deputy Foreign Minister Dekanusov had written to the Swedish ambassador in Moscow, Staffan Söderblom, informing him that Wallenberg had been found on Benczur Street in Budapest and that "measures have been taken by the Soviet military authorities to protect Mr. Raoul Wallenberg and his property."

In February, Alexandra Michaelovna Kollontai, the Soviet ambassador in Sweden, met with Wallenberg's mother, Maj von Dardel. Despite being the daughter of a czarist general, Madame Kollontai had commanded the first Soviet antireligious act of the Revolution, the occupation of the Aleksandr Nevsky monastery, and had held a cabinet post in the first Soviet government. She quarreled with other Soviet leaders when she headed a movement calling for the dismissal of all technical experts trained before the Revolution and the expulsion of all nonproletarians from the Communist party. She lost, and her superiors removed her from the mainstream of Soviet politics by appointing her ambassador to Norway and then to Sweden. She had never abandoned her elegant upper-class manners and taste for fashionable clothes, and in Sweden she enjoyed a comfortable life of diplomatic parties and friendship with such men as Marcus Wallenberg (Raoul's father's banker cousin). Meanwhile, in the Soviet Union, her husband and many of her comrades were disappearing during Stalinist purges.

"Don't worry!" Madame Kollontai assured Mrs. von Dardel. "According to my information your son is completely safe. He will come back."

Madame Kollontai also invited Ingrid Günther, wife of the Swedish foreign minister, to tea at her residence. On this occasion she promised again that Wallenberg was in good hands and under Russian protection.

The Swedish ambassador in Moscow, Staffan Söderblom, became so concerned over Wallenberg's disappearance that he wrote a confidential letter to the Swedish Foreign Ministry in which he said: "One of the troubles that lies on my heart is, of course, Wallenberg's tragic disappearance. . . . I am pursuing an extensive correspondence with the Soviet Foreign Ministry regarding the Budapest Swedes. I have emphasized that all information is lacking regarding Wallenberg."

Söderblom, however, had failed to translate his concern into action, and he wrote that in his dealings with the Soviet Foreign Ministry he did not yet consider it "proper to return to the matter."

The American ambassador, Averell Harriman, offered his assistance, but Söderblom refused. "The Swedish Embassy has no

reason to believe that the Russian authorities are not doing everything within their power," he told Harriman. "We do not require
American intervention."

Söderblom had not consulted with Stockholm before refusing
Harriman's offer. Afterward, he encouraged the Swedish Foreign
Ministry to believe that the United States had itself decided not
to intervene. In April 1945 he cabled that "the U.S. Embassy
has received a long cable on [Wallenberg] from Herschel Johnson
[U.S. ambassador in Stockholm], who must have spoken to some
member of the family. They have apparently replied that the
State Department should approach its representatives in Hungary;
[they] can hardly consider that anything can be done [in Moscow]
from the American side."

Five months later Söderblom reported that "the Americans
have not made any approach to the Soviets." The truth, of course,
was that he himself had discouraged any American action.

Instead of pressing Soviet leaders to explain what had become
of a Swedish diplomat who had been under their "protection"
since January, Söderblom made excuses for their silence on Wallenberg. "What I am afraid of is that the Russians, with the
best intention in the world, cannot inform us what really happened
to Wallenberg," he reported to Stockholm. "The tumultuous situation in Hungary makes it impossible. Troops that were in Budapest in January have surely moved on to Vienna by now. Marshall
Tolbuchin's staff can hardly be expected to give much attention
to such matters under present conditions. It is conceivable that,
if Wallenberg died in an accident or was murdered during the
journey to Debrecen, he might have disappeared without trace
in all the fighting and chaos."

The only action Söderblom proposed proved futile. He recommended that Marcus Wallenberg write a personal note to Madame
Kollontai, the former Soviet ambassador in Stockholm, who had
returned to Moscow several months earlier. Marcus sent a letter
and even a present, a portrait of Prince Eugen. Madame Kollontai
replied in elegant French, full of good wishes to the family, but

admitted that "when one is retired, one does not have the same possibilities to arrange these things."

Throughout 1945 dozens of explanations were offered for Wallenberg's disappearance, and he was "sighted" in a number of different locations.

One Hungarian told a Swiss visitor to Budapest that Wallenberg was living in Buda disguised by a full beard. When he returned to Switzerland, the visitor reported the story to the Swedish Embassy in Berne, but refused to reveal his own name or that of his informant. Nonetheless, the rumor made Söderblom nervous. Fearing embarrassment if Wallenberg should surface in Budapest or Istanbul while he was protesting in Moscow, he delayed delivering photographs of Wallenberg to the Soviet Foreign Ministry.

Professor Albert Szent-Györgyi, the Hungarian Nobel Prize winner who had discovered vitamin C, called at the Swedish Embassy while on a visit to Moscow and reported that he had been at Marshall Malinovsky's headquarters in January when the Russians first learned that Wallenberg had been located. There had been great rejoicing, Szent-Györgyi reported, and the Soviets seemed especially pleased that Wallenberg was the first Swedish diplomat to be liberated.

Even this apparently harmless story angered the Russians, and afterward Szent-Györgyi was removed from consideration as a candidate for president of the new Hungarian Republic. He refused to travel to Sweden to repeat his story and later wrote to the Swedish Foreign Ministry that "I do not believe in the theory that Mr. Vallenberg [sic] is in Russian captivity. . . . The fact that Mr. Vallenberg was liberated by the Red Army does not imply that the Russian authorities could be made in any way responsible for his further fate. There was no reason whatever to give him especial protection because after the withdrawal of the Nazis Mr. Vallenberg was in no greater danger than anyone living then in Hungary. The war has left behind a devastated, disorganized country where death could be met at every corner. Thousands of people died in this period anonymously. Naturally, such a dynamic personality as Vallenberg was especially exposed to danger. It was only too easy to die."

Some believed that there was a chance Wallenberg was still interned in Budapest. In late May of 1945 the NKVD freed most of those arrested during the liberation of the city. Arrow Cross officials, members of the Hungarian police, and neutral collaborators reappeared. Wallenberg was not among them. In September the Langlets arrived in Sweden from Istanbul, where they had gone after being released by the Soviets. They knew nothing of Wallenberg's whereabouts.

The director of the Hungarian National Bank told a Swiss businessman in Budapest that Wallenberg was still alive. He had been captured by the Soviets and they planned to use his notes and papers in the upcoming trials of Hungarians who had collaborated with the Germans. The director recommended that private intervention was more likely than official petitions to secure Wallenberg's release. Soon afterward he was arrested for "sabotage."

A Budapest police officer reported meeting Wallenberg in a Bessarabian camp where he had been awaiting transfer to a prison in Russia. The Swedish government immediately approached the prison administration in Focsani. An official responded by saying: "It is unfortunately impossible to establish if this individual passed through a camp and if he is or is not in prison."

The number of stories filtering through to Stockholm, and their variety, complicated the search. Should the Swedes look for Wallenberg in Hungary or Russia? As a free man or as a prisoner? No one was sure. But almost everyone believed he was still alive.

On April 26, 1945, *The New York Times* published an article describing Wallenberg's actions in Budapest. The article referred to his disappearance, but used the present tense in describing his background.

In July, the board of the Israelite Congregation of Pest sent a letter to Wallenberg care of the Foreign Ministry in Stockholm. They enclosed an extract from the minutes of a meeting at which they commemorated his "immortal achievements and heroic fight to save the greatest possible number of persecuted and oppressed people." The board also voted to name a building of the reconstructed Central Jewish Hospital the "Wallenberg Pavilion."

The official position of the new Hungarian government was that Wallenberg was dead. Kossuthradio, the government radio station, in a broadcast describing Nazi atrocities, stated that "one of the chiefs of the Red Cross work in Budapest during the German occupation was Raoul Wallenberg, who disappeared without trace on the seventeenth of January. All signs indicate that Gestapo agents murdered him."

The Budapest municipal authorities renamed Phoenix Street in the former ghetto "Raoul Wallenberg Street" in his memory, and a delegation from the president of the new Hungarian parliament brought an address of gratitude to Wallenberg's mother, Maj von Dardel. The address overflowed with thanks and praise, but implied that her son had suffered a tragic end.

1946

By the winter of 1946, Wallenberg's mother, Maj von Dardel, had become desperate. A year had passed since the Russian ambassador had assured her that her son was safe and in good hands. Since then she had heard nothing. She expected the Swedish Foreign Ministry to lead the search and therefore visited the Ministry building frequently throughout 1945. At first the diplomats who received her were sympathetic and kept her informed of their efforts. But now, a year later, she could detect a change in their attitude. They were more remote and less friendly; clearly they thought it was time she stopped bothering them and accepted that her son was dead.

The failure of the Swedish Foreign Ministry to press strongly for Wallenberg's release during the early years of his captivity appears, on its surface, to be almost incomprehensible. His continued detention was in clear violation of his rights as a diplomat, and two senior Soviet officials, Deputy Foreign Minister Dekanusov and Ambassador Kollontai, had admitted that he was in Soviet custody.

The excessive caution of the Swedish government probably resulted from a combination of factors. First of all, Swedish leaders must have decided at one point that the Wallenberg incident was not important enough to pursue at the risk of seriously damaging relations with their most powerful neighbor. The fact that Wallenberg was not a career diplomat and had employed unorthodox and controversial methods while in Budapest may also have caused Swedish diplomats to be less forceful than might otherwise have been the case in their protests to Soviet authorities.

There is, however, one hitherto ignored factor which may have had an important chilling effect on Swedish efforts to free Raoul Wallenberg. All previous books and articles on Wallenberg have avoided discussing this crucial factor. Most authorities on Wallenberg have acknowledged their debt to the Hungarian historian Jenö Lévai, whose book about Wallenberg was based on interviews he conducted in Budapest shortly after the war. Yet, all of these authors have chosen to ignore the fact that, as reported in Lévai on the basis of firsthand testimony, Wallenberg left Budapest for Debrecen with a large quantity of Jewish gold and valuables concealed in his automobile.

Lévai does not attempt to explain why Wallenberg took these valuables. One possibility is that he planned to use them to bribe the Russians to liberate the ghetto as soon as possible and to spare the Jews from the acts of looting and raping being committed by Soviet troops elsewhere in the city. He had had great success bribing the Germans and their Hungarian allies; why, he may have reasoned, should the Soviets and *their* Hungarian allies be any different?

Among the other possibilities are that he hoped to buy the Soviets' approval for his relief and reconstruction plans, or that he intended to use the valuables as seed money for the Wallenberg Institute.

The most likely explanation, however, is that he feared that if he left these valuables in Budapest, they would be stolen by Russian soldiers. These fears, it later turned out, would have been well founded. As Budapest was liberated, there were numerous instances of looting and misconduct by Soviet troops. According to Per Anger, there was a rumor "that as a reward for taking Budapest, the Russian soldiers were given free rein for three days of looting and raping in the city."

When, on January 30, Russian soldiers liberated the house on Buda's Rose Hill in which Anger had taken refuge he remembered that "a soldier accosted me with that characteristic phrase we would later hear so often: 'Davay! Davay!' ('Give! Give!')." The Russians looted the house and stole his pen and wristwatch; elsewhere in Buda they took Ivan Danielsson's watch and ripped a gold crucifix off the papal nuncio.

When the Russians occupied the Swedish Legation on St. Gellert's Hill, Lars Berg reported that "the whole Legation was like a madhouse. Singing, laughing, cursing soldiers staggered around everywhere with a bottle in one hand and a pistol in the other. The curtains were torn down, the paintings were used as targets, cabinets and closets were broken open . . ."

According to Anger, "the Legation was totally looted. The building had been ransacked from top to bottom and the safe had been blown up and emptied of its contents. The booty even included the table silver left with us by the former Soviet mission. All furnishings of any value were driven away in trucks brought there for that purpose." Jewish valuables entrusted to the Swedish Legation were among the contents of the safe.

Anger reported that when he, Danielsson, and the other Swedish diplomats were finally permitted to leave Budapest, "we had been unable to save any of our personal belongings and we had, practically speaking, only what we walked around in."

However, despite Danielsson's personal experience, it appears that by 1946 the Swedish Foreign Ministry had in its possession a report written by him which implied that Wallenberg had taken the Jewish valuables to Debrecen not to save them from Russian looters, but to steal them.

After the war Danielsson and Miklós Krausz both took up residence in Switzerland. Krausz visited Danielsson at his home in Lugano on several occasions and found him upset about Wallenberg. According to Danielsson, after the liberation of Buda a number of "Swedish Jews" from Üllöi Road and Jókai Street, as well as the relatives of those who had perished at Jókai Street, had come to him demanding that he return money and valuables which they had entrusted to Wallenberg for safekeeping. He had to admit to them that he had no idea as to the whereabouts of their valuables. Soon afterward he learned that Wallenberg had taken certain Jewish assets with him to Debrecen. He then jumped to the conclusion that Wallenberg had not planned to return them to their owners.

Danielsson told Krausz that after the war he had sent a detailed report to the Swedish Foreign Ministry in which he made it clear that Wallenberg had left Budapest with a large quantity of valuables. (If this report still exists, it may be among the documents on the period from 1944 to 1949 which the Swedish government did not release with other Wallenberg papers in 1980.) The implication of this report was that Wallenberg had taken these valuables for his own use. According to Krausz, rather than holding a grudge against Wallenberg, Danielsson appeared genuinely upset and disappointed by these developments. During an interview on this subject in 1981, Krausz said, "When he [Danielsson] told me this, he was almost in tears."

Danielsson's report can only have been based on circumstantial evidence. Like Anger and the other Swedish diplomats who had taken refuge in Buda, he had no direct contact with Wallenberg during the week preceding his departure for Debrecen. It would have been impossible for him to know Wallenberg's motives. Furthermore, since according to Berg the Russians looted the safe in the Swedish Legation, it is entirely likely that the Russians had stolen many of the Jewish valuables entrusted to the Swedes.

Unless Wallenberg confided in an aide who is still alive, no one can characterize with absolute certainty his motives for removing the valuables to Debrecen. What *is* certain is that there is absolutely nothing in his personality or in his behavior in Budapest to suggest that he planned to keep these valuables. If anything, his record and character, combined with the need to protect Jewish assets from Russian looters and his practice of achieving results through bribery, strongly suggest that his motives were entirely honorable.

Nonetheless, Danielsson's report, combined with the fact that several Hungarian Jews later traveled to Sweden to demand compensation for their losses, must have had a chilling effect on the Wallenberg search. Krausz is not the only source which indicates the presence of such a report. Over the years other evidence has surfaced that this story became known in Swedish diplomatic circles and that it impeded the search for Wallenberg.

In 1952 a Swedish author, Mia Leche Löfgren, wrote to Birgitta de Vylder Bellander, the chairman of a committee of Swedish citizens attempting to secure Wallenberg's release, recounting a conversation she had had over Christmas dinner with a Swedish diplomat in Paris who had once been involved in the Wallenberg investigation. The diplomat had told her that Wallenberg had done something in Budapest that deserved punishment, "a dereliction of duty."

During an interview held in 1981 with one of the authors of this book, Nanna Svartz, a Swedish doctor who had been the personal physician to both Prime Minister Tage Erlander and Madame Kollontai, said that shortly after the war a member of Budapest's aristocracy had told her: "I just cannot fathom why this highly intelligent man [Wallenberg] took all that money over to the Russians." Dr. Svartz also claimed that Erlander and Wallenberg's stepfather, Fredrik von Dardel, also knew about the money.

Prime Minister Erlander and Ambassador Söderblom have indicated during interviews with one of the authors of this book that they were both made aware of the question of the missing valuables. This may be one reason Söderblom made such a halfhearted attempt to secure Wallenberg's immediate release from Russia.

In 1946, when members of the Wallenberg family came to the conclusion that the efforts of the Swedish government were inadequate, they launched their own rescue program.

In the hope of uncovering new information, Wallenberg's brother-in-law volunteered to join a relief convoy bringing food to malnourished Hungarian children. Upon his arrival in Budapest he questioned Wallenberg's former aides, but learned nothing new. The trip was judged to be a failure.

To create more publicity over her son's disappearance, Maj von Dardel shared her papers and reminiscences with a Jewish émigré from Austria, Rudolph Philipp. He wrote a book which was both a eulogy to Wallenberg's accomplishments in Budapest and a polemic against the Swedish diplomats who had failed to rescue him. After publication, relations between the Wallenberg family and the Swedish Foreign Ministry deteriorated still further.

One mysterious middleman promised the family that he could secure Wallenberg's release if they fulfilled two conditions: they must pay the man twenty thousand dollars and promise not to publicize what had occurred during Wallenberg's imprisonment. Fredrik von Dardel, Wallenberg's stepfather and guardian, agreed to meet both conditions, and for days his son, Guy, and Rudolph Philipp waited at the airfield to which the middleman had promised to deliver Wallenberg. He never appeared.

One Swedish woman, Britt Ehrenstråle, told Philipp and Fredrik von Dardel that in 1945 she had met an injured Swede in a Polish partisan camp. The Swede was unconscious and his face was covered with bandages. She whispered in his ear that he should press her hand if he was Raoul Wallenberg. After repeating these instructions five or six times she claimed to have felt "a light pressure in my hand." The partisans told her that the Swede had been a passenger on a Soviet prison train they had recently blown up. The von Dardels persuaded Ehrenstråle that publicizing her inconclusive story would simply serve Soviet interests.

The rumors and theories reaching Stockholm in 1946 were not encouraging. The Swedish chargé d'affaires in Budapest, Lennart Rolf Arfwedson, reported, "It is believed here that either Wallenberg was taken away by the Russians and shot while trying to escape, or he was shot by the Arrow Cross, or he died on the journey to Debrecen. In that case, it was either a car accident, or a bomb attack or robbery."

A Hungarian suggested to a Swedish friend that Wallenberg may have died in a prison camp in Gödöllö (just outside Budapest). People died there "like flies," he said, and the Soviets were unable to identify them.

A Hungarian government representative in Stockholm told a reporter: "It is now certain that Wallenberg . . . was murdered. [He] insisted on driving to Debrecen. . . . He was warned, since the roads there were regarded as unsafe, because bands of Arrow Cross and German troops were still committing their atrocities in the area." (In fact, after a major tank battle that occurred in this vicinity in October 1944, the Red Army completely controlled the road to Debrecen. The region is a plain, and there are no mountains or forests to shield an ambush.)

Swedish journalists published stories stating that they had found Wallenberg's clothes as well as articles belonging to the Russian soldiers who had escorted him to Debrecen. This was meant to prove the theory that they had all been murdered en route.

Only one story inspired hope. A Swedish journalist, Edvard af Sandeberg, who had been a correspondent in Berlin, arrived home during the summer of 1946 and published reports of his wartime adventures. After the German surrender he had been evacuated to Moscow with 137 other people claiming to be neutral nationals. Some had no passports and the Russians had imprisoned and interrogated the entire group. While in prison af Sandeberg met a German who had shared a cell with Langfelder and a Rumanian who said he had been Wallenberg's cellmate.

Ten years later, diplomats at the Foreign Ministry would request testimony from the German, Hille, who had spoken to Sandeberg, but in 1946 they took little notice. They answered one inquiry by saying, "It is probable that [Wallenberg] is no longer alive."

They did, however, act on one clue. An anonymous Hungarian supplied the names of the three soldiers who accompanied Wallenberg from Budapest on January 17. The Swedish Embassy in Moscow relayed these names to the Soviet Foreign Ministry, suggesting that they be questioned. At first the Soviets were silent. Finally they responded mysteriously by saying: "Af Sandeberg has been found and is being returned to his native country." This apparently irrelevant reply encouraged Ambassador Söderblom. He wrote in a "Strictly Confidential" letter to Stockholm: "This could be understood as a hint that Raoul Wallenberg is alive and has been identified in some camp."

In early June of 1946, just prior to his departure from Moscow, Ambassador Söderblom requested the courtesy of a farewell audience with Stalin. Under normal circumstances the Soviet leader only saw the British and American ambassadors, and only if they were bringing personal communications from the British prime minister or the American president. He never received ambassadors from neutral countries. Foreign Minister Molotov, however, promised Söderblom that he would try to persuade Stalin to make an exception. He succeeded, and on June 14, Söderblom was notified that he would meet with Stalin on the following day. He was flattered that the Soviet leader had agreed to break precedent in order to bid him farewell.

Stalin sat at the conference table in the Kremlin reception room wearing a marshall's uniform; Deputy Foreign Minister Lukovsky was at his side. Söderblom and Legation Counselor Barck-Holst took chairs facing them. Söderblom began speaking in Russian: "I am grateful to Your Excellency that you have agreed to receive me before my departure from Moscow. I do not want to take up too much of your valuable time as I have no reason to plead with you on any matters, nor do I wish to approach you regarding any difficult problems." He then transmitted greetings from the Swedish king and prime minister and expressed his country's desire for good relations with the Soviet Union.

Stalin asked: "Have you any particular requests?"

"I have nothing special to take up with you," Söderblom answered, "but as you ask, I would like to mention one matter. When Szálasi took power in Hungary, they began to kill Jews. The king cabled Horthy and explained that this was too indecent. They agreed that the Jews of Budapest would be placed under Swedish protection. Among those who saved twenty-five thousand to thirty thousand Jews was a Swedish diplomat, Wallenberg."

"The name was Wallenberg?"

"Yes, Wallenberg."

Stalin reached for a pad and noted the name.

Söderblom continued: "I informed Dekanusov that Wallenberg went through the front to the Red Army while the rest of the Swedes remained in Buda. Dekanusov informed me that Wallenberg was the first Swede to be found by the Russians. Later he was seen in a car together with Russian soldiers, evidently en route to Debrecen, which was then the temporary capital. Since then, he has disappeared without a trace."

"You do know that we gave orders that the Swedes were to be protected?"

"Yes," Söderblom replied. Then, making a suggestion that was to impede further attempts to free Wallenberg, he said, "I am personally convinced that Wallenberg was the victim of an accident or of robbers."

"Did you not receive any message from us on this matter?" Stalin asked.

"No. I consider it probable that the Soviet military authorities do not have any information regarding Wallenberg's further fate . . . however, I would prefer to receive an official message that all possible efforts have been made in the search for Raoul Wallenberg, even if they unfortunately up to now have been without result. Furthermore, [I would like] an assurance that we will receive further notification if anything is learned with regard to Wallenberg's fate. This would be very much in your own interest, as there are people who, in the absence of such information, will draw incorrect conclusions."

Stalin said, "I promise you that this matter will be investigated and cleared up." The audience was over.

Söderblom was pleased with the meeting. He reported to Stockholm: "The mention in the Russian radio and press that I was received by Stalin has caused great attention here. It is understood as visible evidence that Swedish-Russian relations are excellent."

If the Wallenberg affair had ever constituted a potential stumbling block to those relations, it had now been removed. By inviting Stalin to confirm that Wallenberg was "the victim of an accident or of robbers," Söderblom had indicated that Sweden would be satisfied with a statement along the lines of "efforts . . . made in the search for Raoul Wallenberg . . . have been without result." He had almost suggested that the Swedish government desired that kind of response in order to smooth its relations with the Soviet Union.

In 1980, Söderblom explained his remarks as follows: "The political climate was such that I thought it impossible to provoke the Russians. The Soviet government had been very positive and friendly toward Sweden. I therefore considered it inappropriate for me as ambassador to make unsuitable hints or innuendos."

Tage Erlander was prime minister of Sweden in 1946. He now admits: "It would be better if the discussion between Söderblom and Stalin had never taken place. It was a dangerous conversation, one which may have been fatal and disastrous."

On June 19, 1946, four days after Söderblom's audience with Stalin and while Wallenberg was still in cell 203 at Lefortovskaya, a gala concert was held in Budapest "to the honor and memory of Raoul Wallenberg." The state radio station broadcast the music program and the eulogy. The speaker praised Wallenberg in lavish terms as "a hero," "a pure and unsullied knight," "a resurrected dragon-slayer," and "a worthy follower to the apostles." He concluded: "In the end, the waves of the war carried him away, a moment before victory. Was it the fascists or shrapnel that hit his car? Who knows? . . . If his end seems unfair, it is nonetheless glorious, for it rounds out Wallenberg's story into a true heroic epic. . . . There will always be heroes . . . who appear, fight, and vanish."

In Sweden many still doubted that Wallenberg had come to a "glorious end." Three members of the Swedish parliament tabled a criticism of Ambassador Söderblom and his replacement, Gunnar Hägglöff. The next day Prime Minister Erlander sent a courier to Moscow with a note instructing the Embassy to make a new attempt to locate Wallenberg.

Hägglöff considered the situation hopeless. The Soviet Foreign Ministry advised him that "we cannot do anything more in the Raoul Wallenberg affair. Stalin himself has taken the matter in hand and it is impossible to remind Stalin's office of anything. Further memoranda and representations are useless."

Hägglöff was reduced to suggesting to Stockholm that if no satisfactory answers came from the "highest levels," the Swedish government should retaliate with "a cold reception of the Soviet foreign minister in Stockholm and actions on cultural and economic contacts."

During Hägglöff's frequent absences, the case was pursued by the chargé d'affaires, Ulf Barck-Holst. He visited Madame Kollontai and afterward recommended that the Foreign Ministry send her a Christmas present. He suggested a silver cup decorated with the Swedish crown.

Barck-Holst had an audience with Deputy Foreign Minister Lukovsky, who had also been present at the Stalin-Söderblom meeting, and informed him that Sweden wanted another meeting with Stalin for the purpose of discussing Wallenberg.

He requested the permission of the Swedish Foreign Ministry

to involve the United States in the search. This permission was at first granted but then mysteriously withdrawn.

He encouraged the Swedish foreign minister, Östen Undén, to bring up the Wallenberg case with the Russian representative to the United Nations. Undén apparently ignored this suggestion.

Barck-Holst believed that the Soviets were interested in negotiating over Wallenberg. Earlier in 1946 the Swiss government had exchanged eight Soviet citizens convicted of espionage in Switzerland for five Swiss diplomatic and consular officials then held by the Soviets. Among them was Harald Feller, a Swiss diplomat who had collaborated with Wallenberg in Budapest.

After the liberation of Budapest the Swiss government had repeatedly asked for information about Feller, only to have the Soviets deny all knowledge of his whereabouts. Meanwhile, Feller was in an internment camp for foreigners undergoing repeated interrogations. The Swiss, however, refused to abandon their efforts and within a year secured his release through a prisoner exchange.

In 1946, Sweden had no Soviet spies to trade for Wallenberg. Yet, when Barck-Holst raised the issue of Wallenberg at the Soviet Foreign Ministry, an official asked him, "What information can you give us about Lydia Makarova, or Anatoly Granovsky, or the Balts?"

Lydia Makarova was the seventeen-year-old daughter of a Russian officer. Believing that both her parents were dead, she had joined a party of Russian refugees who had arrived in Sweden in 1945. Since then her father had reappeared in the Soviet Union and had demanded her return. The Soviets were anxious to have her extradited.

Anatoly Granovsky was a former agent of the Soviet secret police who had defected to Sweden and was now in a Swedish prison awaiting a decision on his plea for asylum.

A total of 146 nationals of the Baltic provinces (Estonia, Latvia, and Lithuania) who had fought with the German Army and then escaped to Sweden had been returned to the Soviet Union at the end of the war. The Swedish government, however, had permitted a small number of the most seriously ill to remain. Since then, the Soviets had demanded their return.

Thus, Sweden held several Russian citizens who interested the Soviet authorities. Barck-Holst broached the idea of an exchange with Ambassador Hägglöff, who proposed it to Foreign Minister Undén.

Undén quite rightly vetoed the trade. These Russians were political refugees, not spies. "Sweden will not go in for human barter," he replied. "The actions we have already taken are quite sufficient." Lydia Makarova, Anatoly Granovsky, and the Balts remained in Sweden; Wallenberg remained in Russia.

18

1947–1948

In 1947 the Soviets adopted a new approach. Previously they had professed ignorance of Wallenberg; now, during routine discussions with Swedish Embassy officials, they began to speculate. "Perhaps Wallenberg was killed in street fighting in Budapest," a Foreign Ministry official named Vetrov suggested in early 1947 to Rolf Sohlman, the new Swedish ambassador. This was the first time the Russians had offered this theory.

In Stockholm, Mrs. Birgitta de Vylder Bellander, a well-known author and champion of humanitarian causes, formed a Wallenberg Action Committee and collected 1,600,000 signatures on a petition to Stalin requesting Wallenberg's return.

Maj von Dardel also wrote to Stalin:

> *To Generalissimo Joseph Stalin:*
>
> *As mother of Raoul Wallenberg, legation secretary to the Swedish mission in Budapest, I plead with the powerful rulers of the Soviet Union for help in retrieving my beloved son. In short my son's story is as follows: From July 1944 to January 1945 he fought with all his might and intelligence against the Nazi terror which wanted to destroy the entire Jewish*

population of Budapest. When Budapest was liberated by the forces of the Soviet Union, my son was put under protection of the Russian military authorities in January 1945. This fact was officially communicated to the Swedish Foreign Office by the Foreign Ministry of the Soviet Union on January 17, 1945. In February that year this joyful message was further confirmed to me by Ambassador Kollontai. Since then two and a half years have passed without the Soviet authorities communicating any further information about him. My trust in the powerful Soviet Union is so great that, despite my great anxiety, I have remained convinced that I would see him again. As I presume that the delay with his return home is due to misunderstandings by lower-level officials, I now turn to the ruler of the Soviet Union with a prayer that my son may be returned to Sweden and to his longing mother.

Respectfully,
Maj von Dardel

She handed the letter to the Foreign Ministry and asked that it be delivered by the Swedish Embassy in Moscow. This was never done. Instead, the Swedish ambassador cabled back to Stockholm: "If this is just a matter of calming Mrs. von Dardel we can always conduct a mass at Minindel [the Russian Foreign Ministry]."

On August 18, 1947, several months after Wallenberg had been transferred from Lefortovskaya in Moscow to the Vorkuta camp in Siberia and three weeks after the NKVD had interrogated and isolated his Lefortovskaya cellmates, the Soviet Foreign Ministry broke its official silence on the Wallenberg case. Swedish Ambassador Sohlman received a letter from Andrei Vyshinsky, the deputy minister for foreign affairs, which said: "As a result of careful investigation, it has been established that Wallenberg is not in the Soviet Union and that he is unknown to us."

The letter also explained that the note sent by Dekanusov on January 16, 1945, reporting that Wallenberg had been found on Benczur Street in Budapest was based on "indirect information from a commander of combat troops taking part in the fighting in Budapest. At the time it was impossible to verify the report. Since then, a thorough investigation has been carried out, but has failed to produce a positive result. The Soviet officer who provided the information about Wallenberg has not been found. Wallenberg has not been found in the camps for prisoners of war and internees. . . . The Soviet authorities have worked on the Wallenberg case for a considerable period of time, but their attempts to find him have met with no success. . . . It should be remembered that Wallenberg was in an area where Soviet troops were involved in violent fighting, when anything might have happened. Wallenberg could, on his own initiative, have left the region occupied by Soviet troops, there might have been an enemy air attack, he could have perished under enemy fire, etc."

Stalin had followed Söderblom's advice. He had officially informed the Swedish government that every possible effort had been made to search for Raoul Wallenberg, but without success. To Söderblom's suggestion that "Wallenberg was the victim of an accident or of robbers" he had added the theory that Wallenberg had died during the siege of Budapest or had been captured by the Arrow Cross.

After receiving Vyshinsky's letter denying Wallenberg's presence in the Soviet Union, officials at the Swedish Foreign Ministry in Stockholm and at the Embassy in Moscow stopped pestering the Russians. They had gone to Stalin, the highest authority in the Soviet Union; their consciences were clear—they could do no more. The case appeared closed.

Wallenberg's family and the Wallenberg Action Committee, a group of distinguished Swedish citizens, were not satisfied. They mistrusted the Foreign Ministry and thought that Swedish diplomats had been halfhearted in their efforts because they did not consider Wallenberg a genuine diplomat and believed that his unorthodox methods had endangered his colleagues in Budapest.

The von Dardel family was certain Wallenberg was still alive, and his half brother, Guy von Dardel, begged American politicians to get the State Department involved in the search for him. The response of American legislators was always sympathetic, but emphasized, according to one, "In view of the fact that Mr. Wallenberg acted as a member of the Swedish diplomatic mission in Budapest, the initiative in the inquiries directed toward the Soviet government rests with the Swedish authorities."

Clearly the American legislators as well as the American people were unaware of the full extent of the United States' involvement in Wallenberg's mission. The State Department did not enlighten them, and the papers of the War Refugee Board remained classified. The release of just one of these papers—a cable sent by Herschel Johnson, the War Refugee Board representative in Stockholm, to the State Department on June 28, 1944—might have changed American perceptions. This cable stated: "We should emphasize that the Swedish Foreign Office in making this assignment [of Wallenberg to Budapest] feels that it has cooperated fully in lending all possible facilities for the furtherance of an American program."

State Department officials may have avoided taking an active role in the Wallenberg case for fear that any American interest might confirm Soviet suspicions that he was an American spy. Or, like their Swedish counterparts, they may have decided that the case was not important enough to warrant a major effort. It is also possible that the rumors concerning Wallenberg and the missing Jewish valuables had reached American officials and had restrained them from taking responsibility for his mission.

In 1947 the Wallenberg Action Committee in Sweden scrutinized the evidence collected by the émigré Austrian writer, Rudolph Philipp, and became convinced that Wallenberg had been, and probably still was, in Russian custody. In November 1947 they met with the Swedish government representatives to discuss their findings.

Foreign Minister Undén was shocked by their claims. "Do you think Vyshinsky would lie to us?" he demanded.

"I damn well do," answered Birgitta Bellander.

Although at this time Foreign Ministry officials had ceased to make direct approaches to the Soviets, they did not entirely abandon the Wallenberg case. They filed every piece of information and rumor concerning Wallenberg and followed every lead, however unlikely.

A Finn named Anti Turunen wrote to Marcus Wallenberg, Raoul's father's cousin, proposing to mount an operation to retrieve him from a prison in Estonia. First, however, Marcus Wallenberg would have to send a private car to Gothenburg to fetch Turunen. The car was dispatched, but the Finn never appeared. The Foreign Ministry searched for him in Gothenburg without success.

Swedish diplomats next learned that Lill Träsk, a man known for swallowing nails and forks in bars in northern Finland in exchange for drinks, was offering to sell sketches of Wallenberg made by a Soviet prisoner. By the time the Foreign Ministry tracked down Träsk, he had been sentenced to three years in prison for forgery.

An official of the Swedish Embassy in Rome visited the Varite Florida nightclub in order to befriend the beautiful Hungarian dancer, Vedetta International, who was believed to have confidential information about Wallenberg. He was told that she had recently disappeared from the club. She was never located.

The Ministry even filed a letter from one Waldemar Johanson, who described himself as "forced to accept lifelong internment in the United States of America." He claimed information from a witness "whose credibility could not be challenged," and reported:

The raid on the Swedish Legation in Budapest was made by a large detachment of Asiatic Russian troops under the command of Colonel General Leon Kotliar of the Jewish Red Army.

After the Legation was ransacked and robbed of all monetary values and papers, Kotliar ordered Mr. Wallenberg removed for further questioning by a Russian inquisition committee which was also attended by a representation from the advance guard of the United States forces.

After completion of this inquisition, Mr. Wallenberg was wired and weighted and thrown into the river.

All women employees of the Legation were, by orders of Kotliar, raped—some by as many as 150 drunken and insane Asiatics.

This act was one of the many that were incidentally proposed and approved of in the orgies—conferences—at Teheran and Yalta, by Roosevelt, Stalin, and Churchill, and not an outcome from rivalry and usual underground warfare between different groups of international Jewry.

Although no progress was made in finding Wallenberg during the early postwar years, he had not been forgotten. In 1948 three deputies of the Swedish parliament, supported by an eminent group including Albert Einstein, proposed him for the Nobel Peace Prize. Under the Nobel rules, candidates for the Peace Prize must be proposed by members of the Nobel Committee; members of parliaments, governments, and certain international organizations; university professors lecturing in political science, history, philosophy, or law; or former winners of the Nobel Peace Prize. On this basis Einstein was excluded from nominating Wallenberg. Nevertheless, he wrote to the Wallenberg Action Committee, "I would find it quite justified that Raoul Wallenberg should receive the Nobel Peace Prize and I am gladly permitting you to mention this expression of mine to any person."

In the letter of nomination, the Action Committee wrote: "Raoul Wallenberg has . . . contributed to alleviating the horrors of the war, and to suppressing hate between peoples. The fact that he achieved this feat at continuous risk to his own life is of considerable worth in the comparative distinction with [his] great predecessors."

In Budapest, the sculptor Pál Patzay had labored for two years to create a monument to commemorate Wallenberg. A public fund-raising drive had been mounted to purchase the necessary materials, and Patzay had refused to be paid for his work. Wallenberg had saved the sculptor's friends from deportation.

The completed monument stood eighteen feet high. Patzay had cast a bronze figure of St. George fighting a serpent to represent Wallenberg's struggle against violence and Nazism. St. George stood on a plinth bearing a relief of Wallenberg's face and an inscription in his honor. "This monument," it concluded, "expresses our silent and eternal gratitude to him and should always remind us of eternal humanity in inhuman times."

The Budapest Wallenberg Committee organized a ceremony in St. Istvan Park to dedicate the monument. It was planned that the president of the committee would make a speech and then present the monument to the mayor of Budapest. Members of the Swedish Legation accepted an invitation to attend, but Wallenberg's mother declined. She thought a monument should not be erected until her son was free; a memorial should not occur until he was dead.

Those arriving at the park for the dedication ceremony were shocked. Only part of the plinth remained standing, and the bronze figures had vanished. They soon learned that on the previous night the Russians had tied ropes around the figures and used a team of horses to pull them down. The relief of Wallenberg and the inscription were never seen again.

Years later the bronze figures reappeared on a new base in front of a penicillin factory in Debrecen. The statue was intended to symbolize the battle of medical science against disease. A Swedish journalist asked a factory worker who the man fighting the serpent was meant to be. He replied: "If there had been a name on the statue, nobody would have known who it was; but now, when there is no name, everybody knows. The man was a hero."

Within the borders of the Soviet Union, the Soviets confined themselves to verbal attacks on Wallenberg. In January 1948 the semiofficial Soviet weekly *New Times* used its "Spotlight on Slander" column to publish an article entitled "The Wallenberg Legend." It said:

> *A new campaign of slander against the Soviet Union has been unleashed in Sweden. Delving into the rubbish heap of anti-Soviet fabrications, the servitors of Swedish and foreign reaction have dragged out and revived the so-called Wallenberg affair.*

The article admitted that Wallenberg's fate was unknown, but presented only two theories to explain his disappearance: He had been killed either by "frenzied Nazis" or "Szálasi's bandits." It continued:

> *Swedish right-wing newspapers have suddenly given this regrettable but by no means exceptional occurrence in wartime conditions a sensational, even provocative, character. Fables about the "Soviet secret police" which is allegedly holding Wallenberg in its fearsome clutches are persistently disseminated by the press. It is of interest to note that the circulation of these absurd inventions in print coincides with a visit to the United States of Wallenberg's stepbrother [sic], an engineer named von Dardel.*

Even the Nobel Peace Prize nomination was seen as part of the conspiracy, an attempt to drag Norway into Sweden's "anti-Soviet fabrications." The article concluded:

> *It is obvious that the people who circulate vicious fabrications about Wallenberg are least of all interested in his fate. The whole affair is utilized as a pretext for anti-Soviet provocation by those Swedish circles that cannot reconcile themselves to the development of friendly relations between the Soviet Union and Sweden and are doing their utmost to damage*

*these relations. The Soviet public views such provocatory en-
deavors with profound indignation and hopes that Swedish
democratic circles will draw the correct conclusions, giving
a merited rebuff to the despicable activities of the Swedish
"stepbrothers" of the American warmongers.*

The Nobel Prize nomination, the Budapest statue, Philipp's
new evidence, von Dardel's attempts to involve the American
government, and all of the other ploys and strategies tried between
1945 and 1948 by Wallenberg's family and those interested in
his fate failed. They failed not only to secure his release but
even to force the Soviets to admit they had arrested him. They
failed because of American and Swedish indifference, and because
Wallenberg had become a hostage to the Cold War. Clearly the
Soviets believed that if they told the truth they would be losing
an important propaganda battle to the "Swedish 'stepbrothers'
of the American warmongers." A change in their position could
be brought about only by a change in their leadership, a break
in the Cold War, a more determined campaign by Swedish officials, or a combination of the three. This was not to happen
for almost ten years.

19

1948–1956

In 1948, Wallenberg's friend and colleague from Budapest, Per Anger, took over responsibility for the Wallenberg case at the Swedish Foreign Ministry. Anger shared the belief of the Wallenberg Action Committee and the von Dardel family that Wallenberg was alive in a Soviet prison, and that official Swedish efforts had been inadequate.

The foreign minister, Östen Undén, was in large part responsible for the attitude of the Swedish government. Undén, the author of a learned textbook on international law, viewed validity under that law as the guiding principle of foreign policy, a belief which he enjoyed expounding in lengthy theoretical speeches to the United Nations. He was also a social democrat who took a benevolent interest in the Soviet experiment and wanted to promote friendly Swedish-Soviet relations.

On one earlier occasion Undén had shown himself reluctant to protest totalitarian brutality. In 1944 the Swedish section of the World Jewish Council had petitioned the Foreign Ministry on behalf of the Jews of Hungary. Undén, who was then the Ministry's expert on minority and national rights, replied that it would be meaningless for the Swedish government to approach

221

Germany on the subject, since the action would only provoke an answer humiliating to Sweden. He suggested instead a protest meeting, preferably organized by church leaders of the Swedish State Church, the Lutheran Church. In this case, he argued, the Germans "could not attribute the reason for the criticism and protest to Jews and Bolsheviks."

Undén became foreign minister in 1945, the year of Wallenberg's disappearance. In following years he resisted involving the Foreign Ministry in efforts on Wallenberg's behalf whenever he thought those efforts would harm Swedish-Soviet relations. On one occasion he said, "We cannot declare war just for the sake of Wallenberg!"

Between 1948 and 1950, Anger became increasingly troubled by Undén's attitude toward the Wallenberg case. He later wrote: "I noticed that Undén persisted in his negative attitude, and many times I was ready to give up. I had not gained the slightest attention at the highest level for my conviction that Wallenberg was in Russian imprisonment, or for what I thought should be done to set him free."

Finally, at the end of 1950, Anger had an opportunity to confront Undén when they traveled together by train to attend a meeting in Oslo. Undén invited Anger to sit in his compartment during the journey and at one point said: "You have been in Budapest, Mr. Anger, and are said to have views on what has happened to Wallenberg."

Anger summarized Wallenberg's actions on behalf of the Jews and explained the reasons why he believed that Wallenberg was still in Russian custody: the af Sandeberg testimony and Philipp's evidence. He then argued that the only way to deal with the Russians was to be tough. The Swiss, Italians, and Danes had secured the release of their citizens from Soviet jails through exchanging Soviet spies. Why did the Swedish government not do the same? There were now several spy cases before the Swedish courts which involved Soviet citizens living in Sweden. He also wondered why in 1946 the government had not demanded Wallenberg's release as a condition for the one billion kroner trade credit agreement with the Soviet Union.

Undén's reply was curt: "The Swedish government does not do such things." The audience was over. Soon afterward, Anger asked to be relieved from handling the Wallenberg case.

In 1951, a year after Anger's resignation, the Soviets exchanged some of Wallenberg's Italian neighbors and knocking partners from Lefortovskaya Prison for a group of communists held in Italian jails. Among the Italians freed was Claudio de Mohr, the cultural attaché from Sofia who had communicated with Wallenberg at Lefortovskaya and been so surprised to learn that the Russians had imprisoned a Swedish diplomat.

At cocktail parties in Rome, de Mohr often related anecdotes of his prison life and explained how he had communicated by knocking on his wall. He remembered that most of the prisoners were Germans, but there was also a Swede. When this news reached Stockholm, the Foreign Ministry sent experts to question de Mohr. His story was so convincing that the government had to act.

Between 1952 and 1954 the Foreign Ministry made fifteen written and thirty-four oral requests to the Soviet Union for Wallenberg's return. Swedish diplomats pointed to de Mohr's information as proof that the Soviet government could, if it chose, locate Wallenberg and return him.

Soviet Foreign Minister Rodionov ignored the new evidence. He repeated Vyshinsky's 1947 response: The competent authorities in the Soviet Union had made a thorough search and had concluded that "Wallenberg has not been and is not in the Soviet Union and he is not known to us."

Rodionov's reply did not convince the Swedes. In November 1952, King Gustav Adolf VI decorated Wallenberg with the gold medal *"Illis quorum meruere labores"* ("Those whose works deserve it") for his humanitarian work in Budapest. The Foreign Ministry pointedly announced that the medal was *not* being awarded posthumously.

A new channel for pursuing the search for Wallenberg became available in 1953 when the Swedish diplomat Dag Hammarskjöld was appointed secretary-general of the United Nations. On the day Hammarskjöld assumed his post he promised that, if Swedish representations to the Soviets produced no result, he would himself work "with heart and soul" for Wallenberg's release.

Three years later, before he left for his first visit to Moscow, Hammarskjöld received a telephone call from Carl-Frederik Palmstierna, private secretary to the Swedish king, asking him to raise the issue of Wallenberg with the Soviet government. In his memoirs Palmstierna recalled: "Hammarskjöld answered in a stream of crystal-clear phrases that the fact that he himself was a Swede made it doubly difficult for him to put the case of a compatriot to the Russians. If matters had been different, he would of course, etc., etc. . . . I wondered, however, in my heart of hearts how the matter could have been different. If Hammarskjöld had assumed the case of a non-Swedish citizen, he would probably have been snubbed by an answer that, as secretary-general to the United Nations, he had no right to meddle with the internal affairs of other countries!"

Rodionov's statement that Wallenberg was not in the Soviet Union may not have been convincing, but it did demonstrate the Russian determination to consider the case closed. It also provided the Swedish Foreign Ministry with a new excuse for doing nothing. All this changed, however, with the appearance in Stockholm of Henrik Thomsen in 1953.

"Henrik Thomsen" was the Norwegian alias used by a Russian interpreter at the Swedish Legation in Budapest. In 1944 he had been assigned to handle Soviet affairs in Hungary, particularly contacts with Soviet prisoners of war in Hungarian hospitals and camps. During the liberation of Budapest he was arrested by the NKVD, and it was widely believed that he had been executed.

When he reappeared in Stockholm, the Foreign Ministry lodged him at the Grand Hotel at government expense. Soon after arriving, he approached Maj von Dardel and said that he could assist in the search for her son. He had been in several Soviet prison camps and claimed to have connections he could use to Wallenberg's benefit.

Wallenberg's mother was suspicious, but could not afford to ignore any hope of finding her son. She met with Thomsen and, when he complained of having no watch of his own, even loaned him a gold watch that had belonged to Wallenberg's grandmother.

One night, slightly drunk, Thomsen confided to Mrs. von Dardel that while attached to the Swedish Legation in Budapest he had been spying on the Russians. When he interviewed Russian prisoners of war, he asked not only for personal information but also for important military information. He then relayed his findings to a contact in Stockholm. This was why the NKVD had arrested him. In 1947, while imprisoned by the Soviets, he had signed a confession stating that the Swedish Legation in Budapest had been engaged in anti-Soviet espionage.

Thomsen's story was a great blow to the Wallenberg family. Evidently there was some truth to the Soviet allegation that the Swedish Legation in Budapest had been engaged in espionage; Thomsen's activities must have compromised Wallenberg. Thomsen received twenty thousand kroner, apparently at the instigation of the Swedish Foreign Ministry, and agreed to leave Sweden. Only when customs police threatened him with arrest did he return the watch Mrs. von Dardel had loaned him.

After his departure the family demanded that the Foreign Ministry provide an explanation to the Russians of Swedish espionage in Budapest during the war which would absolve Raoul Wallenberg of any complicity. If the Foreign Ministry refused, the family threatened to publish Thomsen's story of Swedish anti-Soviet espionage. The government capitulated and in the fall of 1953 handed the Soviets a report describing how information had been obtained from prisoners of war and vouching that Wallenberg had had nothing to do with Thomsen's activities. The report did not deny that the Swedish Legation in Budapest was involved in anti-Soviet espionage.

Thomsen's story was a powerful weapon, and Maj von Dardel used it again in 1954 to force Foreign Minister Undén to travel to Moscow and demand the return of her son. Undén left in June on a visit that the Foreign Ministry characterized as "a private vacation." On his return he informed Mrs. von Dardel that the Soviets had again assured him that Wallenberg was not in the Soviet Union.

Soviet Foreign Minister Andrei Gromyko was scheduled to visit Stockholm on March 25, 1955. Shortly before he arrived, Ivan Danielsson, the former head of the Swedish Legation in Budapest, received a letter from Dublin from Count Kutuzov-Tolstoy, who had once been an interpreter at the Legation. Kutuzov-Tolstoy wrote that he had remained in Budapest working for the Russians for four years after the end of the war. During that time he made investigations into the fate of Wallenberg and had discovered that he had either been killed by Nazis or Arrow Cross before he reached the Red Army headquarters, or had been shot by Russian troops "by mistake" because he was dressed in German uniform.

Danielsson passed the letter on to the Foreign Ministry. It was the first time anyone had suggested that Wallenberg might have been dressed in German uniform. The Ministry asked the Swedish Embassy in Dublin to investigate the count. The report came back that he was still believed to be employed by the Russians. Gromyko apparently wanted the Swedes to close their Wallenberg file before he arrived in Sweden.

Kutuzov-Tolstoy was not the only Soviet agent who tried to dupe the Swedish Foreign Ministry. In 1956, Deputy Foreign Minister Lundberg received a letter from an Estonian named Tamvelius who was incarcerated in a prison camp near Vorkuta. Tamvelius asked for permission to live in Sweden after his release and claimed to have met Wallenberg in the Vorkuta camp. He also informed the Swedes that Wallenberg had definitely died while at Butyrka Prison in Moscow.

When Tamvelius arrived in Sweden he changed his story. He

now described how he had visited Wallenberg in the Vorkuta hospital in December 1947. They had talked in German: Wallenberg gave his name and said he had been arrested in Budapest. Wallenberg appeared undernourished, so Tamvelius obtained permission to visit again and bring him some food. But when he returned, Wallenberg had disappeared. The doctor said he had been taken "to the next station."

Tamvelius no longer asserted that Wallenberg was dead, but there was no doubt that this was what his testimony was intended to imply. When the von Dardel family and Rudolph Philipp questioned him further, he was unable to add any details to his story, which he appeared to have memorized. When they showed him photographs, he was unable to identify Wallenberg. An Estonian priest with whom Tamvelius stayed in Stockholm later reported that before writing his letter to Sweden, Tamvelius had been visited at the prison camp by two senior Soviet intelligence officers who subjected him to lengthy interrogation.

In 1960 an individual calling himself Baron von Wetschl arrived in Stockholm, claiming to have been at Wallenberg's deathbed in a camp near Archangel in 1950. A Hungarian named von Wetschl had been mentioned in a recent book entitled *In Beria's Camps*. When its author was shown a photograph of the man who had arrived in Stockholm claiming to be Baron von Wetschl, he pronounced it "very unlike" the man he had met in the Soviet Union. Further investigations revealed that the "baron" had arrived in West Germany from the Soviet Union in 1955 and was living in considerable luxury in a Hamburg suburb.

The Soviets had good reason to attempt to persuade the world that Wallenberg was dead. In 1955, West German Chancellor Konrad Adenauer had secured the release of many German prisoners from Soviet jails. The Russians knew that many of these would bring with them stories of their contacts with Raoul Wallenberg.

Among those who returned to Germany were Gustav Richter,

Wallenberg's first cellmate in Lubyanka in 1945, and Rensinghoff, von Rantzau, and Wallenstein, the neighbors with whom he had discussed the composition of his letter to Stalin by knocking on the walls of Lefortovskaya. They and fourteen others provided sworn testimonies to the Swedish Foreign Ministry that described their contacts and conversations with Wallenberg. These testimonies were crucial in persuading the Swedish government to pursue the search for Wallenberg more energetically. Two former members of the Swedish Supreme Court scrutinized this new evidence and concluded that there was no doubt that Wallenberg had been a prisoner in the Soviet Union from January 1945 to February 1947.

The Swedish government wrote to the Soviet Foreign Ministry on March 10, 1956, stating the new evidence. It was well known that the Soviets often answered inquiries about prisoners with death certificates, particularly if the evidence of imprisonment ceased beyond a known date. For this reason, although the Swedes provided the Russians with a summary of the former Supreme Court justices' report, they were careful to state only that there was evidence that Wallenberg had been a prisoner since 1945.

The new evidence did not change the Soviet position. On March 19, 1956, Soviet officials replied that a thorough investigation had been made confirming that Wallenberg was not on Russian soil. It was impossible, they added, to accept the testimonies of war criminals when these were in disagreement with the result of a thorough investigation by the responsible authorities.

In April 1956, Prime Minister Tage Erlander led a delegation to Moscow for the first official Swedish visit to Russia since the Revolution. He brought with him a letter to Wallenberg from Maj von Dardel that said:

Dear beloved Raoul,
After many years of despair and terrible longing for you, we have finally reached the point where the heads of the coalition government, Prime Minister Erlander and Minister

Hedlund, are going to Moscow to ensure that you will be allowed to return home. May they be successful, and may your suffering finally be at an end. We have never given up hope of seeing you again, even though all our efforts to contact you up to now, to our great regret and sorrow, have been in vain. Through other prisoners who have returned from captivity and who shared prison with you, we have received information about your time in prison in Russia and through Major Richter we received regards from you. There is a room here waiting for you when you return with the prime minister.

The testimonies of the German prisoners and the conclusions of the Swedish justices convinced Erlander, who had been prime minister since 1946, that the Russians had arrested Wallenberg in 1945. He also believed that there was an excellent chance that Wallenberg was still in a Soviet prison. He had decided to use this state visit to undo some of the damage caused by Swedish officials who, by not pursuing the search for Wallenberg vigorously enough, had perhaps given the Russians the mistaken impression that Sweden was unconcerned by his disappearance.

Erlander resolved himself to persuade the Soviet leaders that the Swedish government was serious about the Wallenberg case; serious about its demand for a full and thorough investigation; and serious about wanting Wallenberg returned. To this end he had brought to Moscow the Swedish documents concerning Wallenberg. These papers contained the testimonies of the former prisoners who had come into contact with Wallenberg; they were the most persuasive evidence Erlander could muster to prove that Wallenberg had been in Soviet custody.

During a meeting in the Kremlin with Premier Nikolai Bulganin, Foreign Minister Vyacheslav Molotov, and Party Secretary Nikita Khrushchev, Erlander pulled out the documents and began explaining why his country considered the Wallenberg case so important. Khrushchev and Molotov remained silent. Bulganin, however, flew into a rage at the mention of Wallenberg's name.

He accused Erlander of bringing up this matter in order to poison relations between Sweden and the Soviet Union. "This is a waste of time!" he ranted. "We don't have time for this kind of nonsense!"

"If you won't even accept the material that I have brought," Erlander replied, "how can you be so sure that this whole affair is a falsification, an unimportant sideshow cooked up to embarrass you?"

Bulganin shouted, "I don't want to hear any more of this!"

Erlander refused to be deterred. He said, "At the very least I must demand that you accept this material and appoint someone you trust to investigate it. If you refuse, then I'll end my visit now. I won't go to the south of your country as planned; I won't visit the atomic power facility you have so wanted me to see."

At this Khrushchev, who was sitting nearest to Erlander, reached over, took the file of documents, and then whispered something into Bulganin's ear. When he had finished, Bulganin turned to Erlander and said, "It's a great pity that we have to waste so much time on an affair such as this; however, as a gesture of our goodwill toward Sweden we will accede to your request that we accept this material about Wallenberg, and we will appoint someone to examine it. You will have our reply as soon as possible."

On April 5, 1956, *Pravda* published the communiqué from the Swedish-Soviet meetings which mentioned that the Soviet government had agreed to reopen its investigation into Wallenberg's disappearance. The communiqué said, "The Swedish ministers stressed the great importance attached by them to the fate of Mr. Raoul Wallenberg. The Swedish ministers handed to the Soviet side the material collected concerning Mr. Wallenberg with the request that the Soviet authorities should study and examine it, to which the Soviet ministers agreed. It was also agreed that, if Mr. Wallenberg was still alive in the Soviet Union, he would be permitted to return, and that the Swedish government would be notified of the results of the Soviet investigation through diplomatic channels."

Wallenberg's family and supporters considered these developments to be the most encouraging in a decade. It seemed to them that the combination of a new Soviet regime and the new determination of Erlander and the Foreign Ministry might finally result in the freeing of Wallenberg. They did not believe that the Russians could ignore the overwhelming evidence of these documents.

20

1957–1960

Throughout 1956 the Swedish Foreign Ministry pressed the Russians for the results of their new inquiry into Wallenberg's fate. At last, on February 6, 1957, Deputy Foreign Minister Andrei Gromyko handed a memorandum to Ambassador Sohlman. It said:

At the request of the government of the kingdom of Sweden, the competent Soviet authorities were charged with undertaking a thorough examination of the Wallenberg file received by the Soviet Foreign Ministry from Sweden in March, April, and May 1956.

As a result, the authorities studied the archives for the registration of prisoners. They also examined the reports of interrogations, looking for signs of the presence of Raoul Wallenberg. Similarly, they questioned those who may have been concerned in the circumstances mentioned in the Swedish dossier. No one interrogated recognized the name of Wallenberg. None of these efforts provided the smallest indication that Raoul Wallenberg had spent time in the Soviet Union.

However, in the course of their research, the Soviet authori-

232

THE SEARCH / 233

ties had the occasion to examine the files of prison infirmaries. They discovered in Lubyanka [in Moscow] a handwritten report which may refer to Wallenberg. This report is addressed to Abakumov, minister for state security, from A. L. Smoltsov, the head of the prison hospital service. It is dated July 17, 1947: "I am writing to inform you that the prisoner Walenberg [sic], known to you, died suddenly in his cell last night. He was apparently the victim of a myocardiac infarctus. In view of your instructions to me to supervise Walenberg personally, I ask you to let me know who should conduct the autopsy to ascertain the cause of death. 17 July 1947. Signed: Smoltsov, Colonel, Chief of the Prison Infirmary."

The same report contains a second manuscript note from Smoltsov: "Informed the minister personally. Order given to cremate the body without autopsy. 17 July 1947."

No further information, documentary or from testimonies, has been found. Smoltsov died on May 7, 1953.

The above-mentioned facts lead one to conclude that Wallenberg died in July 1947. Evidently he was arrested, like many others, by the Russian Army in the area of fighting. That he was later detained in prison and that false information was given about him to the Foreign Ministry by the chief of state security over a number of years, is one aspect of the criminal activity of Abakumov. As is well known, the latter was sentenced by the Supreme Court of Justice and executed for serious crimes.

The Soviet Union expresses its sincere regret in relation to these circumstances and assures the government of the kingdom of Sweden, and the family of Raoul Wallenberg, of its profound sympathy.

The Soviets had read the evidence of Richter and the other returned prisoners carefully before preparing their statement. From those testimonies they had learned that no one claimed to have heard from Wallenberg after February 1947. They also knew that those who had shared cells with him and Langfelder had been interrogated on July 27 of the same year. They therefore chose July 17 as the date of his death; it was a date that was as late as possible after the February evidence that he was still alive, but one that also provided an explanation for questioning his cellmates on July 27.

Some in Sweden had feared that the answer to the testimonies would be a death certificate; few had expected the fabrication to be so crude.

The Soviets were claiming that Abakumov, who in January 1945 was head of the Soviet military police in the occupied region (and who only became minister for state security in 1946), had ordered on his own authority the arrest and deportation of a diplomat of a neutral country—the same country that was representing Soviet interests in Hungary.

They were claiming that Dekanusov, the Soviet deputy foreign minister who informed the Swedish government in January 1945 that Wallenberg was under the protection of the Soviet military authorities, had neither the curiosity nor the power to discover that the Swede had been brought to a Moscow jail; and they were claiming that Deputy Foreign Minister Vyshinsky, who undertook a thorough investigation between June 1946 and August 1947, presumably at the instigation of Stalin himself, was unable to find Wallenberg in Lefortovskaya, or the note mentioning his death in Lubyanka.

They were claiming that the prisoner was so important that the infirmary chief had to ask for autopsy instructions from the minister for state security, and yet he twice misspelled the prisoner's name as "Walenberg."

They were claiming that Raoul Wallenberg, a man who had never shown signs of poor health, and a member of a family in which most members lived into their eighties, had died of a heart attack two weeks before his thirty-fifth birthday and only a few months after he had been reported in good health and spirits by his fellow prisoners at Lefortovskaya.

They were claiming that Raoul Wallenberg's body was cremated. Other reports on the Soviet prison system at this time agree that the bodies of prisoners were placed in mass graves or else used as cadavers after their heads had been removed to prevent identification. No prisoners were cremated.

They were claiming that they could find nobody who had seen or even heard of Wallenberg in the Soviet Union. Beria was dead; Abakumov was dead; Smoltsov was dead. They could find no guard or soldier or interrogator or orderly or official who had seen Wallenberg or even heard his name in the thirty months between his arrest in Budapest and his supposed death in Moscow.

The Soviets had to claim that Wallenberg was dead. It was one thing for Soviet leaders to denounce the excesses of Stalin and Beria, but quite another to rectify these excesses by releasing a neutral diplomat who could describe in detail his years of unjust imprisonment and hardship in the Soviet Union. The Wallenberg affair had created its own momentum: The longer the Soviets kept him, the more difficult it became to release him.

On receiving Gromyko's note, the Swedish Foreign Ministry immediately issued a special announcement: "While the Soviet Union now admits that Raoul Wallenberg was imprisoned in that country, it is regrettable that their response contains such meager information. Further information is expected from the Soviet side."

Arne Lundberg, secretary-general of the Swedish Foreign Ministry, said in a radio interview: "Since the Russian materials are incomplete, it is reasonable to assume that the conclusions based on the materials are uncertain. The Swedish Foreign Ministry will continue to consider it necessary to investigate every clue in the Wallenberg case."

Sweden later responded officially to Gromyko's note by saying:

If the Soviet security police was able to act in such an autocratic manner as to make a diplomat of a neutral country a prisoner and to keep him in prison for two and a half years without reporting it to the Soviet government or the Foreign Ministry, this is in itself a situation for which the Soviet government cannot disclaim responsibility.

Expressing its regrets, the Soviet government has admitted its responsibility. To this it added the fact that, while Wallenberg was confined in a Moscow prison, the Soviet government could not, considering the numerous Swedish appeals, have been unable to obtain reliable information in the matter, if they had really undertaken the thorough investigations which they repeatedly assured the Swedish government they had made.

The Swedes also pointed out that Ambassador Sohlman had raised the Wallenberg case with Soviet officials the day before Wallenberg's supposed death. It was difficult to believe that the "thorough investigations" which were conducted at that time failed to produce any evidence that Wallenberg was in the Soviet Union. The note concluded:

We reserve the right to take further steps. . . . [We] call upon the Soviet government to provide more information and to undertake further investigation in the Soviet Union.

As far as the Swedish government was concerned, Wallenberg was still alive. He would remain so until the Soviet Union provided more convincing proof that he was dead.

The next evidence received in Sweden reinforced the belief that Wallenberg lived.

Two Germans, Mulle and Rehkampf, and the Swiss prisoner Brugger, returned to the West in 1958 after many years in Soviet jails. Brugger reported his conversations by "prison telegraph" with Wallenberg in the hospital block in Vladimir during the summer of 1954. Mulle and Rehkampf both told of sharing cells with the Georgian, Simon Gogobaritze, a former cellmate of Wallenberg's in the same prison.

Again the evidence was scrutinized by former members of the Swedish Supreme Court. This time their opinion was only slightly less positive: "The investigation, while not providing absolute proof, would make it probable according to Swedish law that Wallenberg was alive at least in the early 1950s and that he was in the prison in Vladimir."

Again the Swedish Foreign Ministry besieged the Soviets with a series of memoranda and details of the new testimonies. Again and again Soviet leaders, ignoring the persuasive evidence that Wallenberg had been in their prisons long after 1947, replied that they had nothing to add to Gromyko's 1957 note. However, just when the search for Wallenberg appeared to have come to a dead end, and just when the Soviets seemed the most intractable, a startling development gave the family and the Swedish government new hope.

This development was in large part Wallenberg's doing. The hunger strike that he mounted in Vladimir Prison sometime after Kalinski's departure in October 1959 (Kalinski had reported him looking "young and fit") had succeeded. By forcing the prison authorities to transfer him to a Moscow prison it had brought him into contact with a man who would soon relay surprising news of his imprisonment to the West.

1961–1964

Dr. Nanna Svartz is an internationally celebrated Swedish physician, who in 1961 was in charge of the Department of Internal Medicine at the Stockholm University clinic as well as on the staff of Stockholm's Karoline Institute, which was then administered by Wallenberg's stepfather, Fredrik von Dardel. Among her private patients were Prime Minister Erlander and his wife, Aina, and Wallenberg's mother, Maj von Dardel. During the 1940s she had also treated Madame Kollontai, the Soviet ambassador who had informed Wallenberg's mother that her son was in Soviet hands.

Dr. Svartz often traveled abroad for scientific congresses, and she had visited Moscow several times. In January 1961 she was invited to visit Moscow by an old acquaintance, Professor A. L. Myasnikov, chairman of the Soviet Academy of Medical Science. She and Myasnikov had met on numerous occasions. In 1954 they had attended a medical congress held in Stockholm. Svartz, the president of the congress, had told Myasnikov then that she would deliver her speech to the congress in German. He had replied that he too would deliver his speech in German. Since then they had always communicated in this common language.

Dr. Svartz was suspicious of the convenient solution to the Wallenberg case provided by Gromyko's note, and she was well acquainted with the testimonies which suggested that Wallenberg had been in Vladimir Prison during the previous decade. She decided to ask Myasnikov if he knew what had become of Wallenberg. She remembered from their previous meetings that Myasnikov was often called upon to give consultations in different parts of the Soviet Union and maintained contact with scores of doctors throughout the country. She thought it possible that one of these doctors had treated Wallenberg.

When the 1961 Moscow congress ended, Myasnikov invited Svartz to accompany him on his medical rounds at Moscow University Hospital, where he was the chief of internal medicine. She accepted, and after making the rounds they retired to his office to discuss the quality of medical education in their respective countries. After they had talked for several minutes, Svartz interrupted the conversation and said, "I must tell you that I have been asked by the director-general of Stockholm's Karoline Institute, Fredrik von Dardel, to see what I can find out about his stepson, Raoul Wallenberg. This case has become a heavy burden for me, my friends, and many other Swedes."

Myasnikov lowered his voice and said, "As a matter of fact, I know a great deal about the Wallenberg case. The person you're speaking of is in a very bad way. He's been at Vladimir for quite some time, and now he's in the mental hospital. He's extremely tired, nervous, and depressed, and he's also lost a good deal of weight; he needs to rest."

Svartz was electrified. Here, for the first time, was firsthand testimony from a distinguished and credible Soviet citizen that Wallenberg was still alive. It was incontrovertible evidence that Gromyko had lied, or been lied to.

Myasnikov went on to tell her that he had recently examined Wallenberg at the same hospital, Moscow University Hospital at 10 Petro Veridzke Street, where they now sat talking. He said that despite Wallenberg's condition he had found it "enjoyable" to talk with him.

It seemed to Svartz that Myasnikov was struggling with his conscience. He appeared to want to say more, but he was afraid. She began to suspect that Wallenberg might still be in the university hospital. Would she be able to see him during Myasnikov's next rounds?

"I'll be returning to Sweden soon," she said. "Since I'm a doctor, why not let him return to his native country under my care?"

Myasnikov said no. "There are 'things' that have to be completed here before he can go," he added.

For the next several minutes they discussed the best method of repatriating Wallenberg. Svartz suggested that the details should be handled by the Swedish Medical Board and repeated her offer to take Wallenberg under her personal care. Finally Myasnikov rose from his chair and said, "Excuse me, I shall fetch a colleague and ask his advice."

A few moments later he returned with a Dr. Danishevski, who expressed great interest in the case. Dr. Svartz wrote "Attaché Raoul Wallenberg" on a piece of paper and handed it to him. He promised to do everything in his power to help. However, when she mentioned by chance that she had recently renewed her acquaintance with Vladimir Semyonov, the Soviet deputy foreign minister, during his official visit to Sweden, Danishevski reconsidered and said, "Well, if you know someone at the Foreign Office then I think you should approach him. If Wallenberg is alive, he can only be returned through diplomatic channels, not by the intervention of doctors."

Before leaving Moscow, Dr. Svartz met with Semyonov. She had first met him in Stockholm during the 1940s when he had been Madame Kollontai's deputy. Svartz had once saved Madame Kollontai from dying of pneumonia and had even escorted her back to Moscow personally. Semyonov remembered her kindness and they were on friendly terms. Perhaps this explains why he now confirmed Myasnikov's startling report, that Wallenberg was in poor health but alive. He ended their conversation by saying,

"Let's see what we can do." Now a senior Soviet official had admitted that Wallenberg was still alive.

Semyonov had gone too far. The next day, when Svartz called him on the telephone, he stalled and was vague. She called again and was told that he had suddenly gone on an official visit to Egypt and would not return for weeks.

She returned to Stockholm and immediately related her conversations with Myasnikov and Semyonov to her personal friend, Prime Minister Tage Erlander. On the basis of her astounding report, Erlander decided to write to Khrushchev.

"[Dr. Svartz] informs me that [at the end of January] Wallenberg was still alive and was in a psychiatric hospital in Moscow in bad health," he wrote. "Mrs. Svartz received this information from an internationally renowned member of the Soviet medical profession. My foreign minister and I have been discussing how Wallenberg should be transported back to Sweden. We have arrived at the conclusion that it would be best if a Swedish physician were to go to Moscow immediately to discuss his treatment and the best method of transportation with Soviet colleagues."

Ambassador Sohlman delivered this letter to Khrushchev in person on February 25, 1961. Khrushchev had already learned of its contents and received him brutally. Leaving the letter unopened on his desk, he said, "For the third time we now inform you that this subject has been completely exhausted. There is nothing to add to our response, nor will there be. If Sweden insists on bringing up the Wallenberg affair again and again, it must mean Sweden is intentionally trying to worsen relations with the Soviet Union." Instead of wishing Sohlman good day, he simply sat down at his desk and returned to work.

In March 1961, Dr. Svartz returned to Moscow. In the presence of another doctor she asked Myasnikov if she might be allowed to see Wallenberg.

"That can only be decided at a higher level," he said coldly. "Provided, of course, that he is not dead."

Later, when they were alone, Myasnikov said: "Why did you

have to repeat to your government what I had told you in the strictest confidence? We've been good friends for so many years—how could you do something like this to me? Khrushchev himself called me in and shouted at me for saying anything about Wallenberg. In fact he was so enraged that he pushed me and I fell down a flight of stairs."

He concluded: "We scientists are forbidden to discuss anything but science."

After this meeting Dr. Svartz attempted to call Deputy Foreign Minister Semyonov. She was always told that he was "unavailable," or "too tired" to come to the telephone. She wrote, asking him for another meeting, but her letters went unanswered. Again she left Moscow empty-handed.

Khrushchev's anger was not confined to Dr. Myasnikov. There is evidence that in 1961 Wallenberg was transferred from Moscow to Wrangell's Island, a small fragment of icy ground half the size of Long Island located three hundred miles inside the Arctic Circle, a hundred miles north of the Siberian mainland, and two hundred and seventy miles northwest of Cape Lisburne, Alaska. Presumably here Wallenberg would have fewer opportunities for making his presence known to the West.

Despite its location, Wrangell's Island has been the subject of disputes for over a century. It was discovered in 1867 by the crew of a New England whaler, who named it for Baron Ferdinand Petrovich von Wrangell, a lieutenant in the Imperial Russian Navy who had led unsuccessful expeditions in search of it a quarter of a century before. The United States claimed it in 1881 when Captain Calvin Hooper planted an American flag and built a cairn into which he put a record of his visit.

For the next forty years rival American, British, and Russian parties raised flags, hunted, surveyed, and trapped on the island. An Alaskan company finally bought it from the American government and established a trapping operation. Then, in 1924, the Soviet gunboat *Red October* landed. The Soviets arrested the American representative of the Lomen Reindeer and Trapping

Corporation and imprisoned him in Vladivostok, where they reported he died of pneumonia. His Eskimo employees were deported to Harbin.

The Soviets had a use for Wrangell's Island. The hundred miles of Arctic Ocean which separate it from the mainland and its even greater distance from civilization, make it one of the most secret places in the world: the perfect location for an underground military airdrome, a base for nuclear submarines, and a training school for espionage agents—perfect, too, for hiding prisoners whose presence in the Soviet Union might prove embarrassing.

Twenty-five miles from Wrangell's Island's nonmilitary airfield, on the Bay of Rodgers, is a camp holding several thousand prisoners, almost all of them non-Russians. However, Russian prisoners, some of them criminals, are employed in the service units. They carry food, cut hair, and sew prison uniforms. Only they can visit all three parts of the camp: the living zone, the working zone, and the hospital zone. Only they know that few ever return from the "hospital," where foreign prisoners whom the government has already declared dead act as guinea pigs for the Soviet Navy and space program. They are injected with experimental drugs, fed potentially lethal diets, forced to endure long periods under water, and breathe air in which the amount of oxygen is varied.

There are few opportunities for prisoners at Wrangell's Island to communicate with the outside world, but sometimes, miraculously, messages are sent. In 1971 an Italian hunter shot down a goose; attached to it was a rubber tube containing a scrap of paper. The paper was old and washed out and the only distinguishable words were "SOS . . . Italian officers . . . island beyond the Arctic Circle."

In 1958, Efim Moshinsky, a Russian Jew formerly employed by the KGB/NKVD, was sentenced to Wrangell's Island and given the job of distributing food. In the course of his labors he learned the names of several prisoners. He repeated some of them ten years later, after he had been released from prison and had emigrated to Israel. The Italian names he could remember were checked and found to belong to officers declared missing during World War Two.

In the early 1960s, Wrangell's Island also held German generals, Spanish officers, Aleksandr Trushnovich—the leader of the Russian anti-Communist group NTS—and Raoul Wallenberg.

Wallenberg and Trushnovich shared a two-room wood hut. An Italian named Pelgrini delivered their food. One day Wallenberg produced a piece of paper on which he had written a letter to his family in Sweden. He asked Pelgrini if he knew a way of smuggling it out of the camp. Pelgrini shrank back, too frightened to even touch the paper. Nevertheless, much later Wallenberg's family did learn about his imprisonment on Wrangell's Island. Pelgrini had told his fellow worker Moshinsky about Wallenberg, and Moshinsky recounted the story when he emigrated to Israel years later.

While Wallenberg was at Wrangell's Island, Dr. Svartz persisted in her quest for information about him. In 1962 she returned to Moscow for another medical congress and again sought out Myasnikov. At their last meeting he had been apologetic; now he was afraid. When she broached the subject of Wallenberg, he turned his back and pretended not to understand her German.

Two years later, in 1964, Myasnikov broke his silence. A visit by Gromyko to Sweden had resulted in new stories about Wallenberg in the Swedish press. The public was again interested in his fate. Myasnikov wrote to Svartz:

I am writing on the subject of new stories in the Swedish press about Wallenberg. I have been mentioned as a source of information which, it is said, I gave you during your visit to Moscow in 1961. As you must remember, I told you that I knew nothing about this person. I had never heard his name before you mentioned it and I had no idea whether he was alive or dead. I therefore advised you to address yourself to our foreign minister via your ambassador. When you asked me to take up the matter personally with Khrushchev (whose doctor I was, according to you), I replied that our secretary-general is in excellent health and, in any case, I was not his doctor.

As the result of a misunderstanding, my short conversation with you (which was in German, a language which I do not speak well) was misinterpreted by official circles in your country. Since then, I have learned that Raoul Wallenberg died in 1947 and that our government has informed your government and the family of the deceased of that fact.

Khrushchev had scheduled a visit to Sweden for June of 1964. Before he left Russia, the Swedish ambassador in Moscow, Gunnar Jarring, brought up the Wallenberg case at the Soviet Foreign Ministry. Deputy Foreign Minister Orlov was firm: "The testimonies concerning the survival of Raoul Wallenberg after 1947 are either in error," he said, "or else they are simply anti-Soviet machinations." He warned that any further mention of Wallenberg would damage Swedish-Soviet relations.

On the day that Khrushchev arrived in Stockholm, the largest Swedish newspaper, *Expressen,* ran a headline and article in Russian on its front page. The headline said, "THE QUESTION: WHERE IS RAOUL WALLENBERG?" The article, addressed to Khrushchev, said: "You are coming to us empty-handed. Whatever presents you have in your luggage, despite your entourage of fifty people, you are coming too much alone. To be a welcome guest you should have brought Raoul Wallenberg with you. . . . [He was] reported dead by your authorities, although it has been proved that he is still alive in Soviet imprisonment, captured without reason, sentenced without cause, mistreated groundlessly, a living prisoner declared dead in your country."

Khrushchev was furious. He protested to Prime Minister Erlander, "If I had suspected that the subject of Wallenberg would be brought up I should never have accepted your invitation to visit Sweden. It is an attack on my honesty not to believe me. How can I be held accountable for things that happened under the Stalin regime?"

After dinner, coffee, and cognac at his summer residence, Erlander again raised the subject of Wallenberg. Khrushchev repeated his denials and remained irritated throughout his visit.

Erlander was upset by Khrushchev's stubborn refusal to even discuss Wallenberg. An election was only two weeks away and one of his ministers, Olof Palme, was arguing that the public had become so involved in the Wallenberg case that Erlander would be taking a tremendous political risk if he permitted Khrushchev to leave without promising a new investigation into Wallenberg's disappearance. On the other hand, Foreign Minister Nilsson was begging Erlander not to risk damaging relations with the Soviet Union by refusing, because of Wallenberg, to sign a joint communiqué. Dr. Svartz, who had kept her story secret for three years at the government's request, was so incensed by Khrushchev's lies that she threatened to talk to the press. Erlander was afraid the story would leak out before the election, and Palme called Svartz frequently to urge her to remain silent.

On the last day of Khrushchev's visit a ceremonial lunch was held in Gothenburg's Town Hall. Earlier Khrushchev had noticed with displeasure that someone had placed cut flowers at the base of a statue of Charles XII, a Swedish king who had staged raids into Russian territory during the eighteenth century. In the course of his rambling after-lunch speech Khrushchev mentioned King Charles and added that there were ominous parallels. "Sweden today again wants to declare war on the Soviet Union," he said.

Erlander considered this such a "confusing, depressing" speech that he did not bother replying. It was clear to him now that the entire state visit had been poisoned by the Wallenberg affair. The Soviets still did not understand that Wallenberg was a serious issue for Sweden, not simply another American-inspired Cold War plot.

When Erlander was alone with Khrushchev in a limousine

en route to the airport, he said, "I'm terribly upset if you, the head of the Soviet nation, really seriously think that Sweden is preparing to attack your country—that you could imagine that we spend our time planning to invade you."

"Maybe you can't attack us alone," Khrushchev replied, "but you certainly have powerful friends who would help you."

After Khrushchev's departure, the Swedes and Soviets issued a joint communiqué which contained no mention of Wallenberg. However, on the same day, Erlander held a press conference at which he said, "We are profoundly disappointed that the Soviet Union was not able to take the opportunity to clear up the [Wallenberg] case. We will not abandon our efforts in this matter." These efforts were soon to produce results, but not the kind Erlander or the Wallenberg family wanted.

22

1965–1981

In 1965 the search for Raoul Wallenberg came to an end for Dr. Svartz and Prime Minister Erlander. During the preceding decade both had pursued this search with great vigor, and with great skepticism of Soviet explanations. By the end of 1965, however, both believed that Wallenberg was dead. Both kept their conclusions, and the reasons for them, secret from the public and from those researching and writing about Wallenberg until January 1981, when they revealed the truth during interviews with one of the authors of this book.

The denouement of the Wallenberg tragedy began in June of 1965, a year after Khrushchev's disastrous visit to Sweden, when Erlander journeyed to Moscow to meet with Khrushchev's successor, Aleksei Kosygin. He hoped that the new Soviet leader would be more willing to explain what had happened to Wallenberg.

During a meeting which was later reported in the Swedish newspapers, Erlander told Kosygin: "The only shadow over the development of good relations between our countries is the Wallenberg case." He went on to mention the testimonies of the Vladimir prisoners, Dr. Svartz's meetings with Dr. Myasnikov, the opinion of the Swedish judicial panel, and the inadequacy of the "proof" offered in Gromyko's 1957 memorandum.

Kosygin appeared to be inflexible. He said: "There is no other trace, no other document, no indication of the presence of Wallenberg in Soviet prisons [after 1947]. A head of state can easily find a living person, but a dead one. . . ." In private, however, Kosygin agreed to permit Dr. Svartz to meet again with Dr. Myasnikov.

Before the end of the year Dr. Svartz returned to Moscow, where she again saw Dr. Myasnikov and Deputy Foreign Minister Semyonov. From them she learned what she and Prime Minister Erlander now believe to be the solution to the Wallenberg mystery.

Myasnikov and Semyonov both told Dr. Svartz the same thing: Raoul Wallenberg was dead. He had died only recently. He had, they both said, first become "tired and very depressed" and "did not want to eat" (presumably he had gone on another hunger strike). Eventually he had become "weaker and weaker" and had had to be treated in a "hospital." Finally he had died.

Myasnikov spoke about this "hospital" and Wallenberg's death in greater detail than Semyonov, revealing that the "hospital" in which he died was actually more of an asylum where "tired people" were detained. It soon became clear to Svartz that both Myasnikov and Semyonov were either forbidden or afraid to tell her more. At one point each said that Wallenberg's death had been "a mistake," and implied that lower-level Soviet bureaucrats had covered it up. Finally they admitted that he had been tortured while at this "hospital."

If one accepts the account of Efim Moshinsky, that Wallenberg was sent to Wrangell's Island in 1961, then it is possible that he became ill because of the harsh conditions and was transferred back to Vladimir or another prison in the Moscow area, where he eventually died.

During her visit to Moscow in 1965, Dr. Svartz also discussed the Wallenberg case with the Swedish ambassador, Gunnar Jarring. She left her meeting with Jarring convinced that he too knew that Wallenberg had died and that he had been shown factual information concerning his death. When interviewed by one of the authors of this book in 1981, Jarring evaded answering questions on this subject.

As soon as Dr. Svartz returned to Sweden she reported her conversations with Myasnikov and Semyonov to Prime Minister Erlander and to Wallenberg's stepfather, Fredrik von Dardel. Four months later the Soviets announced that Dr. Myasnikov had died of a heart attack. (Dr. Svartz, however, has reason to believe that he was merely "isolated" and continued to live beyond 1965.)

During an interview held with one of the authors of this book in January 1981, former Prime Minister Erlander confirmed that he believed Dr. Svartz's account of her meetings with Myasnikov and Semyonov: that he was convinced that Wallenberg had been alive in Russia all those years and had finally died, in the manner described by Myasnikov and Semyonov, either in 1964 or 1965, and that he had informed Wallenberg's mother of his belief that her son was dead.

Erlander and his wife, Aina, also voiced their belief that senior Soviet officials such as Kosygin and Khrushchev were unaware of the exact circumstances of Wallenberg's illness, his transfer to the "hospital," and his death; and that after he died, lower-level officials, fearful of the consequences, had destroyed evidence in order to cover their tracks. They both said that it was their impression that Wallenberg's death had not been sanctioned by the leadership and that "someone had made a mistake."

During this 1981 interview Erlander did not reveal what additional information, if any, he was given by the Soviet leaders or by Gunnar Jarring which confirmed Svartz's account. There is, however, evidence that he did receive discouraging information about Wallenberg during his 1965 trip to Moscow.

It is important to remember that before 1965 Erlander had pursued the search for Wallenberg with vigor, and with great skepticism of Soviet explanations. In 1956 he had refused to accept

Bulganin's denial that Wallenberg had ever been imprisoned in the Soviet Union. In 1957 he had dismissed Gromyko's statement that Wallenberg had died of a heart attack in 1947. In 1964 he had needled Khrushchev for a truthful report, even when his persistent inquiries risked serious damage to Soviet-Swedish relations. On June 26, 1964, at the conclusion of Khrushchev's visit to Sweden, Erlander had said, "Although our many petitions [for information about Wallenberg] . . . have been without result, we will not abandon our efforts in this matter."

Yet after Erlander's visit to the Soviet Union in June 1965, one Swedish newspaper, *Aftonbladet,* reported: "The prime minister explained at a press conference that 'there is no hope of changing the Soviet point of view . . . they have searched their prisons for Raoul Wallenberg . . . without results.' "

The article continued to say, "When he [Erlander] returns home today, his most difficult task remains: to call Mrs. von Dardel, Raoul Wallenberg's mother, and tell her that this would be the last time he would bring up her son's fate at this high level."

If Erlander did receive information about Wallenberg's death while on this trip, it was later confirmed by Dr. Svartz's testimony. As a result, he called off the search and informed Wallenberg's mother that her son was dead. For a decade Erlander had rejected all Soviet explanations of Wallenberg's fate; now he was accepting the explanation offered to Svartz by Semyonov and Myasnikov. Whatever evidence or testimony he received that confirmed Svartz's account must have been convincing. This time Erlander believed the Russians were telling the truth: Wallenberg was dead.

When Svartz reported to Erlander in 1965 on her conversations with Myasnikov and Semyonov concerning Wallenberg's death, he made her swear an oath of secrecy. During an interview with one of the authors of this book in 1981 she said: "Many years ago I gave my oath to former Prime Minister Erlander that I would tell no one of what I had told him after my conversations in Russia with my colleagues."

Svartz finally decided to break her silence and reveal what she and Erlander believe to be the solution to the Wallenberg mystery in January 1981, after hundreds of journalists had journeyed to Stockholm to attend an inconclusive meeting organized by the Swedish Raoul Wallenberg Association. Dr. Svartz was upset by the manner in which the meeting was conducted and by the fact that it seemed to her that its organizers were attempting to perpetuate what she believed to be a falsehood: that Raoul Wallenberg was still alive. Former Prime Minister Erlander was also disturbed by this meeting, and his dissatisfaction is probably what led him to break his silence and confirm Dr. Svartz's account of Wallenberg's death.

Erlander has not explained why, in 1965, his government did not make Svartz's information public, nor why he asked Svartz to remain silent. One can only speculate.

He may have feared that the story of Wallenberg's death, and the likelihood that he was tortured, would have inflamed Swedish opinion and led to a serious rift with the Soviet Union. Because of their country's location, Swedish leaders have traditionally been careful to maintain good relations with Russia.

Erlander also may have withheld the news from the public out of deference to Wallenberg's mother and stepfather. It is very likely that they did not consider the evidence to be one hundred percent conclusive and thus begged Erlander to keep it secret. They could have made a persuasive argument that releasing this information to the public would make continued international efforts to free their son impossible.

Since 1965 there has been other evidence which tends to confirm that Wallenberg died in the middle 1960s, and because of a "mistake" on the part of his captors.

Inga Piltz is a Swedish attorney who, in addition to being a close friend of the Wallenberg family, has also worked in the same office as Gösta Nisser, one of Wallenberg's cousins and the confidant and attorney of the von Dardels and at one time court-appointed legal guardian for Raoul Wallenberg. Piltz recalls prior to April 14, 1980. During this meeting Greenwald pulled out a picture of Wallenberg. While the picture was still at an angle, and before Greenwald could turn it full face, Vogel recognized it and said quickly, "Long dead."

For the next ninety minutes the two men discussed Wallenberg. Vogel maintained that "any information about his being alive is totally incorrect," and said that he had told this to Wallenberg's half brother when Guy von Dardel had visited East Berlin. He did not claim that Wallenberg had died of a heart attack in 1947 but instead, echoing what Svartz had been told fifteen years before, said: "The time of his death could have been an error . . . there was no reason to kill him . . . it was not necessary . . . somebody made a mistake."

When Greenwald pressed him for some evidence, some proof, Vogel said, "So what do you want me to do—bring the bones?"

The Russians have produced no "bones" to prove Wallenberg's death. Instead, there has been a dramatic decrease in the quality and quantity of Wallenberg sightings since 1965. There have been no reliable sightings during this period which mention him by name (they are usually vague secondhand reports about a "Swede") and none in which a reliable informant claims to have seen Wallenberg or heard him tapping on a wall. The most interesting of the post-1965 sightings is that reported by Jan Kaplan who, after being released from a Russian prison, telephoned his daughter in Israel and told her he had met a "Swede" who had been in prison for thirty years. (It is, however, well known that a considerable number of Swedish-looking and -speaking Finns have been imprisoned in the Soviet Union. In fact, Finn-Swedes whose first language is Swedish make up ten percent of Finland's population.) Kaplan was later rearrested by the KGB, according to his wife, because he tried to smuggle a letter to his daughter in Israel; the letter mentioned his encounter with the "Swede."

The explanation for the sudden decrease in reliable sightings after the mid-1960s offered by those who believe Wallenberg to still be alive is that after this date few foreign prisoners who

that in 1965 Nisser became extremely gloomy and pessimisti
about Wallenberg and said that Prime Minister Erlander ha
just given him a report on Wallenberg that was of "a devastatin
nature."

On October 19, 1965, Fredrik von Dardel successfully petitione
a Swedish court to validate a will made out by Raoul Wallenber
in 1939. It is significant that for twenty years von Dardel ha
neglected to take this routine legal step and that he then finall
chose to act only four months after Erlander had returned fror
his June 1965 visit to the Soviet Union.

Sometime in 1970 or 1971, Gösta Nisser told Inga Piltz tha
he had heard from "the highest government circles" in Swede
that, during his imprisonment, Wallenberg had become so "ir
jured" and "damaged" that, even if they had wanted to, th
Russians could not have returned him.

In 1972, Swedish Foreign Minister Christer Wickman said a
a press conference held in Vienna, "As far as the Swedish goverr
ment is concerned the Wallenberg case is closed."

Further confirmation of the story told to Dr. Svartz in 196!
that Wallenberg had died due to a "mistake," came in the cours
of a secret meeting held on April 14, 1980, between Rabbi Ronal
Greenwald and East German attorney Wolfgang Vogel. Greer
wald has played a crucial role in recent East-West spy and pri!
oner exchanges, including the one in April 1978 involving si
nations that resulted in the release of an American student fror
East Germany and an Israeli from prison in Mozambique an
the return of a communist spy to East Germany. He has als
been involved in negotiations with the Soviet Union for the releas
of dissident Anatoly Sharansky.

For more than two decades Wolfgang Vogel has been an impo1
tant Cold War contact man. He is close to Soviet ruling circle
and has extensive knowledge about Soviet spies and political pri!
oners. In 1962 he arranged the swap of U-2 pilot Francis Gar
Powers (one of Wallenberg's prison mates at Vladimir) for Colc
nel Rudolf Abel.

Greenwald and Vogel had already met on fourteen occasior

might have come into contact with him were released from Soviet prisons. The more likely explanation is that Wallenberg died at the time and in the manner described by Dr. Svartz and confirmed by Prime Minister Erlander.

Nevertheless, during the 1970s a number of factors combined to create new interest in Wallenberg and to fuel hopes that, after thirty-five years of imprisonment, he might still be alive.

In 1978, Abraham Kalinski showed Swedish officials the postcards he had written about Wallenberg from Vladimir in the 1950s. In 1973, Avraham Shifrin, a Russian Jew living in Israel who is an expert on Soviet prisons, disclosed the testimony of Efim Moshinsky which placed Wallenberg at Wrangell's Island in the early 1960s. Both of these sightings were pre-1965, but because they were made public in the 1970s, they created new interest and excitement. They also encouraged and revived hopes within the family that he might still be alive.

Until their deaths in 1979, Wallenberg's mother and stepfather continued to write letters to world leaders and to make public appeals for information and justice. His half sister, Nina Lagergren, made well-publicized trips to the United States and Israel to enlist leaders in those countries in the search. At the same time, groups of Hungarian Jews, out of a delayed sense of gratitude, formed and joined Wallenberg Committees in Britain, Israel, and the United States.

The release in 1980 of Swedish white papers which contained details of the first four years of Wallenberg's imprisonment, the renewed public interest in the Holocaust, the election of Menahem Begin in Israel, and the renewal of Cold War tensions also spurred international interest in the Wallenberg case. Meanwhile, in 1979, the Swedish government, in response to this new interest, sent an aide-mémoire to the Soviet Union asking for an explanation for all major Wallenberg sightings since 1945.

Between 1979 and 1981 the search gained more energy and momentum than at any previous time since his imprisonment. Wallenberg Committees were formed in the U.S. Congress and the British House of Commons; a ceremony honoring Wallenberg was held at the Jerusalem Holocaust memorial; a bill was introduced in Congress to declare Wallenberg an honorary American citizen, the first since Winston Churchill; there was talk of a Nobel Peace Prize (even though the rules prohibit posthumous awards); the state of New York and the state of New Jersey proclaimed a "Raoul Wallenberg Day"; and a million-dollar reward was offered by a coalition of committees for information leading to Wallenberg's being traced and freed. Many of these developments were based on the premise that he was still alive.

The search came to a disappointing climax at a world Wallenberg conference held in Stockholm in January 1981. The sponsors had persuaded hundreds of journalists to attend by promising to produce conclusive evidence that he was alive. They could not. Afterward, in the course of a private conversation, an American who has been prominent in the recent search gave an appropriate epitaph for the conference and for the events of the last two years: "Now, after having all gathered here, we know that he is dead. Now we can work to memorialize his heroic deeds in Budapest."

The recent international efforts on Wallenberg's behalf may have failed to achieve their stated objectives of proving him to be alive and then freeing him from Soviet captivity, but they have not been in vain. They have succeeded so well in publicizing his "heroic deeds in Budapest" that his place in history as one of this century's most important and inspirational heroes seems assured. At one time the story of Raoul Wallenberg appeared to be merely a footnote to the Holocaust; because of those who have pursued the search for him with such dedication, this is no longer the case.

If the Holocaust is to be taken as evidence that human nature is essentially evil, then Raoul Wallenberg's life must be considered as evidence that it is not. The relative numbers—the thirty thousand Wallenberg saved compared with the six million the Nazis killed—are deceiving, for Wallenberg saved more than thirty thousand lives: He saved humanity's reputation. It is no accident that so many of those he rescued have claimed that his actions also rescued their faith in mankind. The Talmud, the collection of writings constituting Jewish civil and religious law, had prepared them for Wallenberg. According to it: "He who saves one life, it is as if he saved the entire world."

Acknowledgments

At the end of a project which has occupied much of my time and interest during the last several years I would like to acknowledge my gratitude toward those who have so generously assisted me. I conducted interviews and consulted archives and libraries in Sweden, Israel, Norway, Denmark, Austria, Brazil, Argentina, France, and the United States and was shown great cooperation and hospitality by those with whom I discussed Raoul Wallenberg. To thank them individually would require many pages. A few of those interviewed have expressed the wish not to be named in this book. The others are:

Agnes Adachi
Ambassador Per Anger
Lucy Kadelburger Arnoldson
Consul General Lars Berg
Anna Bilder
Hansi Brand
Professor Asher Cohen
Professor Guy von Dardel
Aina Erlander
Prime Minister
    Tage Erlander
Edith (Wohl) Ernster

Professor Lars Ernster
Ervin Farkas
Arthur Fried
Tuvia Friedman
Prime Minister
    Einar Gerhardsen
Rabbi Ronald Greenwald
David Grunwald
Judge Gösta Hagströmer
Lennart Hagströmer
The Honorable Gideon Hausner
Rabbi Fábián Herskowits

259

Ambassador Gunnar Jarring

Ambassador Ole Jödahl

Abraham Kalinski

Gustav Kadelburger

Ariel Kahane

Elisabeth Kasser

Rolf af Klintberg

Miklós Krausz

Fred Kupferman

Nina Lagergren

Annette Lantos

Deputy Foreign Minister
   Leif Leifland

Viveca Lindfors

Cronid Lubarsky

Envoy Arne S. Lundberg

Professor Yuri Luryi

Marvin W. Makinen

Magda Wilhelm Mayer

Elizabeth Moynihan

Inga Piltz

Victor Reshef

Livia Rothkirchen

Andre Schimkiwitsch

Shalom Schwartz

Avraham Shifrin

Eric Sjöquist

Gilel Storch

Professor Nanna Svartz

Ivan Szekely

Susan Tabor

Bruce (Boris) Teicholz

Tom Veres

Kate Wacz

Simon Wiesenthal

George Wilhelm

Joseph Yaacov

My sincere thanks also go to members of the Wallenberg Committees in Sweden and the United States, especially Ingrid Gärde Widemar, Sonja Sonnenfeldt, Elizabeth Throne Holst, Elizabeth Moynihan, Lena Biörck Kaplan, Kate Wacz, and Annette Lantos; and to Nina Lagergren for her encouragement during the early stages of my research.

Particular thanks are also due Professor Nanna Svartz for the patience she showed in answering my questions during our lengthy interviews; former Prime Minister Tage Erlander and his charming wife, Aina, for discussing the topic at length—considering the prime minister had been reluctant previously during his retirement to be interviewed on this subject; Miklós Krausz, who shared his intimate familiarity with the subject so generously with me; those at the Swedish Foreign Ministry who gave of their time: Professor Wilhelm Carlgren, Ambassador Ole Jödahl, Eric Pierre, and Göran Berg; Consul General Bengt Fridman and S. Ralph Cohen for making invaluable material available in New York; Larry Baratz and Herman Klurfeld for their sound advice; Arthur Fried for arranging several interesting interviews and using his contacts within the Hungarian community continuously on our behalf; Consul

General Benjamin Avilea for contacting key individuals in Israel; members of the Foreign Ministry of Israel who gave of their time, Joseph Yaacov and Victor Reshef; also Tuvia Friedman; Bruce Teicholz; Professor Asher Cohen; Anna Werbell for her patience and understanding; and Eva and Bent Werbell for their encouragement and helpful criticisms.

I am especially grateful to Rabbi Ronald Greenwald, Michael Schlanger and my agent, Joel Gotler, for their enthusiasm and sound advice.

Frederick E. Werbell

Many thanks to Leslie Meredith and Gail Greene for their efficient preparing of the manuscript for publication; to Ike Sorkin for his guidance; to Julian Bach for his support; and to Antonia, who worked hard.

Thurston Clarke

Chapter Notes

Throughout this book conversations and events have been reconstructed on the basis of interviews conducted by the authors, official government documents, and published accounts by authors such as Philipp, Lévai, and Sjöquist who have themselves interviewed key figures who are no longer alive.

In reconstructing events we have endeavored to find out what a particular street or building looked like at the particular time that Wallenberg was in Budapest. Of course, we can only be certain that, for example, our description of the Arizona nightclub is an accurate portrayal of how that establishment appeared on most evenings during the summer of 1944. We cannot, however, say with one hundred percent certainty that it looked *exactly* this way on the particular evening that Eichmann and Wallenberg met there.

In reconstructing conversations we have employed the words that our various sources remember being used on these particular occasions. It is indeed quite likely, the human memory being what it is, that somewhat different words were actually used, but most likely to express the same ideas and emotions.

—Frederick E. Werbell
Thurston Clarke

262

CHAPTER ONE

Sjöquist describes the meeting between Eichmann and Wallenberg at the Arizona. His source is Elisabet Szel, the wife of one of Wallenberg's drivers. Neither Szel nor Sjöquist dates this meeting. However, according to Berg, the Arizona nightclub was closed by the authorities in September; for this reason and because of the nature of the conversation between Eichmann and Wallenberg, we have placed the meeting in late July. It is possible it occurred in August. The details about the Arizona come from guidebooks to Budapest written during the 1930s, an interview with Boris Teicholz, and an interview with a Hungarian refugee who wishes to remain anonymous.

Sources for the summary of the situation of Jews in Hungary prior to July are Braham, Lévai, Horthy, and Macartney.

Sources for the section about Eichmann are Arendt, Braham, Hausner, Reitlinger, Robinson, and the transcripts of the Eichmann trial.

Sources for the world reaction to the Holocaust are Hausner, Morse, and Reitlinger, as well as papers of the War Refugee Board.

Sources for the background to Wallenberg and his mission are Lévai, Philipp, Sjöquist, and von Dardel, and interviews with Guy von Dardel, Lennart Hagströmer, Inga Piltz, Rolf af Klintberg, Nina Lagergren, and Gilel Storch.

CHAPTER TWO

Sources for the situation of the Jews in Budapest during the summer of 1944 are Braham, Hausner, and Lévai; also an article by Bela Vago, adapted from Ottó Komoly's diaries, entitled "Budapest Jewry: Summer of 1944" in *Hungarian Jewish Studies,* and "Race with Time," a statement by Samu Stern of the Jewish Council also in *Hungarian Jewish Studies.*

Sources for the account of Wallenberg's early days in Budapest, his introduction of the protective pass, and the activities of Section C are Anger, Berg, von Dardel, Lévai, Philipp, and Sjöquist, as well as interviews with Per Anger, Lars Berg, Lars Ernster, and Edith Wohl Ernster.

The story of Wallenberg giving a pass to the weeping woman outside the Legation comes from an article in the *Toronto Star.*

Sources for details of other efforts to rescue Budapest Jews are Braham, Lévai, and interviews with Miklós Krausz.

Wallenberg's agreement with the Swedish government is reprinted in Lévai. The text of his letters and reports are in Lévai and in the Swedish white papers.

CHAPTER THREE

The meeting at Gerbaud's was described by Boris Teicholz during an interview.

Sources for the material about Wallenberg's activities in Budapest during September are Berg, Lévai, Philipp, Sjöquist, and the Swedish white papers.

Wallenberg's reports are reproduced in the Swedish white papers.

Sources for the account of Horthy's attempt to negotiate a truce are Braham, Horthy, and Macartney.

The story of the international work brigades and that of Ernster are recounted in Philipp; Ernster was also interviewed.

CHAPTER FOUR

Sources for the account of the Arrow Cross activities after October 15 and the organization's background are Berg, Braham, Lévai, and Macartney.

Sources for Wallenberg's actions in the first weeks following the coup are von Dardel, Lévai, Sjöquist, Philipp, and an interview with Tom Veres.

Sources for the Eichmann sections are Braham, Hausner, Lévai, and the transcript of the Eichmann trial.

CHAPTER FIVE

The story about Müller, Wallenberg, and Baroness Kemény is taken from an affidavit made by Müller in 1948 and filed with the Swedish Legation in Budapest. It can be found among the Swedish white papers. Material from Philipp has also been used in this section.

Wallenberg's heroics during this period are described by Lévai and Philipp. His letters are among the Swedish white papers.

The Eichmann-Wallenberg meeting at Gestapo headquarters is described in Sjöquist. The date is approximate.

Eichmann's death threats are referred to in the transcript of the Eichmann trial. This transcript indicates that the Swedish Foreign Ministry learned of these death threats and protested to Berlin. Anger related one of Eichmann's threats—"I am going to liquidate him"—during an interview for the BBC program *Man Alive*. Berg describes the attempt to crush Wallenberg's car in his book and in an interview. Lévai also describes this incident, although he places it toward the end of December. It is somewhat unclear exactly when it happened; however, according to Philipp, Wallenberg protested this incident to the German Legation at the beginning of December.

CHAPTER SIX

Sources for the roundup for the death march are Braham, Lévai, and Philipp, as well as an interview with Susan Tabor. Paul Gidaly described his experiences in an article in the *Jerusalem Post;* Katherine Szenes's first-person account is contained in *Hungarian Jewish Studies.*

CHAPTER SEVEN

This chapter is based entirely on Philipp and on the Müller affidavit in the Swedish white papers.

CHAPTER EIGHT

Jüttner's report is in Braham.

The meeting between Batizfalvy and the neutral diplomats was described by Krausz during an interview. He also supplied a copy of the minutes of this meeting; also to be found in Lévai.

Sources for the descriptions of the death march are Braham, the Eichmann trial transcript, Gidaly, Hausner, Lévai, Philipp, and Szenes in *Hungarian Jewish Studies.* Braham and Lévai both contain the text of the Red Cross report.

Sources for Wallenberg's actions during the death march are Anger, von Dardel, Lévai, and Philipp; also the transcript for the BBC program *Man Alive* and an interview with Per Anger.

Eichmann's celebration is described in Hausner; his impression of the march comes from the trial transcript.

CHAPTER NINE

Sources for the episode at Jósefváros Station are Berg, von Dardel, Freed, Lévai, Philipp, and Sjöquist, and an interview with Per Anger.

The Wallenberg-Grell meeting is described by Philipp.

Berg's book gives a good general description of Budapest's stations during this period. Berg, Lévai, Philipp, and Sjöquist also all have material about Baroness Kemény's departure.

The description of the meeting between Vörös and Wallenberg comes from Vörös's book.

The segregation of the Jews into two ghettos is described by Braham, Lévai, Macartney, and Sjöquist.

Wallenberg's last letters and reports are found in the Swedish white papers, as well as in Lévai and Philipp.

CHAPTER TEN

The meeting between Eichmann and Wallenberg is described by Berg, who was an eyewitness; also in his book and as part of the BBC documentary *Man Alive*. Sjöquist's book relates the eyewitness testimony of Göte Carlsson.

Sources for details of the Arrow Cross terror are Anger, Berg, Braham, Lévai, Philipp, and Sjöquist.

Karl Müller describes his abduction by the Arrow Cross in his affidavit in the Swedish white papers.

Sources for Wallenberg's struggle against the Arrow Cross terror are Berg, Philipp, and Lévai, who interviewed Pál Szalai shortly after the war and incorporated Szalai's testimony about Wallenberg into his book. Other sources are interviews with Agnes Adachi, Per Anger, Lars and Edith Wohl Ernster, Miklós Krausz, Shalom Schwartz, and Tom Veres.

CHAPTER ELEVEN

Szalai's warning to Wallenberg is reported in Lévai.

Sources for the Jókai Street massacre are von Dardel and Lévai, and an interview with Kate Wacz.

In his book and during an interview Per Anger gave an account of his attempts to persuade Wallenberg to take refuge in Buda.

Much of the material about Wallenberg's last days at Benczur Street was supplied by a Hungarian who was in the same house. Because he still visits Budapest and has relatives there he has asked to remain anonymous. Lévai also has a description of the days at Benczur Street.

Von Dardel has reproduced in his book the documents that were found in Budapest after the war which appeared to be Wallenberg's plans for his Humanitarian Institute. He also wrote to Kalman Lauer about this institute, and Lévai refers to the institute in his book.

Pál Szalai gave Lévai an account of his conversations with Ernö Vajna and General Schmidthuber that stalled the pogrom planned for the Central Ghetto.

CHAPTER TWELVE

Lévai is the principal source for the account of Wallenberg's two days. Just after the war, when presumably their memories were fresh, he interviewed Petö, Nevi, and many of those who saw Wallenberg. Much of the material is also found in von Dardel and Sjöquist. Miklós Krausz supplied the details of his last encounter with Wallenberg during an interview.

CHAPTER THIRTEEN

The sources for the account of Wallenberg's arrest and transfer to Moscow are the testimonies of the various prisoners who came into contact with him between 1945 and 1947. They reported their sightings to the Swedish government after they were released, and these reports became public with the publication of the Swedish white papers on Wallenberg in 1957, 1965, and 1980. Ernst Huber, who shared a cell with Langfelder, remembered the slashed tires, the restaurant in Iasi, and the trip on the Moscow metro. Other prisoners' recollections were less detailed, but all seem to agree that Wallenberg and Langfelder were taken to Moscow by train.

Other, more colorful stories of the arrest have been told, but they are more recent and the sources are less reliable. Someone using the pseudonym "Dr. Toth" describes two weeks of isolation in Debrecen during which Wallenberg was bound hand and foot and given nothing but a slice of bread and a glass of water a day and was tortured and interrogated under bright lights. Both the identity of "Dr. Toth" and the source of his story are unclear.

Avraham Shifrin, a Russian Jew living in Israel who is an expert on Russian prisons, disclosed the allegations by Yaacov Leontevich Lakhotsky-Menaker as to Leonid Brezhnev's reported role in Wallenberg's arrest.

The descriptions of Lubyanka are based on the recollections of Shifrin and Solzhenitsyn. Wallenberg's interrogation and his mood during the early days of his imprisonment were described by Richter in testimony made to the Swedish government after he was released. Wallenberg's stay in the second cell in Lubyanka and his transfer to Lefortovskaya were described by Loyda to Hille, who reported them after being released.

Claudio de Mohr provided the Swedish Foreign Ministry with a description of Wallenberg's first days in Lefortovskaya. Karl Süpprian, who shared a cell with de Mohr, did not remember Wallenberg being in cell 151, but confirmed de Mohr's account in all other respects.

The Swedish white papers are the source for af Sandeberg's account; they also document the knocking system used to communicate in Lefortovskaya, and the empty water pipes. The conversations with Wallenberg in Lefortovskaya were recalled by Wallenstein, Bergemann, and Rensinghoff and recounted in the white papers.

In August 1981, Yaacov Leontevich Lakhotsky-Menaker, a Soviet Jew now residing in Israel, reported that during his term as a lieutenant in the Red Army fighting to gain control of Budapest, he served with senior officers who participated in the capture of Raoul Wallenberg. In 1975 and 1976, while researching the histories of the army units of the Russian 18th Army, Menaker contacted and interviewed several of the senior officers. He was told repeatedly of a "successful operation" completed by one of the special units of the political branch of the 18th Army. This "successful operation" turned out to be Raoul Wallenberg's capture. The political branch was under the command of Leonid I. Brezhnev, who at that time held the rank of major-general. In this capacity Brezhnev supervised morale, enforced party discipline, and developed party propaganda. He was in charge of intelligence units and collaborators, and planned the political and governmental aspects of the Red Army's occupation of Czechoslovakia, Poland, and Hungary. He also decided what would be confiscated and who would be seized in occupied territories.

In June 1977, Menaker was invited to the sixty-second birthday party of his old battalion chief, Pantelej Jakovlevitch Kolotilo, where he met Colonel Levin, one of Brezhnev's closest aides during the war and the officer responsible for the "window"—a part of the front line that was "opened" to dispatch spies, saboteurs, and partisans. Menaker mentioned a meeting he had had earlier in the year with a former captain and agent in their unit, Aminjev. Levin smiled joyfully on hearing Aminjev's name and said, "He took part in the capture of Wallenberg." Kolotilo later that evening told Menaker, "We hunted for that Swede a long time. Our mission was not easy to accomplish. He was an important person, in close contact with the Gestapo." Menaker asked Kolotilo, "Who was Wallenberg really?" "I am not sure," Kolotilo said hesitantly. "I think he was a Swede in a high diplomatic position. Sweden was a neutral country, which did not take part in the war. We ought not to talk about this. It is a dangerous and forbidden subject. It may cause us great harm. Don't write about this in your history of our unit."

Menaker later in the year had the opportunity to question Aminjev, the captain-agent, directly, and asked him, "How did you capture that man in Budapest?" "You know, my friend," he replied, lowering his voice, "we took those we had to. Special orders from Moscow. We were commanded to accomplish these: first according to plan, and subsequently, as circumstances demanded . . . It is not my business who the Swede was. We looked for him for a long time and finally we captured him. He was a clean type, in a white shirt; he was even wearing a tie. And he fought back. We had to muzzle him to silence him. You must understand it was not easy. We had to pass many public places with him—however, everything had been planned. I thought I would be made a hero of the Soviet Union for this, but that was not the case."

Although Brezhnev is known to have controlled the political branch of the 18th Army, experts in the U.S. State Department doubt that Brezhnev was personally or directly involved in Wallenberg's arrest.

CHAPTER FOURTEEN

Wallenberg's feelings on being transferred to Vorkuta were reported to Joseph Wulf by an anonymous Berliner who spoke with him in the transit room at Lefortovskaya for about an hour. Wulf's testimony can be found in his own book. Richter, Kitschmann, and Huber all testified about their interrogations on their release. Their testimonies and Vyshinsky's memorandum are included in the white papers.

Wallenberg's stay at the Pechora camp was reported by Isaac Abramovich Miller, who left the Soviet Union in 1979 and later answered an advertisement for information about Wallenberg placed in a New York Russian-language newspaper. Miller remembered Wallenberg's interest in architecture and said that he introduced himself simply as "Raoul." Miller also claimed to have subsequently met him at two other camps: in 1948 at Camp 501 Salekhard, east of Vorkuta, where Miller claims Wallenberg had a foot amputated because of frostbite, and in 1953 at a camp near Komsomolsky in eastern Siberia. However, both of these camps were work camps and the weight of evidence suggests that Wallenberg was kept in more special isolation camps. However, the Pechora meeting is more plausible and fits in with the timetable suggested by other sightings.

The description of Vorkuta is based on the accounts of Shifrin and Solzhenitsyn.

The Wallenberg clues which were followed in vain are documented by the Swedish white papers.

The meeting between Dr. Meltzer and Wallenberg is described in Sjöquist.

Wallenberg's brief stay in Butyrka was reported by Zoltan Rivo to

Morgens Carlsen, a Dane with whom Rivo shared a cell in February 1951.

Kalinski's conversations with Vendrovsky and his first sighting of Wallenberg were reported to the authors by him during an interview in 1980.

CHAPTER FIFTEEN

Emil Brugger published his own account of his arrest and detention by the Soviets, including the story of his knocking conversations with Wallenberg.

Schöggl told his story to the Swedish Wallenberg Committee, and it is reproduced in their literature.

The description of prison life in Vladimir comes from books by Brugger and Powers. Kalinski's memories of Vladimir Prison and Wallenberg were recounted during an interview. The authors have seen the postmarked postcards which Kalinski wrote to his sister and are convinced of their authenticity.

Kalinski described in an interview the times when he saw Wallenberg exercising at Vladimir. Other sources for background information about Vladimir Prison are Powers, Shifrin, and Solzhenitsyn.

CHAPTER SIXTEEN

Paul Hegedus described his interrogation by the NKVD to Austrian writer Rudolph Philipp, who reported it verbatim in his book. Other stories of the interrogation of Wallenberg's co-workers were also told by Hegedus to Philipp.

Dekanusov's letter to Söderblom is from the Swedish white papers. Madame Kollontai's conversations with Mrs. von Dardel and Mrs. Gunther are reported by Philipp.

The Swedish white papers are the source for Söderblom's correspondence and contacts with the Swedish Foreign Ministry, the American Embassy in Moscow, and the Russian Foreign Ministry. The various Wallenberg sightings in 1945 were recorded by the Swedish Foreign Ministry and made public with the release of the white papers.

The Kossuthradio broadcast mentioning Wallenberg was made on March 8, 1945, under the title "The Terrorism of the Manhunters."

CHAPTER SEVENTEEN

Maj von Dardel's treatment by the Swedish Foreign Ministry is reported by Philipp and von Dardel. Philipp also tells the story of the mysterious middleman, although he does not mention the request for $20,000. This figure is referred to in a letter from Guy von Dardel to the American Joint Distribution Committee.

Miklós Krausz described Danielsson's report on Wallenberg and his conversations with Wallenberg during an interview in 1981 with one of the authors.

The description of Söderblom's audience with Stalin is based on his own account in an interview in 1981, and is also included among the Swedish white papers. These papers also document Barck-Holst's efforts on Wallenberg's behalf.

CHAPTERS EIGHTEEN, NINETEEN, AND TWENTY

The American response to Guy von Dardel's request for assistance came from Secretary of State Dean Acheson via Senator Vandenburg and was communicated in a letter of April 23, 1947.

Anger describes in his book his attempt to persuade Undén to arrange an exchange for Wallenberg. Erlander also discussed this in an interview in 1981.

Palmstierna described his conversation with Hammarskjöld in his memoirs. The story of Henrik Thomsen was supplied by Sjöquist and Söderblom during interviews.

Count Kutuzov-Tolstoy's claim to have evidence of Wallenberg comes from von Dardel. The white papers are the source for the stories of Tamvelius and von Wetschl.

Erlander described his 1956 conversation with Khrushchev during an interview in 1981.

CHAPTER TWENTY-ONE

The general account of Dr. Svartz's meetings with Dr. Myasnikov can be found in the 1965 Swedish white papers, which, prior to January 1980, had been kept secret from the Swedish public. Many Swedes understood the publication of these papers to be a tacit admission by their government that no successful resolution of the Wallenberg affair was now likely. Twenty-five documents pertaining to Wallenberg's years in prison after 1950 were withheld from publication in 1980 to be released "one year later," according to the government. In January 1981, the government reported that publication of these documents had been postponed "indefinitely."

The fact that Dr. Myasnikov had examined Wallenberg himself and had found it "enjoyable" to talk with him, was revealed by Dr. Svartz during a taped interview with one of the authors in 1981. Earlier accounts, e.g. Sjöquist and Bierman, state that Dr. Svartz was never able to contact Semyonov at all in January 1961. However, during interviews in 1981 Dr. Svartz revealed the true circumstances as outlined here.

The account of Wallenberg's imprisonment on Wrangell Island is to be found in Shifrin and Sjöquist.

Khrushchev's singular behavior and remarks in Gothenburg were told by former Prime Minister Erlander during an interview in 1981.

CHAPTER TWENTY-TWO

As is indicated in the text, most of this chapter is based on interviews and telephone conversations with Erlander and Svartz that took place in January and March of 1981.

The circumstantial evidence confirming that Wallenberg died in the early 1960s comes from interviews with Piltz and Greenwald.

The comment by a member of the Wallenberg Committee about working to memorialize Wallenberg's deeds was made to one of the authors.

Bibliography

BOOKS

Anger, Per, *With Raoul Wallenberg in Budapest.* New York: Schocken Books, 1981.

Arendt, Hannah, *Eichmann in Jerusalem.* New York: Viking Press, 1963.

Berg, Lars, *Vad Hände i Budapest.* Stockholm: Forsners Förlag, 1949.

Bierman, John, *Righteous Gentile.* New York: Viking Press, 1981.

Biss, Andreas, *A Million Jews to Save.* South Brunswick, New Jersey: A. S. Barnes, 1975.

Braham, Randolph L., *Eichmann and the Destruction of World Jewry.* New York: Twayne Publishers, 1961.

Braham, Randolph L., *The Hungarian Jewish Catastrophe.* New York: Marstin Press, 1962.

Braham, Randolph L. (ed.), *Hungarian Jewish Studies.* New York: World Federation of Hungarian Jews, 1966.

Braham, Randolph L., *The Politics of Genocide: The Holocaust in Hungary,* 2 vols. New York: Columbia University Press, 1981.

Cookridge, J. H., *Spy Trade.* New York: Walker, 1972.

von Dardel, Fredrik, *Raoul Wallenberg—fakta kring ett öde.* Stockholm: Proprius Förlag, 1970.

Derogy, Jacques, *Le Cas Wallenberg.* Paris: Editions Ramsay, 1980.

Ehrenstråle, Britt and Hans, *Sju Dagar, Oktober 1947.* Uppsala: Brombergs, 1980.

Hausner, Gideon, *Justice in Jerusalem.* New York: Schocken Books, 1968.

Hilberg, Raul, *The Destruction of the European Jews.* Chicago: Quadrangle Books, 1961.

Horthy, Miklós, *Memoirs.* New York: R. Speller, 1957.

Israeli Government, *Attorney-General of the Government of Israel* vs. *Adolf son of Adolf Karl Eichmann, Minutes of Session.* Jerusalem: Government of Israel, 1961.

Langlet, Waldemar, *Verk Och Dagar i Budapest.* Stockholm: Wahlström and Widstrand, 1946.

Lévai, Jenö, *Black Book on the Martyrdom of Hungarian Jewry.* Zurich: Central European Times Publisher, 1948.

Lévai, Jenö, *Eichmann in Hungary.* Budapest: Editions Pannonia, 1961.

Lévai, Jenö, *Raoul Wallenberg—Hjälten i Budapest.* Stockholm: Saxon och Lindström, 1945.

Levin, Nora, *The Holocaust: The Destruction of European Jewry 1933–1945.* New York: Schocken Books, 1973.

Lindström, Ulla, *Och Regeringen Salt Kvar.* Stockholm: Bonniers, 1968.

Lukacs, John, *1945 Year Zero.* New York: Doubleday, 1978.

Macartney, C. A., *October Fifteenth.* Edinburgh: Edinburgh University Press, 1961.

Masur, Norbert, *En Jude Talar Med Himmler.* Stockholm: Bonniers, 1945.

Morse, Arthur D., *While Six Million Died.* New York: Random House, 1968.

Philipp, Rudolph, *Raoul Wallenberg, Diplomat, Kämpe, Samarit.* Stockholm: Fredborgs Förlag, 1946.

Powers, Francis Gary, *Operation Overflight: The U-2 Spy Pilot Tells His Own Story for the First Time.* New York: Holt, Rinehart and Winston, 1970.

Reitlinger, Gerald, *The Final Solution.* New York: A. S. Barnes, 1961.

Robinson, Jacob, *And the Crooked Shall Be Made Straight.* New York: Macmillan, 1965.

Shifrin, Avraham, *The First Guidebook to the USSR—To Prisons and Concentration Camps of the Soviet Union.* Switzerland: Stephanus Edition Verlags AG, 1980.

Sjöquist, Eric, *Affären Raoul Wallenberg.* Stockholm: Bonniers, 1974.

Solzhenitsyn, Aleksandr I., *The Gulag Archipelago,* 3 vols. New York: Harper and Row, 1973.

Svartz, Nanna, *Steg För Steg.* Stockholm: Söderström, 1968.

Swedish Foreign Office, Utrikes Departementet, *Raoul Wallenberg: Dokumentsamling jämte kommentar rörande hans fångenskap i Sovjetunionen.* Stockholm: Swedish Foreign Ministry, 1957.

Swedish Foreign Office, Utrikes Departementet, *Raoul Wallenberg: Dokumentsamling rörande efterforskninnarna efter år 1957.* Stockholm: Swedish Foreign Ministry, 1965.

Swedish Foreign Ministry, *White Papers—Raoul Wallenberg 1944–1949.* Stockholm: Swedish Foreign Ministry, 1980.

Syrkin, Marie, *Blessed Is the Match.* Philadelphia: Jewish Publication Society, 1947.

Villius, Elsa and Hans, *Fallet Raoul Wallenberg.* Stockholm: Gebers, 1966.

Vörös, Marton, *Även för din Skull. . . . .* Stockholm: Askild & Kärnekull, 1978.

Wulf, Joseph, *Raoul Wallenberg.* Berlin: Colloquium Verlag, 1958.

DOCUMENTARY AND ARTICLES

British Broadcasting Corporation, *Man Alive,* a documentary about Raoul Wallenberg first broadcast on March 20, 1980.

Clark, Gerald, "Wallenberg: The Man Who Saved the Jews." Montreal: *Saturday Night,* July/August 1980.

Freed, G. B., "Humanitarianism *vs.* Totalitarianism: The Strange Case of Raoul Wallenberg." *Papers of the Michigan Academy of Science, Arts, and Letters,* Vol. XLVI, Ann Arbor, 1961.

Lester, Elenore, and Werbell, Frederick E., "Raoul Wallenberg." New York: *The New York Times Magazine,* March 30, 1980.

Marton, Kati, "The Wallenberg Mystery." Boston: *The Atlantic,* November 1980.

McBride, Stewart, "Missing: Raoul Wallenberg, the Hero of the Holocaust." Boston: *Christian Science Monitor,* July 25, 1980.

Meyer, Ernie, "Family's Faith." Jerusalem: *Jerusalem Post Magazine,* January 25, 1980.

Tesher, Ellie, "Is 'Scarlet Pimpernel' Still Alive?" Toronto: *Toronto Star,* October 20, 1979.

Archives

Swedish Foreign Ministry, Stockholm
Central Zionist Archives, Jerusalem
Yad Vashem, Jerusalem
World Jewish Congress, New York
American Jewish Joint Distribution
        Committee, New York
U.S. State Department, Washington
War Refugee Board Section, Roosevelt
        Library, New Hyde Park, New York
Kungliga Biblioteket, Stockholm

Index